JEAN LAFFITE
Revealed

JEAN LAFFITE Revealed

UNRAVELING ONE OF AMERICA'S LONGEST-RUNNING MYSTERIES

ASHLEY OLIPHANT *and* BETH YARBROUGH

2021
UNIVERSITY OF LOUISIANA AT LAFAYETTE PRESS

http://ulpress.org
University of Louisiana at Lafayette Press
P.O. Box 43558
Lafayette, LA 70504-3558

Printed on acid-free paper
Library of Congress Cataloging-in-Publication Data

Names: Oliphant, Ashley, 1978- author. | Yarbrough, Beth, author.
Title: Jean Laffite revealed : unraveling one of America's longest running
   mysteries / Ashley Oliphant and Beth Yarbrough.
Other titles: Jean Lafitte revealed
Description: Lafayette, LA : University of Louisiana at Lafayette Press,
   2021. | Includes bibliographical references.
Identifiers: LCCN 2020043081 | ISBN 9781946160720 (paperback)
Subjects: LCSH: Laffite, Jean. | Ferrer, Lorenzo, -1875. |
   Pirates--Louisiana--New Orleans--Biography. | Lincolnton
   (N.C.)--Biography.
Classification: LCC F374 .L174 2021 | DDC 910.92 [B]--dc23
LC record available at https://lccn.loc.gov/2020043081

To Fred Harrill, beloved father and grandfather. You loved history as much as we do, and you would have been thrilled with every second of this project. We could feel you with us as this adventure unfolded before our eyes.

To Louisa Ferrer. You had no voice during your lifetime, yet yours was the one that called across nearly two centuries and opened the door, more than once, to critical pieces of the puzzle. We honor you and every other enslaved person whose suffering was part of this story.

TABLE OF CONTENTS

AUTHORS' PREFACE

It all started with a persistent local legend that sparked an itch we were never quite able to scratch. A mysterious man—who many suspected was Jean Laffite living incognito—arrived in our hometown of Lincolnton, North Carolina, in 1839 and lived out the rest of his days under a cloud of suspicion. His name was Lorenzo Ferrer. One hundred and eighty years later, the cloud still lingered.

We are Ashley Oliphant and Beth Yarbrough, a mother-daughter team—one an English professor, the other an artist—who became so intrigued with the potential truth of the legend that we could not rest until our curiosity was satisfied. From June 2018 to August 2019, we roamed rural blacktops from North Carolina to Texas in search of answers. What we found was truly astonishing. We are so pleased you have chosen to join us as we share what turned out to be a first-rate adventure. More than once, we jokingly considered calling this book *Two Blondes and a Buccaneer*. If Laffite knew the lengths to which we went in order to figure him out, we think he would approve of that title.

To fully explain the dozens of individual connections that coalesced into our overall theory and to do so in chronological order, it was necessary to break the book into three parts. Part I offers a succinct summary of what is known about Jean Laffite's life as a corsair. It took months to peruse two hundred years of published conversation and distill it into what we think is a reliable account based on the best sources. Part II takes us to Mississippi, where Lorenzo Ferrer first appears at the approximate age of fifty with no earlier records to support his life—no birth records, no port of entry documentation, no prior marriage or family history. He simply materializes out of thin air, unless one chooses to subscribe as we do to the theory that Mississippi was Laffite's first stop under his new identity as Ferrer after what we believe was a faked death in the Caribbean. Here, too, is the first evidence of the Henderson family, a notable band of brothers whose connections ultimately led Ferrer to relocate to Lincolnton, North Carolina, their family seat. Part III brings the theory into full focus, picking up the narrative in North Carolina as Ferrer finally settles and lives out the remaining thirty-five years of his life, during which time the speculation about his true identity as Jean Laffite was present almost from the start. That speculation is what ultimately took hold, putting down the roots of the legend that persists to this day.

You will find that this book is not written in straight academic prose, though scholarly methods were certainly employed throughout the research process. Instead, we opted to use our own voice to chronicle our journey through historical documents, local lore, and old newspaper files. This book is not historical fiction, however. Any places where sources are suspect will be acknowledged.

Rarely does a story as interesting as the one you are about to read contain a cast of characters comprised of real people. These were not fictitious parts created by us in order to devise a narrative that fit our research scheme. If anything, we actually found it necessary due to the constraints of space to abbreviate the roles that they played—and these are just the main players. As it pertains to some of these names, many of which you will recognize, the story runs much deeper.

Jean Laffite: Famous nineteenth-century privateer and longtime Freemason who operated under many aliases throughout his life, including (we argue) the name of Lorenzo Ferrer, the use of which was his longest running and most successful effort.

Pierre Laffite: Jean Laffite's older brother, business partner, known Freemason, and himself a famous nineteenth-century privateer.

Dominique You: Trusted close associate and confidant of the Laffites in all their privateering ventures, possibly even the half-brother of Jean and Pierre, buried in New Orleans as a Freemason.

Andrew Jackson: Hero of the Battle of New Orleans, Freemason, and seventh president of the United States. Also known as "Old Hickory" for his determination on the battlefield.

Edward Livingston: New Orleans power broker, attorney for the Laffites, friend of Andrew Jackson, future secretary of state in the Jackson administration, and a Freemason.

William C. C. Claiborne: Governor of Louisiana, nemesis of the Laffites, friend of Andrew Jackson and Edward Livingston, and a Freemason.

Arsène Lacarrière Latour: French-born surveyor, explorer, engineer, author, Caribbean influencer, spy for the Spanish, close friend of and facilitator for the Laffites, Jackson, Livingston, and Claiborne, and a Freemason.

Napoleon Bonaparte: Emperor of France, friend of the Freemasons.

Barthélémy Lafon: Famous New Orleans architect and city planner—and sometimes pirate with the brothers Laffite. He was a member of the Perfect Union Freemason Lodge in New Orleans.

General Charles Lallemand: French General under Napoleon, founder of the Champ d'Asile colony that Jean Laffite supported, and a well-known Freemason.

Marshal Michel Ney: Napoleon's famed military commander who many scholars believe escaped a French firing squad with the assistance of the Freemasons and ended up living in North Carolina under the assumed name of Peter Stuart Ney.

James Pinckney Henderson: Native of Lincoln County, who resided briefly in Canton, Mississippi, before becoming the first governor of Texas, and a Freemason.

Henderson family: Lawson F. Henderson, George W. Henderson, Charles C. Henderson, and other brothers of James Pinckney Henderson, most of whom left Lincoln County and moved to Canton, all of them Freemasons.

Louisa Ferrer: An enslaved octoroon woman, born in Richmond, Virginia, sometime around 1814 and purchased by Lorenzo Ferrer sometime after 1829, who became his housekeeper, his mistress, and possibly the mother of his son before she died a premature death at the age of forty in Lincolnton, NC.

Wallace Reinhardt: Resident of Lincoln County, former student of Peter Stuart Ney, close confidant of Lorenzo Ferrer's, co-executor of Ferrer's estate, recipient of Ferrer's house and property at his death, and a very vocal and firm believer in Ferrer's true identity as Jean Laffite.

Prepare yourself for one of the most unbelievable yet verifiably true stories you can imagine, a tale complete with international Freemason plots, double agents, explorers charging into open frontiers, jail breaks, miraculous rescues, faked deaths, shady financial scams, and murder—all of it hinging upon control of the Gulf of Mexico and the sustainability of one of the most effective black market operations the United States has ever known. Parts of our hypothesis contradict commonly accepted Laffite historical chronology and challenge long-held beliefs about what ultimately happened to him. Since nothing particularly innovative or provocative has been published about Laffite in a very long time, we are delighted to have the opportunity to push those boundaries.

Hang on to your hat because this is not your mama's sleepy history book.

INTRODUCTION

The old Frenchman was dying. At the age of ninety-three, he understood the inevitable, even if the event itself did not appear to be on the immediate horizon. At the end of a life spent watching that horizon, he knew what it held. Indeed, it was a talent that had served him well for most of his nine-plus decades, saving his life too many times to recall, and, if the account in this book is to be believed, helping to save the United States from a second British invasion as well. The latter, however, is not a story that the old man was eager to have told. In fact, the preceding fifty years had been an exercise in un-telling it, so keen was this man on making sure the threads of the matter stayed buried.

One thing remained. It was a loose end, probably lost to the ages if you were a person prone to complacency and easily reassured that all was well. Lorenzo Ferrer, however, was not that person. He was determined not to go to his grave until the matter was forever settled and the loose end firmly tied.

As it turned out, he would live two more years after this day, though he had no way of knowing that. All that mattered at the moment was his last will and testament, that it be duly and properly recorded, and that it be witnessed by trustworthy friends.

The line items were unremarkable, save for his heartfelt wish to soon be reunited in heaven with two old friends, William Lander and Michael Hoke, both of whom had left distinguished marks on nineteenth-century North Carolina before passing.

Ferrer left substantial, though not excessive, sums of money to those who had shown him kindness, had dealt with him fairly, or had in some other way proven themselves worthy of remembrance in his last wishes. He then appointed executors, men who were friends of many years, and the matter was complete, save for a final paragraph that seemed a bit odd to all those who later read it, though none of them made a serious effort to understand what it meant.

A little more than two years later, at the age of ninety-six, Lorenzo Ferrer died and was buried in a grave marked with a stone of his own design. He died at peace, believing that he had successfully separated himself from the thing he had so diligently tried to hide. And he almost did.

While local suspicions and rumors had swirled around Ferrer during his later life, the first hints of the real unraveling came at the hands of one of his executors, who after the Frenchman's passing began declaring loudly to anyone who cared to listen that he knew the secrets Ferrer had spent a lifetime trying to conceal. Many during that day believed the man's story. Others were skeptical. And that is how the situation settled and rested for 123 years, existing as nothing more than a local legend, told from time to time when somebody took up the cause—unwrapping the old myth to see if it contained any truth. Always, though, the trail went cold.

It remained cold, sheltered, and hidden in long-forgotten file drawers and scarcely-looked-at news articles until a warm June afternoon in 2018 when we began discussing a proposed book during a long road trip home from New Orleans that had seen us consume epic quantities of gumbo. Among other things that transpired in the following weeks, we happened upon the will of Lorenzo Ferrer and read what others before us had read and never understood. Even we had a dim understanding when we first saw it.

Neither of us knew it at the time, but we were reading words that were much more than ink on paper. In fact, the final paragraph of Lorenzo Ferrer's will, the one that he felt compelled to include in an effort to hide the truth once and for all, became the very thread that helped unravel his carefully constructed charade.

Lorenzo Ferrer, as it turns out, lived the last forty-five years of his life under an assumed name. Prior to that, his name was Jean Laffite.

NOTE

Scholars studying eighteenth and nineteenth-century figures are accustomed to the challenges presented by inconsistent spelling, oftentimes the result of careless clerks who may have also been afflicted with poor penmanship. As well, in an era when literacy was not widespread and many people only knew enough about handwriting to sign their names to legal documents, it is not surprising to see any given last name spelled in a variety of ways. Many genealogists, in fact, must acknowledge in their prefaces the myriad ways a single surname has been spelled over time. Further complicating matters is the common practice of immigrants manipulating the spelling of their given names to fit in more easily to the culture in which they are trying to assimilate. In a melting pot like New Orleans in the early part of the eighteenth century, where many languages were spoken concomitantly, variations in spelling are certainly to be expected in the recording of names for newspapers, port records, business documents, land deeds, marriage licenses, and the like.

But what happens if your name is actually an alias? Will you use it consistently to attempt to prove its veracity and thus your trustworthiness? Or will you vary your name to keep your true identity a mystery? Such questions make it incredibly difficult for a book like this one, as we had to decide which spellings to use for the two main names under investigation.

Laffite has evolved as the more conventional spelling of Jean Laffite's name in the scholarly literature, just as it is the more common spelling of the family name today in America. *Lafitte* is also used as the spelling for the Jean Lafitte National Historical Park and Preserve, the Lafitte Blacksmith's Shop (now a Bourbon Street bar), and town and street names honoring the pirate. And there were all kinds of wild spellings from contemporaries of Laffite writing about their interactions with him, including *La Feet, La Fiete, La Fitte, Lafit* and *La Fete*.

For the purposes of this manuscript, the spelling of *Jean Laffite* will be adopted, even though many researchers recognize the more common Americanized version *Jean Lafitte*. A plaque called "Laffite vs. Lafitte: What's in a Name?" in the "Battle of New Orleans" exhibit at the Cabildo Museum in New Orleans asserts, "While there is much we don't know about the notorious pirates of Barataria, we are relatively sure how they spelled their surname. In virtually all of the documents that they are known to have signed, Jean and Pierre Laffite spelled their last name L-a-f-f-i-t-e, often leaving a tiny space between the second 'f' and the 'i.'" This includes documents witnessed by a notary and held in the Notarial Archives Research Center on Poydras Street in New Orleans. Likely for these very same compelling reasons, the Jean Laffite Society in Galveston, Texas, also recognizes the proper spelling as *Laffite*. The readers of this text should note that we will not alter the *Lafitte* spelling when it is used in a direct quote by another author.

Lorenzo Ferrer, a man who lived in almost complete obscurity compared to Laffite, left behind a trail of evidence riddled with variant spellings of his name, including *Lorendzo* and *L. D.* for the first name and *Farrer*, *Farrar*, *Farrier*, *Ferrier*, *Ferrow*, and *Farror* for the last name. Interestingly, after signing predominantly as *L. Ferrer* for most of his life from 1840 to his death in 1875, the name appearing on his last will and testament is his full name, *Lorenzo Ferrer*. However, the tombstone that he took great care to design two years before his passing reads *Lorendzo Ferrer*, with an added "d" in Lorenzo, leaving researchers to wonder if the craftsman of the grave marker simply misspelled the first name or if Ferrer himself specified this spelling.

Similar difficulties arose in determining exact dates and times as they relate to this account. Researchers who have spent any time reading the published material about Laffite from the last two hundred years recognize how much inconsistency there is in the record, even amongst very reliable and well-researched sources. Such informed readers will likely find reason to disagree with some of the dates presented in this volume. When possible, month approximations have been used instead of specific dates to prevent disputes and consternation, though we are aware that both will inevitably arise.

I

LOUISIANA, TEXAS, AND THE GULF

CHAPTER ONE

THE BIRTH OF A PIRATE

As disappointing as it is to admit, the world will likely never know the truth about the first twenty years of Jean Laffite's life. Any claim of the exact city or country of his birth is, at best, an educated guess. Hubert Howe Bancroft writes in the second volume of *History of the North Mexican States and Texas*, a text that was published in 1889—the very century in which Laffite lived—that "so varied and contradictory are the accounts given of his early life that no credence can be attached to any of them."[1] Most of the speculation centers on Laffite's origin in France (with Bordeaux taking the prize for the most likely city), though some posit he may have been born in Spain, Mexico, or the Caribbean (possibly the French colony of Saint-Domingue). A Spanish birth is plausible, especially if he moved into France as a young child and learned the French language as his mother tongue. William C. Davis, author of *The Pirates Laffite: The Treacherous World of the Corsairs of the Gulf*, a reliable and complete biography of Jean Laffite's life, stakes the claim that Bordeaux was his birthplace.[2] But even Davis, whose work is very well-researched, provides no satisfactory evidence to prove that claim. A thorough review of all the extant literature does provide the diligent scholar with at least some hunches about Laffite's genesis, but alas, writers have historically been able to offer only hypotheses, and these vary wildly. No author has ever provided any tangible, *documented* evidence to prove any of the claims about Laffite's place of birth.

The Laffite Society of Galveston, founded in 1994, offers a "Historical Timeline of the Laffites" on its webpage. Though careful to couch the information contained in the timeline as subject to debate and not wholly agreed upon by all members of the society, the document nonetheless offers birthdates for Pierre Laffite (April 12, 1772), Alexandre Laffite, who many say was Dominique You and the brother of Jean and Pierre (May 6, 1774), and Jean Laffite (August 15, 1782)—all in Bordeaux, France.[3] However, no records exist to validate these claims. The general consensus on the date range for Jean Laffite's birth is somewhere between 1778 and 1782.

It is incredibly suspicious that there is no evidence—no baptism records, no census records, nothing—to be found for Jean Laffite's early life. First, he became famous worldwide as a young man with the name Laffite, so it would seem likely that someone who remembered him from his home country or someone who discovered documentation later would have spoken up to claim him and prove his identity. Even in the eighteenth and nineteenth centuries, most especially in Europe, countries documented births and deaths with a good deal of consistency. (Fires and other disasters, of course, have destroyed some records over time.) Considering this, we lean toward the notion that *Jean Laffite* was not his real name at birth. A footnote in Davis's book sheds light on a scenario we think is viable:

> Galveston journalist and amateur historian John Dyer was almost certainly the source for perhaps the most novel origin story of all in a Galveston *Daily News* article on May 9, 1920, which said that Jean Laffite told Warren D. C. Hall, Mrs. James Campbell, Jane Long, J. Randal Jones, and others that he was born in Haute Pyrenees, France, and that Laffite was in fact an assumed name taken from an old servant who brought him to Louisiana in 1807, and that Pierre was the son of the servant, not Jean's real brother. Most of Dyer's sources appear to have been old Galveston loungers with little or no verifiable connection to the Laffites during their days on the island.[4]

Whether the reader believes this particular account or casts doubt on it because of its sourcing, we suspect it would make perfect sense for a man who quickly became known as a renegade to change his name and adopt a new "brother." Indeed, we know from numerous narratives about Jean Laffite during his lifetime that he regularly lied. Rosalie Daniels writes in "Fact and Legend about Jean Lafitte, Privateer of the Gulf of Mexico," "As we see him throughout the pages of eyewitness accounts, he enjoyed telling one story about himself to one ear, only to get on the other side of the room to flash a completely different version to another listener."[5] Jean Garrigoux concurs in his biography of Laffite's friend Arsène Latour entitled *A Visionary Adventurer: Arsène Lacarrière Latour 1778–1837,* pointing out the historical record proves the Laffites "lied a good deal, and often."[6] It would have been absolutely essential for men working outside the bounds of the law to create a smokescreen of mystery around themselves. Consequently, building a contradictory body of facts about oneself is a great way to zigzag and keep folks off your trail.

Scholars have long discussed the request for a privateer's license by both Pierre and Jean Laffite in March 1813 in the office of the French Consul in New Orleans , a document that claimed both were born in Bordeaux. Pierre gave his age as thirty-five, and Jean said he was thirty-two. (If true, this would have put Jean's birth year anywhere between 1780 and 1782 depending on his actual day of birth.) But again, smugglers like the Laffites lied, and they could have been lying about French ancestry in this particular instance to increase their chances of obtaining French privateering papers.

As well, there are several families who claim in their lore that Jean Laffite was really their ancestor, born under a different name and later adopting the name *Laffite* for business purposes. These include the Hix brothers of Baytown, Texas, who gained notoriety for their 2018 Laffite documentary on the Discovery Channel's "Expedition Unknown." We had an engaging conversation with Charles Hix in 2018 shortly after the episode premiered and realized that we agree on many points of contention that divide the Laffite research community. However, we do not put stock in the ancestry research the Hix theory relies on, and we also do not believe as they claim that a pirate would scuttle (or burn) a ship *with treasure on it*. Nonetheless, we do value any ongoing efforts to expose the truth about Laffite, whether those efforts support our theory or not.

We know from the indispensable records of the Laffite Society that Jean used a plethora of assumed names: Mortimer Wilson, Captain Hillare, David Campbell, Jean Thomas, and Wesley Clinton MacOrr, among others.[7] Pierre also regularly used aliases to skirt officials and fly under the radar. Furthermore, during the 1820s, the Laffites served the Spanish crown as spies, an endeavor which constantly necessitated using aliases. As this book unfolds, we will not only reveal a code name they used to conceal their identities for the purposes of letter writing but also a second (heretofore undiscovered) code name that became a pivotal piece of our research. As well, we will explore the final alias that we believe followed Laffite to his grave. For now, it is enough to understand that the use of these aliases and code names began early and continued throughout the history of the Laffite brothers in the Gulf. Because of all this uncertainty of origin, we are not even comfortable concluding that Pierre and Alexandre (who may have been Dominique You) were his brothers. We do, however, feel there is a decent chance Jean could have served as a soldier in the French Revolution, though he would have been a young man and would not have participated for very long. In fact, several Lincoln County sources claim Lorenzo Ferrer served under Napoleon. Some theories go so far as to suggest a direct connection within the French Revolution between Laffite and Napoleon. Lyle Saxon's 1930 book *Lafitte the Pirate* presents the far-fetched theory that Laffite was actually born illegitimately into the Bonaparte family in France and that he took the last name *Laffite* from a foster family.[8]

Many sources include conjecture that Laffite's mother may have been Spanish based on what he told acquaintances. Arsène Latour, whose friendship with Jean Laffite will be discussed in Chapter Five, wrote in a report to Spanish officials that Laffite came from "Spanish descent through his mother, and had a wish to find his family, a part of which lived on the frontier of France and Spain."[9] Indeed many of the cities that scholars cite as possible birthplaces for Laffite are right on the border between France and Spain in the Basque region.

Most compelling in this discussion is that Laffite was definitely a native speaker of French, though scholars squabble about the dialect associated with his language variety. He also was fluent in English and at least capable with Spanish. Some also add that he may have known Italian. Historia Obscura's Aya Katz interviewed the well-known Laffite scholar Pam Keyes, who explained

> Although Jean Laffite appears to have not been able to write fluently in English, he could read it fluently. . . . The fact that he was highly literate in a language not his own demonstrates that either he had had advanced schooling, or was intelligent enough to teach himself. According to historical accounts by contemporaries, Jean seems to have been better at conversational English than the written form, so perhaps he did teach himself by being around English speakers. This ability to do business in three languages plus a knowledge of proper manners helped secure his social status, too, as a middle man bridge between the rough, mostly illiterate ship captains, and the old French and Spanish families of New Orleans.[10]

Many scholars suspect that the extant Laffite writing samples were composed by secretaries or other transcribers, but we have not come across any evidence to prove conclusively who wrote what. Our guess is that a man who had command of at least three languages and possibly more and who built a behemoth illegal financial empire could probably write his own letters. However, Davis suggests Laffite's writing in English was not strong and "even his written French was ungrammatical."[11]

As for what Laffite looked like, sources are generally in line with the details. Inès Murat asserts in *Napoleon and the American Dream* that Laffite was a "physically impressive man with a dark Creole complexion, black hair and beard, and a usually courteous manner, although at times he displayed violent anger."[12] Henderson King Yoakum's *History of Texas 1685–1846* provides a similar description: "Lafitte was a well-formed, handsome man, about six feet two inches in height, strongly built, with large hazel eyes, black hair, and generally wore a mustache. He dressed in a green uniform and an otter-skin cap. He was a man of polite and easy manners, of retired habits, generous disposition, and of such a winning address, that his influence over his followers was almost absolute."[13] Winston Groom, in his book *Patriotic Fire: Andrew Jackson and Jean Laffite at the Battle of New Orleans,* describes Laffite's physical makeup this way:

> In his mid-twenties, Laffite was described as a handsome, dark-haired man about six feet tall with "dark piercing eyes" and a furious vertical crease in his brow—he was "well made," in the parlance of the day—with a physical comportment something like that of a large, powerful cat. He was also recorded as being smart, shrewd, and convivial—if not jovial—and a gambling and drinking man as well.[14]

Other accounts echo these sentiments about Laffite's height, his distinctive choice of clothing, his handsome features, and his dark complexion.

Though very few in number, the paintings and sketches that are claimed as likenesses of Laffite bear out the physical descriptions in the written accounts. The problem is that we ultimately do not know if these images were created by artists from life or if they were merely influenced by details read in a description of Laffite. The Rosenberg Library Collection in Galveston, Texas, contains three oil paintings of Jean Laffite. One of the most well-known images associated with the buccaneer is the piece in which he poses in a red suit, black cape, and large feathered hat (shown on p. 6).[15] However, Rosenberg curator Eleanor Barton cautions that the clothing Laffite is wearing in the portrait "pre-dates the era in which he lived," thus making the image suspect.[16] The painting's date and artist are unknown.

The Rosenberg Collection houses another iconic Laffite oil painting. Its medium is oil on devoe composition board, and the artist is Alyce Martin (date unknown).[17] The portrait, shown on p. 7, depicts Laffite in a dashing navy blue suit and red tie with a black hat. In the digital era, this image has been manipulated and modified in a number of ways for everything from book covers to maps. The third piece in the Rosenberg Collection by artist Paul R. Schumann from 1928 depicts Laffite in a navy blue uniform and hat with gold buttons.[18]

At one time there existed an 1804 portrait said to be of Jean Laffite by Baron Antoine-Jean Gros, an artist working in the service of Napoleon

Portrait of Jean Lafitte (?), *oil on canvas*
Courtesy of the Permanent Collection, Rosenberg Library, Galveston, Texas

Jean Lafitte, *by Alyce Martin, oil on devoe composition board*
Courtesy of the Permanent Collection, Rosenberg Library, Galveston, Texas

Bonaparte, but the painting was lost to fire in 1959. According to Pam Keyes's article "The Laffite Portrait Proves the Authenticity of the Laffite journal," the piece was originally part of the Jean Lafitte Journal collection that will be discussed as a fraud in Chapter Eight. Keyes's argument is that "only the subject of the Gros portrait could have written the Laffite journal, and that person was Jean Laffite."[19] However, there is no way of knowing who the subject of the portrait truly was, and just because a person possesses two items (a journal and a piece of art) does not confirm the identity of the person in the portrait or the identity of the person who wrote the journal.

The Louisiana State Museum houses a painting that was long thought to depict Jean and Pierre Laffite along with Dominique You. The attributed title was *Jean Lafitte Drinking at Dominique You's Bar*, and the piece was said to be from artist John Wesley Jarvis circa 1830.[20] However, according to museum histo-

rian Dr. Karen Leathem, art historian (and colleague) Dr. Richard Anthony Lewis determined several years ago that the painting, which came into the museum's collection in 1917, was not a true likeness. Leathem explained the painting is a genre scene depicting gamblers and drinkers in a cautionary way and is likely connected to the temperance movement. It was not created from life. Furthermore, the determination was made that the artist was not Jarvis but likely New York artist Ezra Ames.[21]

Many scholars give attention to a John D. Telfer woodcut that was used to create art for Saxon's book. Another sketch purportedly from an artist named Lacassinier who worked for the Laffites during the Galveston years is also part of the conversation. A glut of other sketches and paintings that may or may not be of Jean Laffite exist, many of which were produced in the twentieth century at the time when his image became increasingly glamorized due to several books and feature films about his life. Similarly, fiction writers over the years have taken great liberty with every detail of the Laffite mystique, making it nearly impossible to separate the exaggeration from the truth.

SAINT-DOMINGUE

Very many Laffite scholars suspect the pirate was either born in Saint-Domingue or possibly spent his early childhood years there. From 1791 to 1804, the French-controlled colony that would eventually become the nation of Haiti was in the grips of a brutal slave uprising. Depending on the state of the violent revolt, it sometimes became necessary for white families to evacuate quickly to safer locations. Garrigoux writes that "every night privateers, including brothers Jean and Pierre Lafitte, sailed from the island with wealthy white refugees bound for Cuba and Louisiana."[22] Complicating matters was the fact that by 1803, France and England were at war with each other, and the British decided to set up a blockade of the port in Saint-Domingue, so the work of privateers like the Laffites became even more challenging and dangerous.

A footnote in Bancroft's text offers a fascinating nugget about Laffite's life, one that he supposedly offered to a group of men visiting him at his Galveston settlement late in his days as a pirate. Bancroft noted

> Lafitte persistently maintained that he only made war on Spanish vessels. According to an account given by an officer of the *Enterprise,* who accompanied [American Lieutenant Lawrence] Kearney on a visit to Lafitte, the freebooter gave at table the following sketch of his life as a pirate, and the cause of his adopting this career; he stated that 18 years before [that would

be 1803] he had been a merchant at Santo Domingo, and that having become rich, he wound up his affairs, sold his property, bought a ship, and freighted her with a valuable cargo, including a large amount of specie. Having set sail for Europe with his wife on board, he was captured, when a week at sea, by a Spanish man-of-war, and robbed of everything he possessed. The Spanish captain had the inhumanity to set him and the crew ashore on a barren sand key, with provisions for a few days only. They were taken off by an American schooner and landed at New Orleans, where his wife died in a few days from fever, contracted by hardship and exposure. Lafitte, in desperation, joining some daring fellows, and having purchased a schooner, declared eternal vengeance against Spain. "For fifteen years," he said, "I have carried on a war against Spain. So long as I live I am at war with Spain, but no other nation. I am at peace with all the world except Spain. Although they call me a pirate, I am not guilty of attacking any vessel of the English or French."[23]

Herein lies the problem with trying to sift the Laffite facts from the fiction. Was this a tall tale whipped up by a big-talking pirate who wanted to impress an audience? Was he telling the truth in a moment that felt safe to him? Was the narrative a complete or partial fabrication on the part of the storytellers, who after a meeting with an infamous pirate likely recounted their experiences numerous times and with differing details? Without primary documents to support the story, all researchers can do is offer guesses.

This activity in Saint-Domingue by the Laffite brothers marks the emergence of them together as a team operating a daring and dangerous seafaring business that capitalized on an opportunity created by political turmoil. Their next stop was due northwest in the Crescent City, and American officials were not at all ready for the Laffite brothers' next venture.

CHAPTER TWO

THE BAYOUS OF BARATARIA

Before delving into the specifics of the masterful business operation devised by the Laffites in New Orleans, it is necessary to pause and examine the worldwide events that shaped the stage on which their ingenious scheme unfolded. Jean Laffite is often classified as the last of the great pirates, mainly because his emergence as a force in the Gulf occurred so long after the climax of the Golden Age of Piracy, which ran roughly between 1650 and 1720. This span of seventy years premiered swashbucklers like Blackbeard, Stede Bonnet, Calico Jack Rackham, and Captain William Kidd, all of whom were either killed in combat trying to evade officials or executed after trial between 1701 and 1720.

The Golden Age came into existence for a number of geopolitical reasons, almost all of which were connected to global commerce and colonization. As maritime exploration expanded and Europeans began to move about the globe more freely, trade routes developed, creating a new pipeline of ships carrying costly cargo thousands of miles away from the safety of their home ports, each ship an easy target for a properly outfitted pirate crew. At the same time, countries like Spain were moving jewels and precious metals worth millions across the Atlantic from faraway lands. Additionally, as European countries like France, Spain, and England set up colonies in undeveloped territories, it was necessary for them to constantly transport the valuable supplies required to keep settlers alive. All of this activity took place far removed from the protective reach of the governments sponsoring the ventures, and quick-thinking pirates recognized the money that was to be made by those who were not risk averse.

It can be argued that the main reason the Golden Age ended was because the governments—who for decades had been absolutely pummeled with losses from pirate attacks—began to get more organized in their defenses, and this organization made it increasingly more difficult for pirates to operate unmolested. Likewise, savvy governments decided to dispatch well-armed teams to thwart specific pirates, such as the operation of Alexander

Spotswood and Robert Maynard that took down the great Blackbeard on Ocracoke Island in 1718. When pirates were caught, their executions were held in public, and their bodies were displayed for months afterward to serve as an example for any other pirates who thought about plying the same waters. Governments of countries like Jamaica and the Bahamas, whose lax policies and oversight allowed pirate safe havens to form, also got smart and ran the freebooters out, which resulted in the world becoming a much smaller pond for the pirates to paddle in. Additionally, better organized governments and tax collection systems made it more difficult (but not impossible) for pirates to find a port in which they could sell large quantities of obviously stolen merchandise.

By the time Team Laffite joined the game in the early 1800s, much had changed since the glory days of Captain Kidd and Blackbeard, and still more challenging developments were on the horizon for seafaring men operating outside the bounds of the law. Many scholars suggest Jean and Pierre Laffite arrived in New Orleans in 1803 (around the time of the Louisiana Purchase), while others put their arrival a bit later. Garrigoux suggests that a ship called the *Soeur Chérie* commanded by a "Captain Lafette" and detained in New Orleans in 1804 was related to the Laffite brothers, but not all scholars agree.[1] Davis contends that Pierre arrived ahead of Jean in 1803 and "first took rented quarters on Royal Street, probably near the intersection with Dumaine, while looking for a suitable venue to go into business" before moving briefly to Baton Rouge.[2] In "Slave Smuggling by Foreign Privateers: The Illegal Slave Trade and the Geopolitics of the Early Republic," David Head argues that in these early days, Pierre Laffite was without question a slave trader:

> In the winter between 1805 and 1806, Pierre Laffite traveled from New Orleans to Baton Rouge, located on the Spanish side of the Mississippi in West Florida, to buy slaves. Louisiana was not yet a state, and the federal government had outlawed the foreign slave trade into the territory. But it was legal just over the border. Laffite bought eleven slaves and turned them into $5,000 back home. . . . His first attempts to build a merchant business in the Crescent City failed, but in smuggling Pierre Laffite found the work that suited him best.[3]

The Historic New Orleans Collection contains a handwritten document signed by Jean Laffite that shows us that by October 20, 1805, he had relocated to Grand Terre.[4] Whenever it was that the Laffites actually arrived, their business model became even more difficult almost immediately due to a series of legislative acts that crippled activity in what was at the time one of America's most active and important ports.

First came the 1806 Non-Importation Act, which prohibited the entrance of any British goods into American ports. This meant that American harbors were watched much more closely for ships that tried to evade the law. Then came the Embargo Act of 1807, which barred the import and export of any merchandise from any foreign country. Following that came the Act Prohibiting Importation of Slaves of 1807, which was put into effect January 1, 1808. This meant that the only ways for plantation owners to obtain more enslaved labor was 1) for them to be born into slavery in the United States or 2) to be bought illegally from smugglers. Chapter Nine will delve into the details of the contemporary slave economy; suffice it to say here that the timing of this legislation for the emerging American cotton industry, much of which was centered in the Gulf Coast region and fed by the New Orleans port, was absolutely disastrous.

For a city that relied on international commerce for its very existence, this debilitating legislation brought panic to New Orleans. The cumulative effect especially for the Non-Importation Act and the Act Prohibiting Importation of Slaves was the creation of an environment rife for corruption and smuggling. The people were not ready to give up the luxuries they were used to receiving through imports, and the plantation owners were unwilling to let their pipeline of enslaved labor end. Enter Jean and Pierre Laffite.

It appears that even before this time, the Laffites were already busy establishing a smuggling operation. Jean was adamant throughout his life that he was not a pirate, however. In the May 9, 1920, edition of the Galveston *Daily News*, J. O. Dyer published an article called "Jean Laffite in 1820." In it, he claimed "The more truthful histories of the Barataria establishment . . . give not a single instance of Laffite being in command at any time of any one of his privateers or cruisers; nor was a single case of piracy ever proven to have been the work of the Laffite vessels, which, under special letters of marque obtained from countries at war with Spain, were thus licensed by international maritime laws to prey upon the commerce of Spain."[5] While Jean Laffite may have somehow managed to avoid being caught while actively pirating ships, there is ample evidence that he and Pierre ran a world-class smuggling business and were absolutely the middlemen who brought millions of dollars of stolen goods to auction. They capitalized on the market forces at work in New Orleans (including a high demand for goods and enslaved people) along with its very unusual but advantageous geography situated on the Mississippi River. In short, there were wealthy clients waiting to spend money, their customers' other sources for buying goods had dried up, there were plenty of easy targets constantly parading around in the Gulf, and the Crescent City was the perfect place to circumvent the ports with hundreds of other tributaries that could never be fully monitored by local authorities.

By 1809 the Laffites had established their now famous blacksmith shop at 941 Bourbon (at the corner of Bourbon and St. Philip Streets) in New Orleans. The original building still stands today after surviving two fires, and it operates under the claim that it is the oldest American structure that has continually been used as a bar. It is indeed one of the coolest watering holes in America and a highlight of any New Orleans trip. It was here under the ruse that the Laffite brothers were solely blacksmiths that they covertly sold their stolen merchandise to even the most upstanding gentlemen of the Big Easy. Their workers cranked out a few iron pieces here and there while the Laffites conducted the actual business of arranging sales of pirated goods. Here and at another location on Royal Street, the Laffites mingled within New Orleans society and built a client base and network of well-connected friends that would serve them for years afterward. While their business gave them access to the most wealthy and distinguished men of the city, the Laffites still had a reputation. Everyone in New Orleans knew exactly who they were and what they did.

Lafitte's Blacksmith Shop, which sits at the corner of Bourbon and St. Philip Streets in the French Quarter, is known for its signature drink, the potent purple Voodoo daiquiri.

QUADROON BALLS

One part of New Orleans culture that the Laffite brothers fully embraced was the tradition of the quadroon balls, glamorous social events designed to parade beautiful mixed-race women in front of (often married) men who were seeking mistresses. New Orleans was a cultural outlier during the Laffites' day due to its unusual acceptance of racial intermingling. According to Davis, "if a working or merchant class white male wanted to have feminine company on a stable basis, a mulatto mistress offered an acceptable alternative to participating in the heavy competition for the few eligible white women in the city. As a result, color lines blurred in New Orleans more than anywhere else in the young United States."[6] The quadroon balls, which were most popular in the later decades of the eighteenth century and the first decades of the nineteenth century, were so named because of the racial makeup of the girls whose social circumstances brought them to seek stability there. Forming a long-term sexual relationship with a white man provided more security and social standing than these women could ever achieve otherwise. Different names were applied to women with varying degrees of white and black blood. A person with one white parent and one black parent was known as a mulatto. One with a mulatto parent and a white parent was called a quadroon (for being one quarter black). A person of one-eighth African descent was known as an octoroon. Cohen explains these relationships between white men and their placées (or official mistresses) were often long-term. He writes the quadroon

> took her man's name, as did her children. In this way, the wealthy men of New Orleans could lead a double life, one above ground with a white wife and white children, the other subterranean with quadroon placées and octoroon children. The practice continued [until] the Civil War, in the wake of which racial distinctions hardened. No more balls. No more secret families. Most of the quadroons (who, after generations of intermarriage, were more white than most white people in the city) went north, where they vanished into the fabric of America.[7]

Jean Laffite was known to attend the balls, but most accounts depict him as a man much more interested in talking business than in fooling around. Daniels describes him as "nonchalant to the dusky beauties gliding over the floor, each hoping to attract a rich Creole gentleman who had the means of keeping her as his mistress."[8]

In almost all accounts of Laffite in his adult life, he is described as having a quadroon or octoroon mistress. This book will push the Laffite timeline well beyond the 1820s when most scholars assert he died, and even in the places we have tracked him under an assumed name after his supposed death, he *always* had an exceptionally beautiful mixed-race mistress, even in states where such a practice was not accepted. As a trader who trafficked enslaved people in large numbers, he certainly had access to a varied population of girls from which to choose a companion. The published research about Laffite names many of his mistresses and speculates about whether he was ever married or had children. The chances are good for both, but again no definitive proof exists to prove the claims. What is established as fact was that he loved having beautiful mixed-race women in his service, and by all accounts he was an extraordinarily charming and handsome man who drew attention. According to Robert Tallant in *The Pirate Lafitte and the Battle of New Orleans*, Laffite's sophistication was so notable that "it was said that once a person had met Jean Lafitte it was impossible to believe that he was a pirate."[9]

Despite his affinities for women, Laffite was first a businessman, and his next calculated move would forever cement his position among the ranks of America's most famous entrepreneur pirates.

BARATARIA

At the same time that the Laffites were establishing themselves in the French Quarter, a fascinating community south of the city was growing in a bayou called Barataria in Jefferson Parish. The remote set of islands, which included Grand Terre and Grand Isle, were home to a crusty and dangerous crew of pirates who studied the intricate network of bayous and streams and learned to use them to their advantage to unload the prizes taken from their Gulf conquests. Smugglers had used this bayou system for decades to serve their illicit purposes, and at the time Jean Laffite rose to prominence in New Orleans, there were several hundred ne'er-do-wells using the Barataria islands as their base of operations. Local legend says that Barataria was accessed by Blackbeard and other notorious pirates as a hideout, but such legends exist in nearly every coastal locality in America. Cohen writes, "Barataria boomed in 1808 when the American Congress banned the importation of African slaves. . . . Soon after the law's passage, privateers began preying on slow, fat-bellied ships heading for Cuba. They attacked, then carried the human cargo back to Bargainland. This meant serious money: sable coats, silk eye patches, a diamond stud for each ear. The result was more pirates, more pirate ships, more pirate guns, more pirate violence."[10] This violence and lack of order at Barataria threatened the entire enterprise, and sometime around 1811, Jean Laffite was invited to become the leader of the Baratarian rabble. Anybody could steal, but it required skill to manage such a large community of thieves and keep them all out of prison. They could not have chosen a better president for their pirate republic. This invitation likely came because he and Pierre had become very well known among all the people of New Orleans and had conducted shady business with the Baratarians previously. The Laffites had used these remote islands as a place to store and sell their goods. When Jean took command, historians estimate there were several hundred to possibly a thousand or more pirates already encamped there, some of them unemployed sailors whose jobs had been cut because of the embargo, while others were French exiles from the Napoleonic Wars. Many of them were also Freemasons, the significance of which we will explore fully. Jean Laffite became the leader of them all and one of the most successful middlemen the United States has ever seen. He built his house in Grand Terre in 1811 and became a permanent fixture in his little kingdom, though both he and Pierre traveled frequently in and out of the city.

With hundreds of pirates unloading the prizes from dozens of ships, the sheer volume of cargo (including, unfortunately, human cargo) became too much to supervise without a very systematic approach. The operation required several crucial ingredients. First, an expanded network of warehouses beyond those that already existed at Barataria was necessary to store goods until they were sold. These were strategically placed and concealed all over the narrow bayous in locations that only the most experienced navigators would ever be able to find. Groom reveals Laffite's Baratarian hideaway included "more than forty [warehouses] . . . containing the wealth of Spain, Mexico, South America, and the West Indies: fine silks, Moroccan rugs and leather, elaborately carved furniture—beds, chairs, tables—ornate silver flatware, china, crystal, tapestries, lace, clothing, lamps, and kegs of whisky, rum, and wine."[11] The next necessity was a marketplace where merchandise and enslaved Africans could be sold. This was established with the Temple, an auction venue tucked away in secrecy among the live oaks in a location only accessible by pirogues, or small boats used on the Louisiana rivers. In the article "The Short Life of Dominique You: New Orleans' Most Popular Man," Lionel Bienvenue writes, "The Laffites decided in 1812 to hold regular weekend auctions of slaves and goods at the Temple, a large shell mound in the Baratarian swamps, located about mid-way between Grand Terre and New Orleans. The auctions became a huge success, attracting large gatherings of Mississippi planters."[12] Charles Gayarré suggests in the article "The Story of Jean and Pierre Lafitte: The Pirate-Patriots" that the Temple was the point from which the Natchez Indians worshiped their Sun God.[13] The Temple's name is incredibly significant, too, considering the number of Freemasons who were involved in the Laffite operation. This auction area sadly included holding pens for enslaved people, called barracoons or barracóns. Third was the need for monied clientele, which the Laffites were able to find considering the number of plantation owners who were in close proximity to Barataria just a short boat ride north up the Mississippi River. With the importance of cotton as a cash crop increasing, these planters were desperate for slave labor and willing to pay a premium for it because they could no longer legally purchase imported enslaved Africans. Natural reproduction was the only legal means of growing the slave population, though it was much too time-consuming to satisfy their greedy designs. The final ingredient was coordination through advertisements. The Laffites needed to find a way to advertise their available items for sale and their auction dates and times without drawing the attention of local authorities because the entire operation was as illegal as it could possibly be. At least for the first few years, the Laffites used the blacksmith shop as a place to meet with potential customers and inform them of what items would be coming up for sale. Then, according to Cohen, "plantation owners sailed out [to Barataria] for the weekend. They would stay for two nights, drinking and eating, a party, a feast, before walking the aisles" and making their purchases.[14] As time went on, the Laffites became emboldened enough to advertise their auctions in the city.

The people—from residents in New Orleans to citizens all the way up the Mississippi River—loved the Laffites because their operation gave them access to fine things that the embargo forbade. Furthermore, because the goods were all stolen, the pirates could afford to sell them even cheaper than customers would have been able to buy them legally. The people of New Orleans were vehemently opposed to the Embargo Act and had no qualms about circumventing the law and buying what they wanted. And thus, the image of Jean Laffite as the Robin Hood of the Bayou was born. His operation made a complete mockery of those who claimed to maintain law and order in Louisiana. Every penny in his pocket added to the humiliation of those who should have stopped him but did not.

It is estimated that at the peak of his success, with what some suggest was millions of dollars in stock sheltered in his Baratarian warehouses, Jean Laffite was one of the richest men in America.

This, of course, meant that he was a marked man who had to be taken down. And it all started in 1812 with the election of a new governor.

W. C. C. CLAIBORNE

Following the signing of the Louisiana Purchase in 1803, William Charles Cole Claiborne served as the governor of the "Territory of Orleans" until 1812, when Louisiana gained statehood. Being a territorial leader was actually a bit of a lame-duck post. Once Claiborne became governor, one of his first orders of business was to get after the Baratarians, whose actions routinely made fools of him and his underlings. The days of the Laffites openly defying the law were numbered. Claiborne's job and that of his team of officials was intensely complex. The first problem was that the general populace had a very positive opinion of the Laffite operation, and many of them did not view him as a pirate at all. Even exorbitant rewards for Laffite's capture were not enough to entice citizens to flip on him. Indeed, the customs agents who were tasked with reining in such lawlessness were of minimal help. Davis writes, "People in New Orleans suspected that the customs agents did not want to put the Laffites out of business, for the agents were making too much money from their shares of the proceeds on the confiscated goods they seized."[15] Secondly, the river system, with its hundreds of tiny waterways, made it incredibly difficult to catch the Baratarians in the act. Only those with intimate knowledge could navigate them, and the pirates could easily escape pursuit due to their familiarity with the area. Finally, the heathen city Laffite and his men had established in the bayou was well fortified, and every man was armed to the hilt. (There is some speculation amongst scholars that maybe the Baratarians were not the best fighters, but we find that quite hard to believe considering their line of work.) Law and tax enforcement officers were rightfully terrified to go there and clean the place out. However, Claiborne was determined and desperate to make Laffite pay.

Considering how lax the Laffites felt Louisiana's enforcement of its laws was, they likely saw no end in sight to their scheme. Their profits were staggering, and because they paid their employees well, absolutely everyone in Barataria was happy with the status quo. The Laffites and their band of merry men also had letters of marque from places like Cartagena, so they likely felt secure and justified in their "privateering" being several rungs above what they would otherwise consider "pirating." As long as they did not attack American ships and focused their attentions primarily on British and Spanish assets, they could continue with relative security. There were likely many who had been paid off in the city to ensure their business operated without interruption.

This room at the Cabildo, known as the Sala Capitular (or council chamber), is where France handed over the Louisiana Territory to governor Claiborne and General James Wilkinson. According to Louisiana Museum historian Dr. Karen Leathem, the furniture is not original to the room but was instead recreated based on an inventory of the room at the time of the transfer. Courtesy of Louisiana State Museum

That all changed in November 1812 when John R. Grymes, the United States district attorney, filed charges against Jean Laffite for violating tax law. Three days later, Claiborne's men stormed Barataria and captured Jean and Pierre as they were moving stolen goods on the river. While they had not been caught in the act of piracy, they had been caught with pirate spoils. Dozens of Baratarians were arrested, and over the course of several days, their visible warehouses were raided. All involved posted bail and predictably skipped their hearings. Hindsight is twenty-twenty as they say, but Louisiana officials should have known that giving pirates bail was ill-advised. After their predictable failure to appear, Jean and Pierre Laffite were wanted men.

Approximately a week later, pirates associated with the Laffite fleet attacked an American ship. This crossed a line. The people of New Orleans, who heretofore had been tolerant and even complicit in the Laffite game, began to rethink their position.

The drama—and the quite comical cat-and-mouse game between the Laffites and Claiborne—dragged on for months. In March 1813, Claiborne issued a formal demand for the Baratarians to vacate and urged the people of the city to avoid any contact with them—especially business dealings. The Laffites were unfazed. After a swamp skirmish with local officials in October of that year, Claiborne upped the ante by warning the citizens of New Orleans that they would be arrested if caught interacting with the Laffites in any capacity. On November 24, 1813, wanted posters seeking the arrest of Jean Laffite and boasting a $500 reward were posted all over the French Quarter. Davis points out that Laffite was actually in New Orleans when the notice was made public, and yet nobody turned him in.[16]

By daylight the next day, someone had composed, printed, and distributed flyers advocating the arrest of Governor Claiborne and offering a $1,000 reward for *his* capture.

The Laffites continued their pursuits unabated. On New Year's Day 1814 they had the gall to pepper the streets of New Orleans with ads for a massive auction in the bayou later that month. Around this time, several Louisiana officials were injured, and some killed, in another skirmish with the Baratarians. It looked like Claiborne would never be able to get the upper hand.

The turning point was the arrest of Pierre Laffite without the option of bail near St. Louis Cathedral in New Orleans in early July 1814. He was shackled and placed in a tiny, heavily guarded cell in the Cabildo. The arrest was a critical shock for Jean, who had come to rely on his partnership with Pierre. History tells us that Jean did absolutely everything in his power to facilitate his brother's release, to no avail.

September 1814 turned out to be a pivotal juncture for the Laffites—and indeed for America as a whole. Pierre Laffite managed to escape the wretchedness of his Cabildo cell on September 6, 1814, though some speculate that he was essentially let go. Michael Poll, a member of the Texas Freemason Lodge of Research, writes in "The Battle of New Orleans: A Masonic Perspective" that Pierre's escape was totally orchestrated by the Brotherhood. He explains

> I mentioned that the jailer guarding Pierre Lafitte in the Cabildo was a Mason. That's not conjecture. That's fact. He was the one who seems to have put doing what was necessary for the 'greater good' ahead of what was the technical law. He was a man who was concerned with doing what was right, not easy or safe. In fact, if it were not for him, we can look at the whole of the Battle of New Orleans with a very different ending. . . . The "escape" of Pierre Lafitte allowed everything else to happen. I firmly believe that the forgotten hero of the Battle of New Orleans was that jailer. The jailer was not only a Mason but would end up serving as Grand Master of the Grand Lodge of Louisiana as well as play a rather significant role in Texas Freemasonry. The young jailer's name: John Henry Holland.[17]

Situated at the back of picturesque Jackson Square, the Cabildo stands as a reminder of centuries of New Orleans history. The Spanish colonial structure now houses the Louisiana State Museum. In Jean Laffite's day, it housed the cell where his brother Pierre was kept after his arrest in July 1814. Courtesy of Louisiana State Museum

Davis suggests the escape was "embarrassing" for Holland, which it might have been after the local papers insinuated that he was involved.[18] But this embarrassment does not negate the fact that the Freemasons were likely the only ones able to extricate Pierre Laffite from his confinement. The actual cell where Pierre was held is no longer standing. According to Dr. Leathem, that cell was part of a jail complex that was modified and rebuilt many times.

Pierre immediately headed out to Barataria to rendezvous with his crew. Just days before that, however, the British ship HMS *Sophie* arrived outside Barataria and sent representatives inland to have a talk with Jean Laffite.

Storm clouds had been forming on the horizon for a good long while, and they were just about ready to dump rain.

Chapter Three

The Battle of New Orleans

To borrow an apt Southern phrase, the shit was about to hit the fan on numerous fronts in New Orleans in late 1814. Winston Groom's *Patriotic Fire: Andrew Jackson and Jean Laffite at the Battle of New Orleans* offers a solid account of the build-up and crescendo of the culminating conflict of the War of 1812—along with an outstanding synopsis of the situation faced by the young United States when the British navy began to pace in the Gulf. Groom explains that by 1814, the country's

> treasury was empty, most public buildings in Washington, including the Capitol, the White House, and the Library of Congress, had been burned to ashes by a victorious and vengeful British army. . . . American seaports from the Atlantic to the Gulf of Mexico were blockaded by the British navy and the economy was in ruins because of it, with goods and crops piled up and rotting on the wharves. The U.S. Army was stymied and stalemated; the navy, such as it was, had fared little better.[1]

The British had their sights set on the ultimate prize that would bring the United States to its knees: control of the Mississippi River and the port of New Orleans. Numerous military scholars have pointed out what a terrifying situation this created. The city was not set up to defend itself in any way. Estimates suggest the British had 20,000 soldiers at the ready, while New Orleans had maybe 2,000. The saving grace (if there was one) was the fact that the potent British military was fabulously overextended fighting Napoleon and blockading French-controlled ports all over the globe. By the time Old Hickory himself, Andrew Jackson, arrived in New Orleans on December 1, 1814, he was well aware of the uphill battle he was facing. But a great deal had to happen on the timeline before Jackson's strategy would be revealed.

The British Visit Barataria

In the first few days of September 1814, the British ship HMS *Sophie* threw down anchors at Grand Terre. The British had a packet of letters and a proposition. Captain Nicholas Lockyer and Lieutenant Colonel Edward Nichols were ready to make a deal with Jean Laffite. (Amazingly, these letters are still in existence as part of the Bibliotheca Parsonia collection and can be viewed at the Dolph Briscoe Center for American History on the campus of the University of Texas at Austin. It is worth a trip to Texas from wherever you are just to see the letters, but we can attest to the fact that the state's barbeque is an equally compelling reason to travel there.) The British naively expected that they could convince the Creoles to rise up against the American government and fight for the British. It was the first of a series of major errors in thinking. The British were also aware of the strength of the Baratarian operation and the asset Jean Laffite could be to their geographical understanding of the bayous and rivers that might be used to launch a sneak attack on New Orleans. They felt they could persuade him with an offer of 30,000 British pounds and a commission in the British navy to command the Baratarians to join England's side. Thinking the Baratarians would go along with such a scheme was Miscalculation Number Two. Frank Lawrence Owsley Jr. points out in *Struggle for the Gulf Borderlands: The Creek War and the Battle of New Orleans 1812–1815* that while the offer might have piqued the Baratarians' interest, "they would have lost too much as allies of the British because Nichols had insisted that they should give up their raids on the Spaniards. Whether or not the Baratarians were as pro-American as they claimed is a moot question, but it is certain that they had no love or trust for either Britain or Spain. Support of the United States in this critical time would present them with an excellent chance to receive a full pardon for their past offenses."[2] Finally, the British soldiers who came to shore to begin negotiations were captured by the Baratarians and placed in jail overnight. It was terribly unwise to think they could arrive unannounced on a pirate-controlled island in fancy red coats and come away unscathed.

Laffite made a good show of it, pretending to be on board with the proposition and asking for fifteen days to make arrangements. Then he promptly notified New Orleans officials about the British plot. Even if he did measure the risks and rewards of making a deal in the moment, he ultimately decided against double-crossing what had become his home country, a fact that the scholarship about the battle does not fully recognize.

NEGOTIATIONS

When Jean Laffite came forward with the packet of papers from the British as proof of the deal extended to him, New Orleans authorities had a decision to make. That is when, according to Edward Alexander Parsons, the owner of the collection of documents known as the Bibliotheca Parsonia, a "council of state (i.e. committee of defense) was held to determine the genuineness of the letters and whether the council should deal with the pirate leader. The decision was against having any intercourse with the Lafittes."[3] Jean Laffite's offer to Governor Claiborne to bring his fellow Baratarians to the side of the American defenses was firmly rebuffed. Jackson, who famously called Laffite's men a rabble of "hellish banditti," would have nothing to do with him. Laffite was seen as a man who was simply angling to get his brother out of jail. At the time of Laffite's offer, Pierre had not yet made his clandestine escape from the Cabildo. Davis also writes that at the beginning of negotiations, "Laffite surely knew from his informants in the city that [Commodore Daniel] Patterson was preparing an expedition to destroy the Baratarian establishment. Anything that delayed this would give him more time to prepare the shift of base to the Mexican coast."[4] Louisiana officials had tolerated Laffite long enough. Knowing that his time in Barataria was nearing a close (whether the Americans won the battle or the British overtook the city), Laffite made plans for a new center of operations before his current island paradise went belly-up.

These days of great uncertainty when Jean Laffite did not know if the British were going to lose patience and attack, if the Americans were going to accept or reject the offer, or if New Orleans officials were going to proceed with their impending raid of Barataria must have been intense.

The answer finally came on September 16, 1814, as Commodore Patterson and Colonel Robert Ross invaded Barataria. They took Dominque You and Barthélémy Lafon, another Laffite associate, prisoner, and they cleaned out the merchandise in the warehouses. They also confiscated the Laffite fleet of twenty-seven ships. And then they burned Barataria to the ground.

Both Jean and Pierre Laffite (who had just escaped from jail ten days before) managed to evade capture by fleeing two days before the attack in a pirogue, making a beeline for the home of friend Alexandre Labranche on the German Coast,[5] a place that served as their safe house for the coming days.[6] As with most details surrounding Laffite's life, the estimates about the value of the seized goods vary considerably. Davis estimates conservatively that there was around $200,000 in merchandise, and this does not take

*Visitors to the Louisiana State Museum exhibits in the Cabildo have the chance to
see several artistic representations of former United States President Andrew Jackson,
including this whimsical bust. Courtesy of Louisiana State Museum*

into account the fact that the Laffites had the opportunity before the raid to
evacuate all manner of valuables.

Even though the worst reality had been realized for the Baratarians, the
British still circled New Orleans, and they expected a response from Jean
Laffite. Tellingly, while his main bargaining chip was off the table with Pierre
out of jail and his offer had been rudely rejected by leaders in the city, Jean
persisted in extending his services to Jackson, this time with the help of two
very well-connected friends: lawyer Edward Livingston, who was an aide to
the general, and Arsène Latour, Jackson's chief engineer.

The people in Jackson's inner circle—including Livingston and Latour—
were becoming increasingly wary of the position of the Americans, who were
in a vulnerable city with a much smaller and less capable military. They urged
him to reconsider Laffite's offer, and thankfully they came to agreement on a
solution. Remember, a whole host of Laffite's men were stuck in prison after
the raid, and all kinds of unresolved charges had followed the Laffites for years.
If local authorities agreed to get the pending charges dropped, accepting their
help in such a critical situation might not look like such a dirty maneuver.

Laffite had one more ace up his sleeve that finally encouraged Jackson to
relent. Not only were the Americans facing a shortage of troops, in addition
they did not have enough flints for their guns. It is very likely one of Jean

Laffite's well-placed friends notified him of this critical shortage and encouraged him to make known the fact that he just so happened to have a massive stockpile of flints, acquired earlier that year from arms dealings in Mexico. The deal he made was pure genius: 7,500 flints and the fighting power of the Baratarians in exchange for prisoner releases and pardons. Jackson and Laffite finalized the negotiations in their now notorious meeting in the French Quarter, a gathering that was probably arranged by Livingston and Latour.

On December 18, 1814, the state government pardoned Laffite's men and gave Jean a "safe conduct pass" to come into the city unmolested. Davis reports the Laffites were in New Orleans by December 22, at which point Jackson immediately issued both of them orders.[7] While not given lofty titles or uniforms (Jean was simply named "aide-de-camp"), American commanders absolutely recognized and utilized Jean and Pierre's expertise. Military leaders consulted the Laffites on all sorts of details, from fortifications to geography to the placement of artillery.

Jackson's first order for Jean was to go to the Temple to set up defenses there in case the British tried to use that as a point of attack. Pierre was to remain in the city.

THE BATTLE OF NEW ORLEANS

Accounts differ about the extent of the involvement of the Laffites in the Battle of New Orleans, which took place on January 8, 1815. Most at least acknowledge the artillery help provided by the Baratarians on the front lines. The Baratarians were put into two artillery detachments under Dominique You and Renato Beluche,[8] and most of the narratives conclude that they mowed down the British like beasts. Owsley reminds us that the "Baratarians were well-trained cannoneers," and as such, they were placed at strategic positions to shore up the city's defenses.[9] The Laffite flints are also widely regarded as an essential element of the American victory. While much was made about the Americans' lack of necessary weapons, when it came time for battle, Jackson had everything he needed to succeed, thanks in large part to Laffite.[10] Then there is a whole spectrum of opinions about how involved or removed Jean and Pierre Laffite were from the actual battle. Groom gives Jean a great deal of credit, which we think is deserved. Davis, on the other hand, downplays the role of the Baratarians a lot more than other sources, claiming they comprised only 50 of the 5,000 soldiers at Jackson's disposal.[11] Where Davis does give the Laffites credit is in their service as a "moral force" that likely persuaded the locals to join the effort in larger numbers.[12]

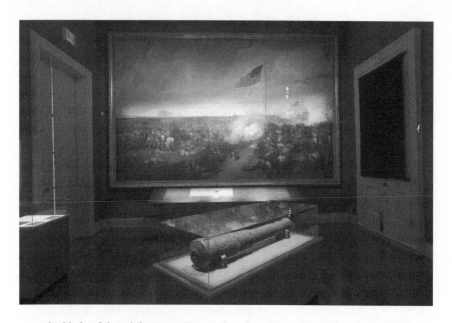

A highlight of the exhibit From "Dirty Shirts" to Buccaneers: The Battle of New
Orleans in American Culture *at the Cabildo is this gorgeous painting of the battle scene.*
Courtesy of Louisiana State Museum

It does not appear that Jean Laffite was on the front lines. Groom contends that he "was returning from an inspection of his stores of powder and
flints at the Temple" when the battle ended, and he arrived not knowing
which side was victorious.[13] However, we did read several accounts from
widows attempting to claim pensions for their deceased husbands years after the battle that indicated Jean Laffite was there.[14] In the days after the
Americans won the decisive battle, Latour biographer Jean Garrigoux says
Livingston was the one who negotiated the terms of surrender with the
British, and Latour ran reconnaissance of the bayous to make sure English
troops were actually pulling out of town.[15]

The feeling of victory on the streets of New Orleans after the improbable American triumph must have been absolutely incredible. On January
21, 1815, Jackson publicly thanked Jean and Pierre Laffite and all of the
Baratarians for their assistance. Then a grand parade and ball at the French
Consulate were held on January 23. The infamous ball has been responsible
for all kinds of mythmaking about Jean Laffite. He was in attendance, and
apparently many of the dignitaries and influential families did not welcome
his presence. Garrigoux claims it was only "after Jackson and Claiborne ap-

A visit to Jackson Square at sunset is the perfect way to conclude your New Orleans day. Notice the statue of the victorious Andrew Jackson on horseback in the center of the square. This piece is just one of many ways the city remembers the valiant efforts of "Old Hickory."

proached the corsair and warmly shook his hand, it was recounted, did the other guests hasten to do the same."[16] Gayarré's article includes the critically important letter Jackson wrote to Jean Laffite dated January 23, 1815, that demonstrates the general's level of gratitude and his feeling of indebtedness for all the Baratarians offered:

> Before I leave the City, I do an act of justice, and at the same time one very agreeable to my feelings, to state the services you have rendered during the late Invasion of your country. Gen'l [John] Coffee has communicated to me that on the 23rd of December your personal courage in action was not less conspicuous, than the judgment with which you availed yourself of your local knowledge in advising the proper position of the troops. From that time, to the end of the campaign, I have had frequent occasions to avail myself of your activity and zeal for the service which always was exerted with the utmost cheerfulness and with the most beneficial effect, sometimes in very hazardous expeditions. Considering you, Sir, as one of those to whom the country is most indebted on the late trying occasion, I feel great pleasure in giving this testimony of your worth, and to add the sincere assurance of my private friendship and high esteem.[17]

Once pardoned by President Madison on February 6, Jean and Pierre Laffite could again walk about the city freely, and Jean now had the glowing written recommendation of a future president in his pocket.

Jackson's performance sealed his status among the ranks of America's finest war heroes. Interestingly, statues, monuments, and paintings immortalizing Jackson are visible everywhere one turns in New Orleans, even to this day. However, aside from the names on the Lafitte Blacksmith Shop and the Jean Lafitte National Historic Park and Preserve Visitor Center in the French Quarter, visitors have to look fairly intently to find any acknowledgement of Jean Laffite's significance to the city. In fact, on our first visit to the French Quarter, we were shocked to see very little trace of him anywhere. What little public recognition of Laffite that exists today in New Orleans and surrounding areas has a lot to do with myths of piracy and buried treasure and very little to do with the fact that he assisted the city in such a significant way.

The reason for that might be due to a major fall from grace after the Battle of New Orleans that quickly overtook any glory the citizens might have felt compelled to bestow upon him. It is true that many people continued to be suspicious of his character even after his support with the Battle of New Orleans. There were people who did not like him before, and his assistance with the military effort did nothing to change that. But for many whose minds about Laffite were changed after his war contribution, they were again suspicious of him after Patterson and Ross began auctioning (for their own profit, we might add) the seized goods from the Baratarian raid back in September of the previous year. Several participants in the auction were able to identify items as having belonged to a New Orleans woman whose ship disappeared on the way to Europe and was never heard from again. Her grim fate was assumed to have been sealed by pirates, and there on the auction block were her things—having last been in the possession of Jean Laffite in Barataria. Any of the hundreds of pirates operating anywhere between the Gulf, the Caribbean, and Europe could have been responsible for her demise, but to the people of New Orleans, that did not matter. Jean Laffite was the easy target for their ire.

The Laffites were once again in a sticky situation. With their fame from the battle waning, they were still faced with the reality that their island hideout had been burned, their stores and their fleet had been seized, and they were out the money for the flints they donated to the war effort. As the Laffites' lawyer, Livingston began working to try to recover their seized wealth. Another attorney, John Grymes, resigned his post as district attorney and joined the Laffite legal team. These efforts most likely required that the Laffites pay substantial sums in bribery money, placing a further strain on their near-empty pockets. Despite the legal wrangling and the case going all the way to Washington, the government never relented, and the Laffites never got their full value back, nor were they compensated for the flints. As a side note, this will not be the last mention of Livingston's assistance in aiding the Laffites. A much later account of Livingston's involvement proved to be a moment of high drama in our research and a pivotal point of fact.

The combined indignity of these circumstances at the end of the war had to be overwhelming. Jean Laffite had the opportunity to double-cross the American government and take the British offer, but he did not. He was insulted when officials rebuffed his bid to help, but yet he persevered. Now his reputation was thoroughly ruined, he had no base camp to continue his operations (and setting up shop anywhere near New Orleans was out of the question), and it is up for debate about how much money he had left. He was at a crossroads. The path he chose was nothing short of stunning, with implications that would echo in Texas, Mexico, Cuba, Spain, and beyond.

CHAPTER FOUR

THE EMPEROR AND THE BROTHERHOOD

To fully understand the complexities of the early nineteenth-century landscape in which Jean Laffite operated, one must recognize two critically important power dynamics at play on the world stage: passionate sentiments about the exile and potential reclamation of glory by Napoleon Bonaparte and the worldwide power grip of the Freemasons. While these two forces were not necessarily linked, their complementary relationship certainly allowed each to reinforce the other.

LOYALTY TO THE EMPEROR

There is no need here to rehash Napoleon's biography, but a few details are exigent as they intersect with many of the characters in our story and several of the personalities who are still to come. Born in 1769, Napoleon made a name for himself as a critic of the elite and a champion of the poor during the French Revolution. After seizing power in France, he was eventually named emperor and served in that role from 1804–1814 and then again for the short span in 1815 known famously as the Hundred Days, a timeframe that paralleled the rise to prominence of Jean Laffite as well.

This "death mask" is reported to capture the Emperor Napoleon Bonaparte's face shortly after his death in 1821 on the island of St. Helena. It is currently housed in the collection of the Louisiana State Museum.

Napoleon negotiated the Louisiana Purchase with the United States in 1803, selling more than 800,000 square miles of land and opening the gateway for Western expansion for the bargain basement price of $15 million. The land in question had been under French control beginning in 1699 before it was granted to Spain in 1762 (as part of the treaty ending the Seven Years' War), with France reclaiming it in 1800. American politicians were fully invested in buying the Louisiana Territory because controlling the Mississippi River and the port in New Orleans was becoming vital to American commerce, particularly with cotton exploding in the international marketplace. At the time of the Louisiana Purchase, France was overextended due to a long history of wars and subsequent debt. Ironically, the $15 million was never paid but only applied to the balance of France's debt. In December 1803, all of Louisiana fell permanently into American hands.[1]

Perhaps the most fascinating component of Napoleon's character is the level of devotion he somehow managed to inspire in the men who served with him directly on the battlefield and even in those who simply believed in the cause of improving life for the French lower class. For French citizens, their passion for Napoleon never wavered even years after the emperor fell from his throne. As for the soldiers, many of them exhibited the same willingness to lay their lives on the line in defense of Napoleon's honor even off the battlefield and after many, many years had passed from their time of active duty. For these troops, Napoleon's banishment to the island of Elba in 1814, his second banishment to Saint Helena (out in the absolute middle of nowhere off the African coast in the South Atlantic) in 1815 after his defeat at Waterloo, and his death on May 5, 1821 were crushing blows to their enduring hope that one day he might return to his rightful position as emperor. In *The Bonapartes in America,* Clarence Macartney and Gordon Dorrance point out that "Napoleon's death in 1821 forever put an end to the dreams and the plots of his followers in America to rescue him from his prison and place another crown on his head. So great had he been to them that it did not seem possible that any prison could hold him."[2] For some, his passing was devastating. The man who they had risked their lives to follow would never be able to bring their collective dreams to fruition.

This hope that Napoleon could somehow regain his position manifested itself in two ways in our story. The first was in the organization of settlements on American soil that included hundreds of exiles from the French Revolution who escaped to save their lives but also with hopes of regrouping as an army. The second was in the rescue plots, some designed by the settlers and some crafted externally, to free Napoleon from captivity. "As long as Napoleon lived," Macartney and Dorrance explain, "the possibility of his escape to the United States was in the minds of all his old officers and followers, many of whom had already found asylum there."[3] The history of these settlements is extraordinarily interesting, especially so because many of the groups organized with a specific plan of action in mind once Napoleon was rescued. Some plots involved Napoleon fighting Spain and taking over Mexico. Many felt a big enough army might be able to gain a stronghold in South America. It was the belief of others that the almost completely undeveloped territory of Texas could be the site of Napoleon's new kingdom. Still others envisioned a regrouping of forces in North America that could be relaunched back into Europe for a triumphant return to the homeland.

Some of these plots were bizarre, including one that planned to use submarines at a time when that technology was not evolved enough to be safe, let alone effective. Other plots to relocate Napoleon in North America seemed much more plausible. During the time before his abdications when Napoleon suspected that his time in power might be coming to an end, he had already contemplated the move stateside. It was apparently a well-known fact among the emperor's inner circle that he ultimately wanted to get his whole family out of Europe. Murat claims that establishing a new territory was not necessarily on his agenda but that instead, "together with the famous scientist, Gaspard Monge, he planned to study the flora, fauna, and climate of the North American continent"[4] as an amateur naturalist. In essence, he wanted to retire.

The Vine and Olive Colony

This retirement is not what the French exiles from his army wanted, however, and their strategy in advance of his anticipated deliverance from Saint Helena was to form settlements in uninhabited parts of North America where they could live and where Napoleon could potentially land once one of the various rescue operations was complete. Former French General Charles Lallemand, who served with Napoleon, was imprisoned in Malta after Napoleon's final exile, but he escaped and managed to get to the United States. In 1816 his team coordinated with the US government to take over several undeveloped towns for their proposed settlements. The group arrived to settle the Vine and Olive Colony in Alabama—named so because they planned to grow olives and grapes—in 1817. Among the settlers was Count Charles Lefebvre-Desnouettes, whose name will factor into our story later.

The colony did not succeed—mainly because the land was not suited for the crops they wanted to harvest. Macartney and Dorrance claim even though he was "president of the Society for the Cultivation of the Vine and the Olive, [Lallemand] never went himself to Alabama. He had a grander project in mind than vineyards and olive trees on the banks of the Tombigbee River."[5] That grander project was Champ d'Asile.

The Champ d'Asile Colony

Meaning "Field of Asylum" or "Field of Refuge," Champ d'Asile was a settlement on the Trinity River in Texas founded by roughly twenty members of the Vine and Olive Colony in 1818 that later grew to around four hundred members. The original purpose of the colony was threefold: A) to provide a strategic position when either Napoleon or his brother Joseph were able to join them and thus have a conducive geographical location to fight the Spanish in Mexico and possibly take over that territory; B) to gather military forces all in one place for training; and C) to mount a mission to Saint Helena to rescue the emperor.

When the initial settlers arrived in the spring of 1818, they pulled into Galveston—which at the time was occupied by none other than Jean Laffite and his band of merry men numbering approximately one thousand. As we will learn, Laffite, after having been run out of Barataria, set up his new headquarters in Texas. Some of the French exiles were alarmed when they got there and realized they had fallen in with buccaneers with such tarnished reputations. Macartney and Dorrance report one of the settlers described Laffite and his men as

> freebooters gathered from among all the nations of the earth and determined to put into practice the traditions of the buccaneers of old. They gave themselves up to the most shameless debauchery and disgusting immorality, and only their chief, by his extraordinary strength and indomitable resolution, had the slightest control over their wild and savage natures. Thanks to him, the pirates became harmless neighbors to the exiles, with whom they often exchanged marks of political sympathy, crying amiably, "Long Live Liberty."[6]

Whether all the recently landed French exiles liked their new friends or not, they needed their help, as they were about to disembark into the harsh environment of the Texas wilderness alone. They needed boats, and Laffite provided them. One of the boats got stuck on a sandbar, and Laffite's men

Sitting handsomely on the corner of Chartres and St. Louis Streets, Napoleon's House is now a lovely restaurant and bar. In the time of Jean Laffite, it was intended by French exiles to be the house for the emperor himself once he was rescued from his imprisonment.

came to their rescue and gave them a push. Their troubles did not end there. On the way to the settlement site, they were hit by a huge storm. They ran out of food. They were not at all prepared for the climate. They did not know what to eat from the land and what would make them sick. A massive hurricane pummeled their camp. And so they abandoned the settlement after just a few months there, some of the settlers returning to Galveston with others dispersing.

While history may make it seem like the Champ d'Asile settlers showed up and happened to find Jean Laffite and company in Galveston, the truth is that their meeting was no accident, as Laffite and Lallemand had been in communication about the settlement. And as we will explore later, Laffite was in Galveston for more than just pirating. He was involved in an incredibly sophisticated web of international intrigue involving many countries and likely influenced by Masonic goals, a network so elaborate and secretive the depths of it may never be fully known.

While these settlements temporarily provided space for Napoleon's men to congregate and wait, there were numerous simultaneous designs by many outside factions to physically rescue Napoleon from his exile in Saint Helena. If you ever have an afternoon free, it is worth a few hours to read about all of the plots and actual attempts to free him from captivity. Some of these proposed escape maneuvers were fantastical and clearly not feasible. However, some of the plans seem quite reasonable and are fascinating (though they are largely not acknowledged in the scholarship), especially considering how many of them have names like *Laffite* and *Lallemand* attached to them.

There were active plots in New Orleans to contrive a rescue scenario that would bring the emperor to the Crescent City. Many suggest Dominique You, other Laffite pirates, and maybe even Jean Laffite himself were the masterminds behind this plot. Several sources point out that Laffite had always been a passionate supporter of Napoleon and was not ashamed for that fact to be public knowledge. This group was so sure of its success that it built a grand home designed specifically for the emperor. However, they never carried out the plot because Napoleon was reported to have died right before the ship was to set sail on its voyage.

Rumors of plots also ran wild in Philadelphia, where Joseph Bonaparte had found refuge. Joseph managed to make it out of Europe under the fake name "Bouchard" after Napoleon abdicated for the second time in 1815. After coming into port in New York, Joseph settled in Philadelphia, where he ran interference for the cause as much as possible in hopes that his brother could be saved. Many plots aimed to find another kingdom elsewhere in the world for Joseph Bonaparte to take over and rule. The trip Laffite took to Philadelphia in 1815, which will be explored in Chapter Five, is incredibly suspect within this context.

Another thread of the Napoleon rescue mythology involves a plot by a son of Marshal Ney, Napoleon's beloved general, who will re-enter our timeline in a big way in Chapter Fourteen.

And then there are the stories about Laffite actually carrying out the rescue of Napoleon himself. Though this seems far-fetched, this part of the Louisiana folklore is still quite striking. Murat's articulation of one of the narratives provides a good synopsis:

According to this legend, the famous pirate set off one day aboard the *Comète*, the fastest of his ships, for St. Helena. Pierre Laffite, his brother and accomplice, arrived at the same time at the port of Jamestown on a schooner flying the Spanish flag and landed a Malaysian slave who, one stormy night, managed to convey the escape plan to Napoleon! Napoleon followed instructions; at seven o'clock on the evening of February 28, 1819, he sat, wearing his largest greatcoat, with the collar turned up, on a cliff overhanging the sea. In the shadows someone—Jean Laffite—tugged at his sleeve, then slid a big wooden cross into the coat and put the hat on top of it, while Napoleon glided away, replaced by his dummy. . . . With much difficulty and emotion, Napoleon arrived aboard the *Comète*. But at the end of the voyage he fainted away across the carriage of a cannon, spat blood, and died without saying a word. Jean Laffite buried him in the place he had chosen for his own grave.[7]

Other sources claim the plot did not involve a dummy, but that Laffite left a man who looked like Napoleon as a double and that is actually who died in his place in 1821. According to this dubious version of events, the grave is supposedly somewhere in the Barataria swamp. One name associated with this double theory is Francois Eugene Robeaud. The claim is that Robeaud actually died on Saint Helena on May 5, 1821, not Napoleon.

Over the years, folks have twisted the Laffite rescue theory and spun it to involve a place called Berthoud Cemetery outside New Orleans. Some in the area allege this graveyard actually holds the tombs of Jean Laffite, John Paul Jones (the great Revolutionary War commander), and Napoleon all side by side. The proponents of this theory claim that at some point Jones joined the Laffite pirates and that is how he came to be buried in that spot. The problem, as Saxon, Dreyer, and Tallant point out, is that Jones died in 1792 before Laffite actually became a pirate.[8]

Naysayers may point out that with the incredible security by British forces set to guard Napoleon at Saint Helena, escape would have been out of the question. We argue that such a plot would have been challenging but not impossible, especially considering the number of people seriously working on multiple plots, the amount of money they had access to, and the number of people all over the world (including likely on the island of Saint Helena) who were sympathetic to Napoleon's cause. One also must consider the fact that there may have been another potent force applied to the situation—a group that had a proven track record of rescuing people under seemingly impossible circumstances.

THE FREEMASONS

It is abundantly clear that Napoleon's grip on his followers was astonishing in its strength and that the energies of his believers—when properly harnessed—had the potential to be an incredibly influential source of power. Running parallel to this narrative, though, is an equally powerful pulse— one made even more significant by the fact that many if not most of the men who were unflinchingly devoted to the reemergence of Napoleon's power were also Freemasons.

The Freemasons are a fascinating secret society, chiefly because they are a global presence while also lacking a worldwide governing body. Organized instead in Grand Lodges or Grand Orients by country or even by state, Freemasonry has survived hundreds of years of turmoil, cataclysmic internal feuds, and subsequent splits and external attacks from the Anti-Masonic political party organized in the 1820s as a protest against the stronghold of power and money that the Freemasons exercised in every facet of public and private life worldwide. The Freemasons' scope and reach cannot adequately be put into words. In *Revolutionary Brotherhood: Freemasonry and the Transformation of the American Social Order,* Steven C. Bullock contends Masonry had its "greatest power and prestige from 1790–1826."[9] Jean Laffite—even if not an official member of the Brotherhood—would have certainly been cognizant of its force and would have been unlikely to get anywhere in the world of business without some connection to it.

There is no physical proof that Napoleon was a Freemason, though many scholars feel very strongly that he likely was. Freemasonry certainly thrived in France while he was in charge, but that does not necessarily mean that surge in growth can be attributed to Napoleon officially being part of the fold. We know for sure that Joseph Bonaparte was a high-ranking Freemason, and some even say Napoleon teased him for it. Most of the men who surrounded Napoleon—including his dear friend and general Marshal Ney—were also Freemasons. It appears that even if Napoleon was not a Freemason, he knew how to manipulate the network of Freemasonry to his advantage. Suffice it to say, if we were handed evidence today that suggested the Freemasons successfully rescued Napoleon from Saint Helena and left a double in his place, we would view that as a totally plausible outcome.

New Orleans in the early decades of the nineteenth century was one of the most prominent cities for Freemasonry in the United States. In *Outline of the Rise and Progress of Freemasonry in Louisiana,* James B. Scot presents an overview of the synergy of the Brotherhood in the Crescent City. He says that up until 1812, every lodge in the state of Louisiana—twelve in all—was located in New Orleans or very close to the city. Jean Laffite could have been a Freemason in any one of these lodges. Unfortunately for outside researchers trying to find answers, representatives of the Grand Lodge of Louisiana are very tight-lipped about any Laffite connection.

While Freemasonry was proliferating at this time in America, it was under stress due to the War of 1812. Glen Greene explains in *Masonry in Louisiana: A Sesquicentennial History 1812–1962* that "about the time the Grand Lodge was organized in New Orleans, the War of 1812 began; critical events soon tested the effectiveness of the organization as well as the solidarity, loyalty, and dedication of its members."[10] As we saw in Chapter Three, the conflict brought Claiborne, Livingston, Jackson, and a number of significant figures together with the unified goal of protecting the United States. The fact that *all* of these men were Freemasons is critically important. Claiborne was a Brother before the Grand Lodge of Louisiana was even formed, and he eventually joined Perfect Union Lodge #1 in New Orleans.[11] Bullock describes Livingston as "one of the oldest [Masonic] brothers in Andrew Jackson's cabinet" and mentions Livingston served in New York as a Masonic deputy grand master.[12] Greene describes Jackson as "a great Mason [who] had many Masonic friends in New Orleans. He had become a Mason about the year 1800. Later, just prior to his election as president, he served two terms, beginning in 1822, as Grand Master of the Grand Lodge of Tennessee."[13] The Freemasons were firmly in control of New Orleans when the British began stalking the city. Greene clarifies that "the British machinations, which ran counter to Masonic sympathies in New Orleans, met with rebuffs as they sought to subvert the Creoles and to win over to their side the Lafittes and their Baratarian confederates."[14]

It is astounding to consider how much of an impact a secret society could have on a war, a government, or the trajectory of a country, but Freemasonry during this time period was in a position to shape even the most powerful and seemingly independent entities in the world. As we will see in the next chapter, the Brotherhood was not the only hand controlling the gears of the international machine.

CHAPTER FIVE

ARSÈNE LATOUR AND THE WEB OF INTRIGUE

The written record of Jean Laffite during the early 1800s paints an undeniable picture of a man whose fortunes did not rise in a vacuum. To fully understand the breadth of his power in the workings of the Gulf nations during this time, it will be helpful to explore the pivotal personal relationships that made it all possible. These relationships were with men of economic, social, political, and cultural influence, and the list of names reads like a nineteenth-century Gulf of Mexico *Who's Who*.

While many of those connections involved Laffite working in concert and sometimes behind the backs of many of these men, his relationship with French architect, engineer, and surveyor Arsène Lacarrière Latour stands apart. Latour is a name that Laffite scholars know because of his participation in the Battle of New Orleans and his expedition with Laffite up the Arkansas River, which will be examined in this chapter, but his scope and impact on Laffite's life beyond that time have not been fully appreciated. In fact, one of the major turning points of our research was the discovery of Jean Garrigoux's 2017 biography of Latour, *A Visionary Adventurer: Arsène Lacarrière Latour 1778–1837*. Garrigoux's volume is still one that is likely not on the radar of most researchers, but its pages contain a wealth of new knowledge not only about Latour but also about Laffite as well.

The various accounts of Laffite's life would seem to indicate that he was truly loyal to very few people. Aside from Laffite's obvious loyalty to his brother, Pierre, his friendship with Latour seems to have been uncharacteristically devoid of any double-dealing. In fact, the case can be made that none of the Laffite relationships was more influential than his close friendship with Latour. Whether that influence was a result of Laffite's dedication or whether the loyalty was born of his recognition of the advantages it provided is hard to say, but our guess is that the friendship was true, and that the fidelity preceded the benefits. In actuality, both men were the winners.

Born in 1778 in Aurillac, France, Latour traveled to Saint-Domingue, the French colony where the Laffites capitalized on the slave insurrection. By the time Latour arrived in 1802, the situation had deteriorated significantly, and men like Jean and Pierre Laffite were using their ships to transport residents out of Saint-Domingue to safer locations. According to Gene A. Smith in the edited collection *Colonies to Countries in the North Caribbean: Military Engineers in the Development of Cities and Territories,*

> One story posits that Latour fled Saint Domingue for Cuba in late 1803 with [Lallemand] aboard a privateer. He supposedly remained with Lallemand in Havana for a short time before traveling on to Louisiana. . . . Even if Latour did not meet the Lafittes prior to his arrival in Havana, he probably did while in the Cuban city, which had become a hub for privateering activity.[1]

Scholars disagree on when Latour actually left the island and when he arrived in New Orleans, with dates ranging all through the first decade of the 1800s. History tells us that he fell into business with Barthélémy Lafon, who Garrigoux describes as a man "with many important contacts, not all above question. [Lafon] was involved in politics, various plots, and even armed a privateer—the *Carmelita*—which he occasionally commanded as its fighting skipper."[2] Lafon had also been in Saint-Domingue with Latour and likely escaped around the same time. As well, as a member of the Laffite posse, Lafon was captured by Louisiana officials during the Baratarian raid in 1814. The connections that bound these men began forming very early in the 1800s.

Both Lafon and Latour became friends with attorney Edward Livingston; Garrigoux reported Livingston actually helped Latour sell some Saint-Domingue property after his departure.[3] It appears that at least for Latour, his personal foray into the world of intrigue began quite early in his life, as he served as a spy for Napoleon in America from 1804–1814 and possibly ran surreptitious operations between Baton Rouge and the Big Easy from 1806–1810.[4]

As you have already seen, the Battle of New Orleans was pivotal in that it provided the Laffites a degree of legitimacy that Jean especially had craved. Latour, too, made a name for himself traveling with General Jackson as his engineer, which afforded the opportunity for him to write his still very important *Historical Memoir of the War in West Florida and Louisiana in 1814–15.* (Interestingly, Latour's book included a "Barataria" chapter in which he defends the Baratarians, pointing out they had legitimate commissions from places like Cartagena, Colombia, then under Spanish rule. While he acknowledges they were wrong in smuggling stolen goods, he says charging them as pirates without proof of them capturing ships was inappropriate. He goes so far as to blame the local government for its pathetic response to the Baratarian settlement.)[5] The outcome of the battle also ushered in a new wave of opportunity for those wealthy and powerful New Orleans businessmen whose financial futures now seemed brighter than ever. All of them were ambitious, and many of them were not afraid of back-door business. And as we know, they were all Freemasons. Garrigoux writes, "At the *Parfait Union* [Perfect Union] could be found a large number of persons— including, soon, a number of Americans—with whom Latour maintained excellent relations."[6] Latour, like Laffite, was thoroughly in the mix with all the major players.

To what degree the Freemasons were involved in the events that unfolded in the Gulf region we cannot say for sure, other than to note that they appear at critical junctures all along the way. This is not to say, however, that there is evidence of any lawless conduct associated with the group. To the contrary, their involvement appears most often to have been benevolent and helpful.

AN "ASSOCIATION" WITH AN AGENDA

As to the group of New Orleans businessmen who now found themselves facing the dawn of a new day that did not include the threat of a British invasion, common interests increasingly drew them toward a shared target— the wealth and influence of Spain and their potential to gain financially by going after it. Davis writes, "Never a formal organization, the 'association' had a fluid membership in which the constants were [Edward] Livingston, [Livingston's brother-in-law Auguste] Davezac, [John Randolph] Grymes, Abner Duncan, [Vincent] Nolte, Lafon, merchant John K. West, and of course the Laffite brothers.[7]

To advance these plans, which would take the form of various plots and schemes over the coming decade, the group sought the assistance of numerous revolutionaries who led, or attempted to lead, private armies in an effort to help Mexico gain independence from Spain. The exact location of the border between Texas and the United States was a matter of ongoing negotiations between Spanish and American officials anyway, which made the situation even more attractive for disruption. With as many potential new ports along the shores of the Gulf in play, to the mind of these insurgents (also known as filibusters), as well as to the mind of the "associates," Texas and Mexico were prizes well worth the trouble.

Although the "associates" contracted with others over the course of roughly five years between 1814 and 1819, two names stand out as they relate to Laffite. One is Jean Joseph Amable Humbert. A former commander in Napoleon's imperial guard, he came to North America in 1812 as a result of having asked Napoleon (now emperor of France) to send him over for the purposes of recruiting arms and men to go into Spanish territories and disturb them, thereby distracting Spain from trying to unseat Napoleon's brother, Joseph, from their throne and reinstate their own King Ferdinand II. However, once here, Humbert's military prowess failed to translate successfully. For one, he talked too much, eagerly spilling his own beans in far too many untrustworthy circles with the end result being that virtually every plan he ever conceived was accompanied by watchful Spanish eyes almost from the moment of its inception. Still, in the early years, Humbert managed to assemble a small army and attract the attention of men such as the "associates." At one point he even succeeded in naming Latour as one of his early officers,[8] though it does not appear that connection was very fruitful or long-lived. By the time Napoleon was ousted from power, most of the French exile community in the United States was concentrated in either Philadelphia or Baltimore. Within this community of Frenchmen, Humbert, who was now operating out of New Orleans, maintained many friends.

A second insurgent leader, José Álvarez de Toledo, also came into play as an operative for the group. Toledo was born in Cuba and led a military uprising against Spanish control of Texas that ultimately failed. Both Toledo and Humbert, separately and with the backing of the "associates," would become factors in the future of Jean Laffite—especially as it pertained to his second run of privateering in the Gulf at Galveston.

Padre Sedella

Other forces were also aligning at the same time, forces that looked in the *opposite* direction toward protecting Spain and her interests. This is the juncture at which the literature can become confusing, as multiple secret factions were operating in the same cities as competing groups while developing plans to control the same contested areas. In New Orleans, those forces included a man commonly referred to as Padre Sedella. The Padre was a shadowy figure that seemed to pop up just about everywhere, and he was known to be fiercely loyal to Spain. Along with former insurgent-turned-Spanish-spy Juan Mariano Bautista de Picornell, he coordinated closely with authorities in both Cuba and the United States, not the least of which was Luis de Onís, Spanish emissary to the United States by day and head of the Spanish spy service by night. And, notwithstanding his strong connections to many of the "associates," it appears that at some point right after the Battle of New Orleans, Latour began working with the Spanish as well. Many also speculate that the Laffites were in secret deals with Sedella before 1815.[9]

However, as the year 1815 drew to a close, the lines of demarcation between pro and anti-Spanish forces were still blurred and quite hard to delineate. It found the Laffite brothers in dire financial straits. Having won pardons from James Madison for all past deeds and infractions, they were nonetheless engaged in an ongoing and increasingly hopeless struggle to reclaim property seized from them during the raid on Barataria. What is more, they did not exactly have the option to head back down that way and pick up where they left off. The confluence of these two facts found the brothers between a rock and a very hard place.

Long before the eventual settlement of Galveston by the Laffites in 1817, Jean and Pierre had been looking to that island as their future—a Plan B, if you will. Having seen the writing on the wall at Barataria even before Patterson and Ross raided them in the fall of 1814, the Laffites, who were nothing if not street-smart, knew that they would eventually need a new base of operations. Preferably, that base would be just beyond the reach of American authorities who seemed increasingly hell-bent on making their lives miserable.

Now with the rise of new energy in New Orleans and the prospect of gainful (if not legal) employment by the "associates," the time seemed to be at hand. The Laffites began making preparations to outfit new ships in anticipation of their partnership but with an ultimate long view toward Galveston.

A TRIP NORTH

For his part, Jean decided to travel to Philadelphia, Baltimore, and Washington, DC. His public purpose was twofold: to purchase new equipment for the Laffite privateering enterprise, and, while there, make a last-ditch appeal directly to Madison to restore the property that was taken from him. The trip started in August 1815 in Philadelphia, with Laffite eventually traveling through Baltimore before his rodeo with the president.

Humbert and Laffite were acquainted by virtue of common circles in New Orleans and now by common interests with the "associates." In advance of the trip, Humbert, Napoleon's former soldier, provided him with introductions to contacts within the growing community of French exiles. Indeed, almost at the same time of Jean's visit, Joseph Bonaparte, now departed from the throne of Spain, arrived in New York. Along with his arrival, word of French subterfuge, plots to rescue Napoleon, plans for a new France on this side of the Atlantic—rumors that had already been circulating among the exiles—suddenly grew even more prevalent. The Philadelphia leg of the trip may have also included meetings related to a fascinating Freemason plot to make Cuba an American territory by inciting a slave insurrection there.[10]

Whether Laffite met with any of these displaced Frenchmen to discuss any of these various designs is unclear, but the likelihood is certainly there considering the political climate of the cities he visited on the trip. We also make note here of Laffite's ongoing connections with the French community (via Humbert, or the Philadelphia exiles, or the later failed French colony at Champ d'Asile fronted by another of Napoleon's ex-generals, the same Charles Lallemand who sailed from Saint-Domingue with Latour). Any blame that he may or may not have deserved for the failure of French efforts in North America could have been reason enough for the heated exchange that nearly came to blows between Marshal Michel Ney and Laffite (now known as Lorenzo Ferrer) on the streets of Lincolnton, North Carolina, many years later, an event that is detailed in Chapter Fifteen.

Returning to the subject of the trip, Livingston also provided a helpful Philadelphia connection, possibly because the Laffites were now aligned with the "associates," of which Livingston was an integral player, or possibly because he was now one of their attorneys.

Latour, on the other hand, was in Philadelphia in November of 1815 for the publicly stated purpose of checking progress on his book, copies of which were being printed there—with, of all people, Edward Livingston "acting as surety for their delivery."[11] However, a much more likely (but secret) purpose for Latour's trip had to do with his newly minted interest in helping the cause of Spain. We have no firm record of how many times Latour and Laffite came together during the several months of this trip, but we do know that at some point Latour must have advanced the notion of the Laffites going to work as spies for Spain. We also know that the two men met at least once with Onís, the aforementioned head of Spanish intelligence in the United States. The likely case that Latour made to Laffite centered around the fact that while the "associates" were well-funded, the insurgents were unpredictable, with a track record that was, so far, a mixed bag at best. Rather than beg trouble in that regard, Latour may have argued, why not consider another route that had the more reliable backing of Spain herself? Indeed, Davis writes, "Rather than risk themselves and their means on wild schemes of conquest, the Laffites could earn sure money by feeding Spain information on the insurgents' plans. With no vessels of their own at the moment, they were out of the privateering business, but they could reestablish their fleet with what they earned from Spain, who might even allow them to privateer as a cover for their espionage. In short, they might have it both ways."[12] Taken in concert with the brothers' long-term goal of a self-sufficient port they controlled, the route utilizing assistance from Spain obviously seemed like a less-risky straight shot to success and a much better deal, and Jean quickly agreed. Unbeknownst to either he or Latour, Pierre Laffite had come to the same agreement in New Orleans with Padre Sedella and Picornell. Jean and Pierre were now officially Spanish spies 13-A and 13-B.

Washington, DC

Jean Laffite's trip to Washington in December 1815 was a total belly-flop. His pleas to the Madison administration did absolutely no good. In short, the message to the Laffites since the end of the war had been that they should consider themselves lucky to get the pardon and move on down the road. Part of this attitude came from the local officials in New Orleans who were at that very moment sticking a tidy profit from the sale of those seized goods into their own pockets. Whatever the true reason, we know that Madison ignored the Laffites's pleas. And while Jean did make arrangements with a Baltimore ship's chandler for a new rig, the benefits of his trip in the fall of 1815 turned out to have come from something much more secretive. Looking back, it appears that Jean went north with a veritable "Open for Business" sign around his neck, available to the first taker, and the second, or both. And Arsène Latour was with him.

Small wonder, then, that historians view what came next as a mission of dual purposes, both of which would benefit Spain.

Laffite and Latour both returned to New Orleans in the winter of 1816 with plans to leave on an expedition up the Mississippi River into Arkansas. The purported reason was to map the territory on behalf of Spain, with Latour in his capacity as a surveyor and Laffite in his capacity as a navigator.

Bear in mind that for all anyone yet knew, the Laffites were still at the service of the "associates." Maintaining that front was paramount to their ability to funnel information about the insurgents to Spain, but it was also critical because most all of these men were long-standing business associates of the Laffites and would likely have them killed if they knew their moves were being reported to Spanish officials.

ARKANSAS RIVERBOATING

For both of those reasons, the Arkansas expedition of 1816 was billed as a surveying project with some potential gold prospecting on the side. The underlying purpose, though, had everything to do with reporting to Spain on the various areas of weakness and vulnerability on the country's increasingly important western boundaries. Spain wanted to know every bend in the river, every pass through the mountains, every possible encounter with un-inhabitable terrain or unnavigable waters—and—most importantly—they wanted to take the temperature of the people beginning to flood into those territories as settlers. Were they potential friends or foes? Their trip lasted eight months, and the resulting report given to the Spanish government by Latour is well-documented elsewhere. They traveled on the "Red, Sabine, Trinidad, Arkansas, and Colorado Rivers"[13] using aliases—*John Williams* for Latour and *Captain Hillare* for Laffite.

If not already cemented, it seems to us that the bond of friendship between Latour and Laffite was made permanent during this expedition. To our knowledge, there is no record from this time forward (if there ever was) of any sort of double-dealing between either Laffite or Latour. As you will see shortly, the friendship endured until very near the end of Latour's life in 1837—a statement that we do not make lightly in sight of the fact that most people believe Jean Laffite died way back before that.

Before we get there, however, we would also observe the importance of what Laffite learned about the upper Mississippi during this trip. When we first discovered Lorenzo Ferrer's paper trail in Mississippi (documentation that was the first and only evidence we found of him living anywhere on earth before arriving in North Carolina), we immediately wondered how someone as notorious as the pirate Jean Laffite could have pulled off a re-entry in that neck of the woods without recognition. While we will go into great detail about this theory in a future chapter, it is enough to say here that once we understood his relationship with Latour and the eight months they spent combing every nook, cranny, bayou, and bend of the Mississippi, it was clear to us that the land on both sides of the river would have been well known to Laffite, based on nothing more than the knowledge he gained during the year 1816. Did he make contacts during that trip who possibly aided, sustained, and shielded him from discovery fifteen years later? We do not know, but it is certainly possible. For this reason, we view the Arkansas expedition as having served a third purpose. It quite possibly created a literal road map for a man who, more than a decade later, would find himself in need of a new name and a place to hide.

As for the "associates," after casting their lot with unpredictable insurgents such as Humbert and Toledo, the pirate Louis-Michel Aury (sometimes spelled "De Aury" or "d'Aury" in historical sources), as well as Spanish revolutionary Francisco Xavier Mina, a man who had never supported the Spanish crown, their dreams of Spanish riches never came to fruition. For one thing, most all of the insurgents were victims in one way or another of self-destruction. Aury was a loner, a hot head, and a man who generally could not get out of his own way. Mina fared not much better. Therefore, in spite of the fact that the "associates" were the original backers of the Galveston settlement, and in spite of a mound of money and other resources aimed at taking that prize and others along the Texas coast, they eventually failed and gave up. The end of Mina signaled the virtual end of the "associates" as well.

A brief word is also in order about a man named William Mitchell. We insert him here simply for the purposes of letting you know that his specter may have resurfaced many years later in North Carolina. The theory is valid enough that his name is worth remembering. During the volatile years between 1810 and 1820, when plots, schemes, and alliances came and went as swiftly as a Gulf hurricane, Mitchell made a very bad name for himself. Pam Keyes's article "The True Tale of Mitchell, the Zombie Pirate" describes him as a horribly disfigured man, one who had endured all kinds of physical wounds from his work as a privateer, sometimes alone and sometimes in concert with the Laffites. In this capacity, he also engaged with the "associates" as a minor player, running a small fleet of privateers between New Orleans and Galveston. Mitchell, however legitimate his talents at privateering may have been, was, as we say in the South, batshit crazy. History records that he not only killed at will, but the manner of execution was often brutal and cruel in the extreme, and done seemingly for his own pleasure. How he avoided capture for murder (multiple times over) we are not sure, but we do know that he (not unlike Laffite in later years) is reported to have died not once but twice. The first report of his death at sea in 1821 turned out to be a farce when he showed up alive and well a few years later. Following that, he reportedly died—again—this time in Mobile, Alabama.[14] Afterward, he continued his reign of terror before vanishing from view around June 1841, *vanishing* as opposed to *dying*. Because of a later story as it relates to Laffite and his dealings with Mitchell both directly and indirectly, we make note of this man and ask that you remember his name.

As for Latour, sometime around 1818, he moved to Havana. According to Gene A. Smith in the edited collection *The Human Tradition in Antebellum America*, in Cuba Latour "continued his association with Lafitte, Lafon, and with French operatives such as [Lallemand]."[15] His placement there would become very important, as Jean Laffite was planning to relocate. Their friendship was far from over.

CHAPTER SIX

RECLAIMED GLORY AT GALVESTON

Most sources jump to 1817 when talking about Jean Laffite's transition to Galveston, Texas, like it was a clean break and a fresh start. In actuality, he had been dabbling in all kinds of Texas schemes at least as early as 1814 when he was still in Barataria. His connections with the "associates" meant that his hands were part of the secret collective constantly stirring pots all over the Gulf and well beyond. Good businessmen never become complacent and satisfied with their current means of income no matter how lucrative. Instead they plan for the eventuality that their industry will die or their market will dry up and continually keep their eyes on future opportunities for investment and growth. Some sources report that at least for a time Jean Laffite attempted to set up a new base in Port-au-Prince but was quickly run out of town. He had also scoped out Texas for quite some time and recognized the likelihood that he would eventually need a softer place to land.

Before Laffite got to Galveston, his predecessor, the French pirate Aury, was already in command of a band of buccaneers in a village there. Barker's article "The African Slave Trade in Texas" sets the stage:

> In the fall of 1816 . . . with some twelve or fifteen small vessels, of the self-styled republics of Mexico, Venezuela, La Plata and New Granada, he [Manuel Herrera, who had in 1813 been appointed Mexican minister to the United States] sailed to the island of Galveston and by the authority of his office as plenipotentiary of the Mexican republic, set up a government, in which Louis de Aury [*sic*], . . . sometime commandant-general of the naval forces of New Granada, was appointed governor, commander of the fleet, and judge of the court of admiralty. This extraordinary combination of powers De Aury wielded with the greatest facility and convenience: as governor of the province, he issued privateering commissions to his flotilla; swept the Gulf for Spanish merchantmen as commodore of the Mexican navy; and adjudicated the prizes of his own court of admiralty. He plied a

brisk business, and among the vessels captured off the coasts of the West
Indies were many fully laden slavers. The disposition of these unfortunate
cargoes became an urgent problem; for at Galveston there was no need of
them, and throughout the rest of Texas, inhabited as it then was, chiefly by
Indians, there was no better market. The difficulty was settled by some of
De Aury's recruits from the United States, who smuggled the negroes into
Louisiana and sold them even in the suburbs of New Orleans. Thus Texas
began her novitiate in the traffic as a kind of supply house for Louisiana.
Other than human merchandise, too, was introduced in this way; and per-
haps there was collusion between De Aury's men and the revenue officers.[1]

Essentially, Aury had set up an operation very much like Barataria in
Galveston, though selling merchandise (especially enslaved people) was much
more difficult due to the vast distance between the pirate base camp and the
nearest solid American market in New Orleans.

Make no mistake: Aury was not in control of Galveston by chance.
Everything that happened in Texas and throughout the Gulf was being carefully manipulated by the "associates." In fact, Jean Laffite was sent to Galveston
for two weeks in March of 1817 to meet with Aury about the group's plans.

Shortly thereafter, on April 5, Yoakum reports Aury left the settlement,
having "burnt and destroyed all the houses and cabins, leaving only an ad-
vice-boat and his collector, Pedro Rousselin."[2] Other writers suggest that
maybe the encampment was destroyed in a battle with a warring faction of
pirates. We found a copy of Jeff Modzelewksi's translation of Rubio Mañé's
The Pirates Lafitte in the Laffite Society files in the Sam Houston Regional
Library in Liberty, Texas. In it, Mañé suggests that there

> could have been a serious confrontation between d'Aury and Lafitte, dis-
> puting the rule of Galveston and perhaps going so far as combat. This
> incident perhaps happened in Matagorda, a port that d'Aury frequented
> and on the adjoining islet of which he had built some huts. Not only could
> the conflict have originated between these two corsair chiefs through an
> argument of the Galveston base, but also because Lafitte was in the service
> of the King of Spain and in New Orleans Fatio [authorized agent of Spain]
> had offered him one hundred thousand *pesos* if he took control of d'Aury's
> establishment at Galveston, where there functioned a sham government
> under the support of the Mexican insurgents.[3]

Days after Aury left, Jean Laffite took control of Galveston. Many
sources offer narratives of the takeover that depict it as a coup. Yoakum
claims Aury returned to Galveston May 10 to see "the Lafitte government

in 'full blast,' and his collector Rousselin occupying the same office in the new administration."[4] Subsequently, Aury "addressed a letter to . . . Herrera . . . dated July 21, 1817, informing him that he had for the present determined to abandon Galveston, that he had taken Rousselin the collector with him, and that all proceedings there after the 31st of July would be without his consent. He addressed a similar letter to Beverly Chew, the collector at New Orleans, on the 28th of the month."[5] This letter was clearly intended to wash Aury's hands of any liability should future calamity ensue, and chances were good that it would.

In contrast, the Laffite overthrow was carefully orchestrated by outsiders and therefore not just a power grab. Davis argues the switch in leaders was necessary because "Aury had been disavowed by the 'associates,' who were now backing the Laffites."[6] We likely only know a tiny fraction of the influence this group actually exerted in the early development of Texas, but we suspect it was significant.

While Laffite's starting crew in Galveston was initially quite small, word quickly spread throughout the Caribbean that the pirate lord was back on the throne in a new kingdom, and his former Baratarians began to reconvene. Many estimate that his army was in the hundreds, while others are bold enough to argue he may have had over one thousand men under his command once again.

Like Aury before him, Laffite claimed allegiance to the Mexican republic and set up his own government, choosing the role of governor for himself. He put some familiar faces in charge, including Lafon, who became his deputy. His new realm was christened as *Campeche*, and he quickly set to work rebuilding a livable village after the destruction that befell the island upon Aury's departure. Most importantly, Laffite built a fine house for himself and painted it candy apple red, a structure thereafter known as *Maison Rouge,* the French term for "red house." According to Eleanor Barton, the curator for the Rosenberg Library, Maison Rouge stood at 1417 Harborside Drive in Galveston, a piece of property that currently includes the ruins of the Hendricks House, which was built by sea captain F. W. Hendricks around 1870. The house, which is also known as "Hendricks Castle" or "The House of Twelve Gables," was torn down in the 1950s.[7] The ruins that remain are of that structure, not of Maison Rouge as some people report. Laffite's red house was completely destroyed before he left Galveston Island. In any event, put a pin in the name Maison Rouge because it will factor into our story in a significant way in Chapter Eight.

The community Laffite built in Galveston mirrored the village he established in Barataria. Campeche was its own functioning town, and surpris-

ingly, women settled there. It is known that Laffite enjoyed female compan-
ionship during his Texas years. Just like all the reports from everywhere he
lived as an adult, he had with him in Galveston a gorgeous octoroon woman,
one whose striking beauty was noted by visitors to Campeche.

The Laffites refused to let the geographical challenge related to the distance between their base and their market in New Orleans thwart their business. Head explains that "at some point, buyers must have balked at the
travel time, since the Laffites built a temporary shelter for slaves near the
Sabine River, inside the so-called Neutral Ground, a zone between Louisiana
and Texas claimed by both Spain and the United States."[8] Enslaved people and merchandise were also shuttled into New Orleans through similar
backchannels that were utilized under the Barataria model. Barker speculates most of the purchases in New Orleans were conducted by agents, and
then the enslaved people were delivered, though some buyers wanted personal inspections and came to Galveston.[9] During these years, Pierre Laffite
stayed in New Orleans to act as the broker. The operation required someone
to maintain business contacts there so that sales could be expedited. The
Laffites were also still on the rolls as Spanish spies, and their positions in
different locations (Pierre covering New Orleans and Jean watching Texas)
were advantageous.

Some of Jean's most consistent customers were the famous Bowie brothers: James, John, and Resin. James, of course, is Jim Bowie of Bowie knife/
Sandbar Battle/Alamo notoriety. The Bowies, who were land speculators and
slave traders, hooked into the Laffite operation and applied their own cun-
ning twist to maximize profits:

> Shortly after the War of 1812, Jean Laffite transferred his base to Galveston
> Island, and there the Bowies went to buy Negroes at the standard rate of
> one dollar per pound. Under the law, when Negroes smuggled into the
> United States were discovered by government officials, they were sold at
> auction. Any informer who brought about their discovery was to be re-
> warded with half the proceeds of the sale. This law was the cornerstone
> of the Bowie scheme. After bringing a coffle of bewildered Africans across
> the Sabine River, the Bowies took them to a point near a United States
> Marshal's station, left them tethered in the woods, and became the in-
> formers. The United States Marshal—and one suspects that he connived
> at this chicanery—then held an auction as the law demanded. At this legal
> sale in the wilderness the Bowies were the only bidders. They bought the
> Negroes at a low price, received half that price as the reward for informing
> on themselves, and, most important of all, got to sell the negroes anywhere
> in the United States where slavery was legal.[10]

US officials in the Texas backcountry might have been amused, but the tax collectors and port officials in New Orleans were not smiling. They had mistakenly believed the raid on Barataria in 1814 was enough to stop smugglers from circumventing their system. Revenue officers like Chew launched a vendetta against the Laffites and did everything they knew to thwart Campeche's success.

Chew had legitimate reasons to have his feathers ruffled. The Laffite fleet was absolutely killing Spanish commerce in the Gulf, the peak of their Galveston success coming in 1818. Jean and Pierre were becoming rich again, and the New Orleans market was once again flooded with Laffite contraband. After the Baratarian utopia collapsed and the fleet and warehouse goods were confiscated and after Jean and Pierre realized the US government was never going to repay them for their service, they were clearly in a precarious financial position. The calculated move to relocate to Galveston, and the profits they earned just a year after the move, had the potential to put them right back on top.

But just like Barataria, the scheme was too good to continue without interference. The first blow was a wicked hurricane in September 1818 that leveled Campeche and scared the bejesus out of the Champ d'Asile settlers, who were already on their last leg. Laffite and his men immediately began to rebuild their settlement afterward, but they never got back on their feet fully. It was around this time, too, that Laffite was reportedly beginning to lose control over his men. While he claimed his privateering fleet only preyed on Spanish interests, one of his crews was caught attacking an American ship. Responding the best way he knew to emphasize his leadership when rumors of mutiny were circulating, Laffite decided to hang the responsible captain. Shortly thereafter, though, another Laffite-sanctioned crew attacked an American vessel, which trained the eyes of the US government firmly on Campeche.

The prospect of intervention at Galveston by US officials was extremely convoluted, the nuances of which involved multiple powerful nations, double agents, and a pirate army. Parsons writes, "Spanish diplomacy kept the United States from molesting [Laffite's] little kingdom, as the Spanish Minister to the United States, Luis de Onís, feared that if the United States Navy should dispossess Lafitte of Galvez-town it might be indisposed to surrender it back to Spain (as the boundary was still undetermined between the two countries). Also, it is now revealed that Lafitte was playing the game of triple-cross with Spain, the insurgents of Texas, and the Americans."[11] However, the tenuous protection this situation offered for Laffite was shattered when America and Spain settled the dispute and Texas was firmly in the grasp of the Americans. Only then was the United States in a position to act.

The heat was applied on February 27, 1820, when the USS *Enterprise* with Lieutenant Lawrence Kearney arrived to have a talk with Laffite at his Galveston clubhouse. The American government weighed its military options against Campeche and made it clear that Laffite and his men had to vacate. Kearney cruised through to make sure Laffite was packing his things and readying for departure.

J. O. Dyer's "Jean Laffite in 1820" includes a section called "Dinner with Lafitte" that describes the elegant dinner Kearney and his men enjoyed with the buccaneer during their visit. Dyer's writing also puts an interesting twist on the predominant theory that Laffite was forced out of Galveston by US officials, suggesting that he was looking for a way to extricate himself from a potential overthrow by his own men. Dyer explains,

> Laffite . . . had informed the United States collector of revenue at New Orleans of the probability that the men in the [Galveston] camp would mutiny and take up piracy. It was probably a present sent to the collector at New Orleans which saved the lives of Laffite and of his officials, for a revenue cutter was sent to San Louis Island [*sic*], and while written history has it that Laffite was coerced into evacuating the island the hitherto unpublished history contained in material gathered by the writer would indicate not only willingness on the part of the Laffite officials, but a desire for United States intervention to save their faces and enable them to get away from their turbulent and mutinous forces.[12]

At the same time that the clock was expiring on Campeche, the Laffites learned they had been dumped by the Spanish as spies.[13] In the moment of their Galveston departure, the picture for the Laffites was about as bleak as it had ever been. The world was changing, and the landscape of piracy was shifting perilously close to extinction. When Laffite pulled away from Campeche for the last time on his cherished *Pride* in May 1820, having set the whole place afire, he adjusted his compass for yet another new horizon.

CHAPTER SEVEN

THE (FAKE) DEATH
OF A PIRATE

After the May 1820 departure from Galveston, Jean and Pierre Laffite and their remaining loyal men were on walkabout in the Gulf. They apparently still visited the area's islands from time to time, but most sources place both Jean and Pierre in the Yucatan Peninsula (in the vicinity of Isla Mujeres), some even suggesting they made a base there and had homes. There were reports too that the Laffites might try to settle in Charleston. Pierre even turned up there trying to use the alias "Mr. Francisco" in 1820 and was recognized.[1]

The year 1820 also marked another critical turning point for the Laffite business model when Congress declared that illegal slave trading was a violation of piracy law and thus punishable by death.[2] There was no time for the brothers to set up another thriving empire, even if they had been willing to take a chance. Then, Pierre Laffite died from fever in November 1821 in Mexico while Jean was away. He was said to have been buried in a town called Dzilam de Bravo on the northern tip of the peninsula halfway between Mérida and Cancún. No known conspiracy theories exist concerning his demise, so it appears that his was that rare case of a pirate who was truly dead once his passing was reported.

Most of the subsequent pings for Jean Laffite place him in Cuba. In early 1822, he was captured by Cuban officials while trying to come into port to collect a ransom from a ship he had commandeered off Jamaica.[3] Jailed for weeks in Porto Principe, he became ill (or more likely faked an illness) and was transferred to a local hospital, where, as luck would have it, he escaped on February 13, 1822. It was said that when exiting the hospital room Laffite "[left] his handcuffs hanging on the back of the door as an insult,"[4] a flourish that sounds exactly like the man who drew up a wanted poster with double the reward for the Louisiana governor to counteract the one issued for him.

Without his brother and with traditional piracy running out of daylight in a Gulf that was now much more well managed by international officials, it appears Laffite began to get a little sloppy—and desperate. It is truly remarkable that throughout all his seafaring days from Barataria onward, it was never actually proven that he was responsible for capturing an American vessel. However, in April 1822, that changed when he seized an American ship called the *Jay* off the Cuban coast. American officials were on the case and arrested Laffite a few days later. Then, inconceivably, they made the decision to turn him over to Cuban authorities—the same Keystone Cops who two months earlier had allowed him to escape from the hospital. You have probably already guessed that Laffite escaped custody once again.

He scooted down to Colombia, where he was declared an official privateer. Davis explains that by this time in 1822,

> most of the surviving old corsairs who had not become outright pirates had been commissioned regular navy officers for Colombia, their vessels nationalized as public property. Jean's notoriety spoke for itself. A commission from Colombia would give him legitimacy and protection, and if he did not make his fortunes from prize goods by observing [Simón] Bolívar's rules, what he did at sea outside the gaze of officials could reward him handsomely.[5]

With his privateer status now granted, he returned to sea and began working the waters near Cuba and Florida. Garrigioux suggests Cuba in 1822 was a very hospitable place for Laffite to come inland because of friends like Latour who were in residence. Laffite may have even bought a house "in the area that is now Correa y Calzada street in the Jesus del Monte neighborhood."[6] Ironically, it does not look like all of Laffite's dealings with ships at sea during this time were piratical. In November 1822, newspapers and eyewitnesses reported that he served as an escort to help an American ship get through pirate-infested waters. Considering his personal connections with so many businessmen and his strong ties to Freemasonry, it is not beyond belief that Laffite discovered a friend in need on that vessel and felt obligated to assist.

THE DEATH HOAX

The vast majority of published scholars assert Jean Laffite's story ended in the 1820s. If you choose to believe that he died somewhere in the Gulf after leaving Galveston, Texas, then you have multiple accounts of his death to choose from. One thing is for certain, however: A man can only die once. That hard fact alone renders all but one of the stories that follow as false. And given that, it is not impossible that they all are. We are not inclined to believe a single one of them.

Yucatan

The most widely accepted death theory is that Jean Laffite died somewhere around the Yucatan peninsula in the 1820s. The accounts vary widely, and the only documentary evidence associated with any of the related theories is a *Gaceta de Colombia* newspaper article that appeared on April 20, 1823—a full two and a half months after Laffite's death was said to have occurred. The full translation of that article from Spanish to English is provided here:

> The Colombian corsair, General Santander, weighting at 43 tons, under the command of Captain Juan Laffitte; started pursuit of a brigantine and a Spanish galleon at 5am on the 4th of February, some 20 leagues from the 'wind of Omoa' in front of the 'triumph of the Cruz' until 10 at night. One hour into the battle and really close to surrendering, the brigantine signaled the galleon with its lamps. The galleon turned immediately and engaged the corsair. At this time, while mortally wounded, Captain Laffitte continued to invigorate his crew's ardor, and entrusted the corsair's command to his second, who suffered his same fortune. After the death of the second in command, petty officer Francisco Similien continued to maintain the battle until 1am that night; at which point it was impossible to continue and turned the corsair around. It was apparent the other two ships were heavily damaged by the corsair's fire, since they did not take pursuit. Captain Laffitte died from his injuries the next day. The loss of such a brave naval officer was regrettable; the courage he showed by confronting a much stronger and larger force that defeated him, manifests the honour that chose to following him in the valley of death, before abandoning him during retreat. The brigantine had 12 cannons on board, and six the galleon.[7]

The problems associated with this account are numerous. The first is that it is clearly based on the eyewitness accounts of people who had to be on Laffite's boat—these witnesses were his very own men. The article states the two other ships "did not take pursuit" after the conflict. If Laffite had made the decision to abandon a life of piracy and slink off into oblivion, his crew would have certainly been complicit in corroborating this tale for him.

Without Pierre as his business partner, the operation as they had been running it for more than a decade was certainly going to be negatively affected. It is reasonable to envision Jean deciding to step away from the spotlight, especially considering the factors that were making their business model more problematic by the day. Secondly, the nature of the article's narrative is very strange, as it romanticizes his position as a "brave naval officer" and highlights his courage and honor. These are odd characteristics to report of a man who according to this account died while trying to overtake another ship and steal things. Perhaps we should consider that the newspaper was published in a country for which Laffite was technically a naval officer. This article was written on very friendly turf, which rouses our skepticism. The time gap in the reporting is also suspect: from February 5 to April 20. Finally, most theories based on this account suggest Laffite was buried at sea, which would be a very convenient circumstance for a faked death. Given all of this, the details related to the interaction that happened with the other two ships could be completely true while the conclusion that he died from it completely false. The whole story could also be a farce.

From this one article has sprung a whole host of alternate versions of the story, with dates ranging from 1821 to 1826 and the manner of death morphing from death by injury to death by unrelated illness. Some texts also take the same story and transplant it in other locations, including as far south as Honduras. Any source that marks Jean Laffite's death in 1821 is obviously false because he was commissioned by Cartagena in the following year. The timeline for the Jean Laffite Society is one source that pushes the death date to 1826, saying, "Jean Laffite is reported to have died of a sickness at Silan, near Merida or on Isla Mujeres,"[8] though not all members of the society agree with the particulars of the timeline. Such a late death date is especially problematic because it leaves a suspiciously large block of time in which there is no documented Laffite sighting. And then there are sources that figuratively throw their hands up, like the normally reliable *Encyclopaedia Britannica*, which lists his death date as "1825?"[9]

The second most popular theory is that Jean Laffite died in the Yucatan from an illness. Dyer's "Dinner with Laffite" describes the story this way:

> The *Pride* did not meet with a British warsloop in the gulf, and the *Pride* was not boarded by British marines, and Laffite did not fall in single combat with the chief of the boarders, nor did the *Pride* pursue a piratical course, but sailed straight for Yucatan, where the vessel and her cargo were sold and the proceeds were divided, and where Laffite parted from his friends excepting two, who cast their fortunes with him, and remained his

business associates as traders until his death from yellow fever at a small place fifteen miles from Merida. . . . [B]oth were present at his deathbed, and whereas one of them lived in Galveston County later from 1842 to 1900 (attaining the age of a centenarian), and whereas certain officers of the navy of the Republic of Texas saw the tombstone of Laffite inscribed with his name in 1841, the readers of history may conclude that Laffite did not die as a pirate.[10]

Schaadt's article "The Journal of Jean Laffite: Its History and Controversy" cites a source who said he attended Jean Laffite at his deathbed in a village near Mérida, though the man cannot remember the year.[11] Similarly, a letter from S. R. Fisher to Texas diplomat and military leader General Mirabeau B. Lamar dated February 26, 1838, gives an account of another old man from Mexico who told his version of Jean Laffite's death. Fisher wrote, "He said he knew him well . . . and that once he went with him to Galveston Island—he Spoke of him in high terms, and observed he helped to bury him, that he died (I think about ten years Since) of fever near Teljas, a small village on the main, and where he himself resided with his family—and was buried in the neighborhood."[12] There are plenty of other sources that cite eyewitnesses to Jean Laffite's death from some sort of fever in the Yucatan, though the dates are all over the map or the eyewitnesses admit that they actually do not remember particulars. We cannot speak for you, but if an internationally known pirate died in our hometown during our lifetime, we would remember when it happened and where we buried him. This state of affairs has prompted many Laffite scholars to suspect that the locals propagating this narrative simply mistook Pierre Laffite for Jean, which in our view is the best explanation for this canon of stories.

Other outlier tales about Jean Laffite's death also exist, including that he was killed onboard his ship by one of his own men in Cuba after an attempted mutiny. But again, many of these tales involve the testimony of Laffite's men. They were pirates, and there was no way to know if they were lying so their leader, who had led them on adventure after adventure and who had rewarded them handsomely, could make a clean getaway.

Numerous authors also cover the as yet unsuccessful quest to find his grave. Many Mexican natives claimed to have either attended him in death or been aware of his burial, yet no grave has been located—despite active searches. Emmet Collins's article "Pirate Jean Lafitte: Blue-Eyed Natives May Hold Key to Demise of Legendary Buccaneer" offers up the claim that Mexican natives found a grave marker with the pirate's name on it. Collins explains,

Now word has returned to Houston from Mexico that the actual graveside of the famous 19th century pirate probably has been determined. Only recently a group of Yucatan natives—some who claimed to be the descendants of Lafitte—led an exploration party to a small grassy burial ground in the port of Dzilam de Bravo. A weathered and almost illegible wooden marker was removed for examination and found to bear the dim lettering of "Jean Lafitte." It is believed that Laffite left the Isla de Mujeres during his last days and came to this village on the mainland to die.[13]

Remember Dzilam de Bravo is the place where it is fairly well established that Pierre Laffite died in 1821, so the chances of this grave actually marking the spot where Pierre was interred are pretty solid.

An article called "Lafitte, the Pirate," which was published in the *Newark Daily Advertiser* on February 12, 1840, was a very early source that questioned the veracity of the Laffite death legend. It says, "No authentic account has ever been given of his death, and some of those who knew him believe that he is still alive. Nearly all published in relation to him in the *Lives of the Pirates*, as well as in the novel bearing his name, with the exception of what relates to his conduct at the battle of New Orleans, and his operations in Louisiana, is said to be fabulous by those who knew him."[14] Russell Guerin, a historian with the Hancock County, Mississippi, Historical Society, asserts that a faked death was entirely possible. He writes,

At first blush, the most convincing argument is to [be] found in a book published in 1843, *Incidents of Travel in the Yucatan*, written by an American explorer. This was John L. Stephens, who had hacked through Mayan jungles in the Yucatan for some time before the publication date. The objective of his travel had nothing to do with pirates in general and certainly not Lafitte particularly, and it is for this reason that evidence that Stephens gave might be considered trustworthy. . . . Stephens reported that the Isle of [Mujeres] had been the home of the pirate Lafitte, known locally as Monsieur Lafitta, where he was well respected by the townspeople. In the area, he met a local patron who had been a "prisoner" of Lafitte for two years. It was suspected that he actually had served with him in his piracies, as he was certainly fond of his memory. He told Stephens that Lafitte had died "in his arms, and that the widow, a senora del Norte from Mobile, was then living in great distress in Silan." After journeying to Silan, Stephens sought out the local padres, who did not know whether Lafitte "was buried in the campo santo or the church, but supposed that, as Lafitte was a distinguished man, it was the latter." But the grave was not found in the church, and so the padres inquired of some of the locals who had been there at the time of Lafitte's burial. It is here that Stephens' testimony, while believable, curiously lends to the possibility that Lafitte may have mysteriously vanished. It is therefore in order to quote directly the passage: "The sexton who officiated at the burial was dead; the padres sent for several of the inhabitants, but a cloud hung over the memory of the pirate: all knew of his death and burial, but none knew or cared to tell where he was laid." And so a new question arises out to Stephens, and causes one to ponder whether Lafitte's death and burial may have been faked, thus allowing him to continue his life elsewhere without notoriety.[15]

The death issue is a point of contention that has divided Laffite scholars for more than a century. Those resting comfortably on the 1820s death theories have built their arguments on unstable notions. A significant number of researchers agree with us that these death stories are just too unreliable to trust.

So, if, like us, you do not believe Jean Laffite died in the 1820s under any of the circumstances detailed above, the question of where he went naturally arises. It is beyond reason to believe that he could have continued as a working pirate in the Gulf or Caribbean under his same identity. He was simply too well known to get away with that, though some have tried to follow that trail. We found references to potential Laffite activities both on the Georgia and South Carolina coasts—possibly with Dominque You, who did not die until November of 1830. None of these suppositions come with proof.

To date, the most prominent and elaborate faked death theory is espoused by believers of the "Jean Laffite Journal," and there are many of them. The next chapter offers our analysis of the journal. We will go ahead and toss in a spoiler, however: there is no way on God's green earth that Jean Laffite wrote it.

The controversial "Journal of Jean Laffite" is housed at the Sam Houston Regional Library
in Liberty, Texas. Visitors to the library can view the volume through a glass case. While
scholars have debated its legitimacy for decades, the research presented in this volume
demonstrates that there is no way it could have been written by Jean Laffite.

CHAPTER EIGHT

THE "JOURNAL" OF JEAN LAFFITE

In the 1940s, a man named John Andrechyne Laffite, who claimed to be a great-grandson of Jean Laffite, began circulating a "journal" and other materials that he supposedly inherited in a trunk from his grandfather Jules. The journal reports that after the world thought Jean Laffite was dead, he actually changed his name to John Laflin, resurfaced in the United States, got married to a woman named Emma Hortense Mortimore, lived in St. Louis, had children, and then died in Alton, Illinois, on May 5, 1854. What we have as the "journal" is a reprinted translation from French creole to English of the original text found in a small leather notebook. John A. Laffite informed Laffite experts and even the Missouri Historical Society about his alleged find, and he began traveling to seek information about his family history and learn more about the man he argued was his great-grandfather.

Those who interacted with John A. Laffite in the years after his "discovery" reported that he seemed to be very interested in gaining notoriety—and a paycheck—from the archive and that he expressed interest in finding Laffite's treasure. Many of them described him as sketchy character and con man. According to Robert L. Schaadt's article "The Journal of Jean Laffite: Its History and Controversy," John A. Laffite also used a family Bible included in the trunk to get a notary in Atchinson, Kansas, to "certif[y] a birth information sheet" that established his ancestry.[1] He claimed to be the son of Leon Jean Laffite, who was the son of Jules Jean Laffite, who was the son of Jean Laffite and Emma Mortimore. The archive claims a birth date for Jean Laffite on April 22, 1782 in Port-au-Prince, Haiti.[2] The astute reader has probably already noticed that the Laflin/Laffite naming does not make sense. If Jean Laffite had changed his name to Laflin to live undercover, why were his son and grandson using the name *Laffite*? As well, we would pay good money to see the Haitian birth records for a Jean Laffite in 1782.

A footnote in the Schaadt article also points out research that indicates John A. Laffite used the last name Nafsinger from 1913–1947, switching his name conveniently just before coming out as the great-grandson of Jean Laffite.[3] Interestingly, John A. Laffite was known to use the names John A. Laflin and John Mateka/Matejka as other aliases, a fact that does not inspire confidence in his character. Schaadt also cites letters from people who had personal interactions with John A. Laffite during the time the journal was circulating who called him "a collector of old paper" and described his visits to "old bookstores trying to buy end papers from hundred year old books they are tearing up for one reason or another."[4] Aya Katz, writing for *Historia Obscura* in the article "Jean Laffite and the Laflin Connection," characterizes John A. Lafitte as "a person with a shady past and a reputation as a forger."[5] Several print sources report he had even been involved in other forgeries of historical documents, including one related to the Alamo. In short, there are numerous credible reasons to disbelieve the John A. Laffite charade.

Ultimately, the journal was published by Vantage Press in 1958. Since its publication, the authenticity of the text has been hotly contested, and its

The Sam Houston Regional Library and Research Center is a worthwhile stop on any history enthusiast's Texas road trip. The Jean Laffite Collection is one of the library's centerpieces, and the staff there are so generous with their time and expertise.

veracity continues to inspire vibrant debate among scholars in the business of early American document verification. The collection of materials (including journals, photos, clippings, family Bibles, and artwork) was purchased by former Texas Governor Price Daniel in 1975 and then donated to the Sam Houston Regional Library and Research Center. The collection (including the journal, which is kept in a glass box) is currently available for scholarly examination there. We traveled to Liberty in January 2019 to view the collection in person and determine whether the materials were authentic.

Over the years, there have been scientific examinations of the journal's paper and ink along with comparisons to known Laffite handwriting samples in an effort to bring resolution to the debate. The problem with these studies has been that for every expert cited who believes the journal is the real notebook of Jean Laffite there is another expert who disagrees. Likewise, even a modern-day paper expert with designs to forge a document can gain access to old paper and ink. Handwriting analysis is also a very tricky business, with experts often disagreeing with one another about the authorship of specific samples. Conclusions are offered with only a percentage of certainty. There is simply no way for one expert's opinion to provide conclusions that will satisfy every proponent and skeptic simultaneously.

What we are left with then to settle the debate is an analysis of the *content of the words on the page,* a process that for whatever reason has not been undertaken with this journal. Luckily our research team included a rhetorical expert in Dr. Ashley Oliphant, an English professor with twenty years of teaching experience in the college writing classroom and a doctorate in rhetoric and composition. By reframing the debate about the authenticity of the journal through the lens of rhetorical construction, we can gain valuable insights that have not been fully discussed in the literature to date. Putting aside the questions about ink, paper, and handwriting and temporarily suspending the glaringly obvious problems with the character of John A. Laffite, let us consider what the writer actually included in the journal and apply some common-sense rhetorical questioning to our inquiry. Through this framework we will explore how the content of the journal does not work with the stated and implied purposes of the writer.

Beginning with the "To the Reader" section that opens the journal, even a casual reader should note the immediate exigence problem: Why would a man who worked so hard to conceal his identity and start a new life decide to record the truth in writing while he was still alive and able to compose it? The writer of the journal explains, "Since my retirement some years ago, many people have repeatedly urged me to write my memoirs."[6] "Many people" then knew the truth about his past—presumably people he had already told about his identity. Therefore, he had a community of people around him while he was alive who knew who he was. Where is the body of family stories then, stories from someone other than John A. Laffite more than half a century after the journal was said to have been written? Where are the St. Louis legends about Jean Laffite living out his life there that would have naturally formed with such a historically significant figure trying to exist in the city with anonymity?

The journal writer then goes on to claim the reason he wrote the document was to "leave a true account to my descendants, with the understanding that they would not release it until one hundred and seven years from this date."[7] In the next paragraph, he notes how much "research" he will have to do to "collect the necessary proofs of authenticity" required to combat the critics, who he rages against for writing "slanderous conjectures and erroneous fairy tales" about him.[8] If this stated premise was his true rhetorical reason for writing, why would he direct his descendants to delay the release of this document until the middle of the twentieth century? If in 1850 Laffite was already concerned with the many false portrayals of him that had been published during his lifetime, surely he was aware of how many more false portrayals would be written about him in the next century. Furthermore, why would anyone need to do research about his or her *own life* to write a memoir? In the 1850s, in the absence of an email, text message, or social media record to peruse and without access to an international database of newspapers and books, the only way for Laffite to research the dates, locations, and events of his life would be to look through a personal log he kept from childhood—because this journal claims to offer details from that far back in Laffite's history. Where are the logs that he consulted while writing the journal? Certainly, he would have kept them to include in the trunk he would pass down to his descendants, if indeed his ultimate goal was to leave behind a "true account" of his life.

The journal also has an etymological problem that discounts its authenticity single-handedly. The writer explains "At the age of fourteen, I was sent with my brother Pierre to the island of Martinique to continue my studies. The Cruger brothers taught us. When we had finished our studies in our private school, we went to Saint Croix Island to take a course in psychology in order to acquire better comprehension of human nature."[9] The journal says Laffite was born in 1782, so this course would have taken place between 1796 and 1797, yet the usage of the word "psychology" in the behavioral sense did not emerge until the early 1890s. The *Oxford English*

Dictionary etymology entry for the word makes that clear. As well, in the late eighteenth century, psychology was not regarded as a science *among scientists,* so it certainly would not have been something that would have been studied by the mainstream population. The evolution of psychology in the sense of a phenomenon worth studying would not come until the middle of the nineteenth century. Many credit Wilhelm Wundt with creating the academic discipline of psychology in 1879 at the University of Leipzig in Germany with the establishment of his laboratory[10]—*one hundred years* after Laffite supposedly experienced this course and more than *thirty years* after Laffite was said to have written this journal. Even if a course in psychology somehow had existed in the late 1700s, a young boy during this time period would not have had access to it—much less one taught on a tiny underdeveloped Caribbean island. Considering the family's purported business (leather making for the father and seamanship for the older brother), why in the world would the boys need to be sent away for training in psychology? What possible career application could that have had for them in the late 1700s? And according to the journal, Jean and Pierre left Martinique where they were already in a private school their family was paying for to go to St. Croix—for one course. No part of this passage rings true.

Another major problem with the narrative is that its voice does not square with the level of Jean Laffite's intelligence, which can be deduced from all that is known about him and from what he wrote. Voice is defined as an author's unique style—the structural, grammatical, and rhetorical characteristics that make each person's writing unique. Experts who teach writing are skilled at identifying the markers of an individual's work, characteristics that are extremely obvious especially when they are placed next to the words of others. This is essentially how a reader can detect plagiarism: the words on the page do not match the voice of the writer's known work. The astute reader of the journal should apply what is known about Jean Laffite's intelligence (gleaned from his decades of brilliant negotiating, financial maneuvering, and geographical strategizing) for comparison against the intelligence of the writer of this journal. We will not attempt here to undertake a consideration of Jean Laffite's known letters (even if they were transcribed or translated by a secretary), as such an examination would be a book-length endeavor on its own. What we are confident in asserting here is that anyone who has read anything Laffite actually wrote would see that the content of the journal—start to finish—does not sound like him, nor does the act of writing the journal sound like something he would have done. Laffite was a rhetorically savvy man. He had to be to survive and thrive in the way he did through all of the historical turmoil he experienced in his lifetime. Numerous reliable accounts from contemporaries who interacted with him include remarks about his intelligence, and we put stock in a unified body of literature that asserts the fact that he was a very smart man. Even if he was an old man in failing health while he wrote this journal, his ability to think critically and attend to the basic details of this narrative would not have been lost. He had an uncanny ability to outrun the law. He was adept at navigating social circles that included calculating elites. He repeatedly reinvented himself as the social, legal, and business landscape changed. Jean Laffite was astute, yet this journal was written by a less capable thinker. The structure and content are disjointed and choppy. The diction and word choice are not sophisticated. The narrative jumps backward and forward in time. The essential story is not interesting or compelling in any way. None of this squares with who Laffite was.

Jean Laffite, the last of the great pirates, had a magnificent story to tell. If he was using this journal as a way to come clean to his descendants about his real identity, he would have told the true story of his life. This journal is filled with absolutely useless details that nobody cares about (direct ancestors or not), and it often glosses over what would have been astonishing stories about what really happened in his life. The early part of the journal up to page seventeen offers pages of *copious, tedious, boring* details about Laffite's brother Alexander, leaving the reader to question how this information would ever serve to inform his ancestors about Jean's actual life or combat any Laffite biographers with ill intentions. Then on page seventeen, the writer explains, "When I was sixteen years old my brothers Alexander Fréderic, Pierre Antoine and myself made a voyage from Port-au-Prince to New Orleans, Louisiana, on the 19th of January, 1798. We saw very much sickness during the three months we stayed there. We returned home in March 1798."[11] This voyage is something readers very much want to learn about, yet all the detail we get about *three months abroad* is that they saw sickness. If the birth dates for Laffite in the journal are to be believed, he would have been sixteen years old when this happened. This would have been a formative experience for a boy that age living in a different country within a very distinct culture, yet all the writer provides in this journal about the experience is one phrase with no details. Why mention the trip at all other than to include a date—for journal provenance perhaps? In the next sentence, the writer goes on: "When I was seventeen we left our country to take some ships to New Orleans, but we encountered robbers who took all our belongings."[12] Here again, he completely skips over being *robbed by pirates*.

Also bizarre is that as an old man he would still have the dates of the voyages he took when he was so young. Even if he had the dates written down, it is odd he would think his descendants really needed to know that, especially in a work of such short length where other details would be more pertinent. There are numerous other examples of random facts included in the journal, such as on page thirty-seven, where the writer lists dates of meetings, dates of building construction, etc. These sections read like a writer desperate to establish provenance—not a writer interested in telling the fantastic story of his life to his children's children. Similarly, he describes an instance when he took forcible command of a ship in 1801, claiming he remembers the coordinates: "88 degrees 14' west longitude and 22 degrees 12' north latitude, if I remember correctly."[13] He was supposedly nineteen years old when this happened. Who would remember those coordinates in old age? And why would the writer think his descendants would want to know this?

The reader of the journal also notices many passages with unclear rhetorical motives, sections that actually just read as weird. On page eight, very early in the story, he writes that his ancestors "have the reputation of having been able to create around them an atmosphere of peace, contentment and well-being."[14] What a strange thing to say. Also unsettling is a section on page thirty-nine where the writer describes himself in what can only be characterized as an outlandish way: "I have never pretended to be anything but an errant liberator of the suffering masses, with the reward of undergoing periods of exile, imprisonment, mendacity, false judgments and sufferings caused by despotic men. I was young, handsome, generous, honest and ambitious, and unresponsible for the deeds committed by others."[15] Does this sound like something you would ever write down—much less distribute to your family—as a way of remembering you? As well, our guess is that anyone with the word "mendacity" in his vocabulary would be capable of writing better sentences than are presented in the "journal." The forger clearly went to the thesaurus.

Any researcher willing to accept the journal as authentic should also require *primary documents* to back up the claims made in the narrative. Where is the proof of John Laflin's death in Alton, Illinois, on May 5, 1854, as the journal claims? Where is the evidence of him on the tax rolls in the various places the journal claims he lived? Where is the marriage certificate for John Laflin and Emma Mortimore on June 1, 1832? Where is the birth record for Jean Laffite in Saint-Domingue along with brothers named Alexander Frédéric and Pierre Antoine? The writer claims on page eighteen that his brother Alexander enlisted in the service of Napoleon. Do we have a military record of Alexander Laffite serving under Napoleon? The French were excellent record keepers in those days.

Also problematic is the anti-Spanish bent of the journal, which creates a tone that feels manufactured and performative. The writer explains, "We [Pierre and I] decided that when we grew up we would capture all vessels flying the Spanish flag."[16] Yet, we know in the 1820s that both Jean and Pierre became paid Spanish spies along with Arsène Latour. Did Laffite's deep hatred for the Spanish dissipate in adulthood long enough for him to become an agent working for Spain, only for that same hatred to re-emerge in Laffite later in life? There are numerous places in the narrative that the writer could have supported his reasoning for hating the Spanish, yet he chooses to gloss the stories. On page eighteen, he writes about Alexander taking him in September 1798 to "the fortress of Cartegena [*sic*] where we saw many sailors of French, English, Danish and Dutch descent. Pierre and I witnessed many tortures and executions under the Spanish regime at Cartegena."[17] This passage presented the ideal opportunity to expose the "tortures and executions" he witnessed, but the story moves on swiftly with the next sentence: "I missed Grandmother a great deal and she wept everytime I went aboard a ship."[18] The decision was made here to essentially skip over legitimate, historically significant events that offered the canvas for him to present descriptive details that would prove he experienced these things. Instead he shifts to a more detailed description of his grandmother's emotions, which were quite frankly irrelevant. This does not sound like a writer who wants to set the record straight for biographers. Likewise, the writer's anger at the British is felt throughout the text, including with his decision to conclude the piece with "Down with the British Dragon!"[19] It is beyond credulity that a writer with a life as significant as Laffite's would want that sentiment to set the final tone of his testimony.

Several scholars have also pointed out that information related to all of the major historical events used in the journal was readily available to any individual with access to old newspapers and books. No new details that would have been exclusive to a firsthand participant are revealed in the journal. Others have tried to bolster their belief in the journal by suggesting that it is written in a specific dialect of French that John A. Laffite did not speak. However, any forger who expects to make a profit from a falsified document can find and pay an expert in any language variety. As well, we suspect Jean Laffite was more likely born in France, which would have meant that he would have spoken and written in a more standardized version of French, not French creole. While Laffite would have certainly been capable of using the French creole dialect to conduct business in New Orleans, and while he likely became very adept at using that language variety over the years, his writing would have more than likely been influenced by *the formative years when he was learning the language.* Dialect influences in adulthood usually do not have a strong enough influence to impact the way a person writes. Writing, after all, is a learned skill, the fundamental basis of which does not change dramatically much after puberty. Aya Katz also points out in "Was the Journal of Jean Laffite an Original, a Copy or a Forgery?" that the journal that exists in the Sam Houston Library is a copy of the original document because it is written by hand without any mistakes, as it was being copied from another document. While the journal writer could have intended to produce multiple copies to give to several descendants, this fact still creates suspicion because it seems unlikely that an old man would have the energy to transcribe multiple copies of a book, when one book would have been sufficient to tell the story.

With all of this considered, it is truly astonishing that roughly half of the Laffite experts who have examined the journal believe it is authentic. Our research team concludes without reservation that the document is indeed a forgery, and not a good one at that. None of the arguments made by the journal advocates—and there have been many published over the years—offer a convincing case that can override the problems with the character of John A. Laffite/Laflin/Mateka/Nafsinger, let alone the problems outlined in this short chapter that is by no means comprehensive. The content of this journal does not hold up to common sense questioning; therefore, our research team is confident in our determination that the journal was not written by Jean Laffite.

****

So, our story brings us to the mid-1820s and stalls at the point when Laffite is supposed to have died one of the many deaths outlined earlier. While we knew as researchers that another alias theory that had not been fully explored could offer the appropriate answer to our query about what happened to Jean Laffite, we were unsure how much evidence we would be able to find to prove that Jean Laffite was still alive and kicking after reports of his death were circulated.

Our first lead came on a sunny Sunday afternoon as we read Garrigoux's Latour biography. Mention of an otherwise unremarkable letter caught our attention. Garrigoux described very matter-of-factly an uncovered piece of correspondence between Latour and Livingston that made mention of a man called "Redhouse." The letter, which is part of the private Fonds Martine Bardon Collection, is dated April 4, 1829, from Latour (living in Havana) to Livingston. The translated paragraph of interest reads:

> Redhouse has been striving here to recover [some money due for work . . . he will visit you in Washington] . . . he wants to talk with you about assets he may be able to recover in France . . . We have seen that you should be named ambassador to that country from which situation it would be easy for you to provide him with that favor.[20]

As Garrigoux's focus was not on the life of Jean Laffite but was instead trying to tell the story of Latour, he simply made note for the reader that the passage in the Latour-to-Livingston letter was curious given that there was no record of either man knowing someone named *Redhouse*. Garrigoux wrote in the footnote "We have not been able to identify this friend of Arsène and Livingston; perhaps an alert reader will be able to discover who he was."[21]

Not unlike a person who buys a scratch-off lottery ticket and uncovers a winning number, we stared blankly at the footnote for a second or two before fully absorbing what we had just read.

In essence, the letter demonstrated evidence of two of Jean Laffite's closest friends and long-standing partners corresponding with each other in code in the year 1829 about their mutual friend, Redhouse. Redhouse had money in France, and he needed the man who was about to be the French ambassador to help him recover it. Redhouse would come to Washington to visit about it. Redhouse clearly knew Livingston well enough to call in a favor and pay a visit.

Attempting to curb our excitement, we quickly began checking all available records for anyone with the surname Redhouse. We could not find a single one in the United States at the time. The original letter was in a private collection in France that other scholars could not access. Hoping to communicate directly with Garrigoux to learn what else he may have to offer, we were sad to hear of his passing the year before. Following this, we tracked down the American translator Garrigoux had worked with only to discover that the author's notes were gone, and the translator did not know anything about the reference to Redhouse.

While disappointed, we were not deterred. If anything, we were energized by the possibility that other correspondence with a Redhouse reference might be waiting for us in an archival collection somewhere else.

As it turns out, we did not have very long to wait for that answer, which showed up in New Jersey. The Department of Rare Books and Special

Collections at Princeton University's Firestone Library houses the Edward Livingston papers, and among them is a letter written in French from Latour to Livingston dated May 23, 1829, from Havana. Below is a French-to-English translation of the letter. The pertinent paragraph is the final one. We have added italics for emphasis.

Havana, May 23, 1829
Edward Livingston, Esquire
Washington

My dear friend: A few weeks ago, I had the honor of writing to you and sending to you a letter of congratulations with a request to forward it to our dear General Jackson thanks to whom the American nation has just been formed. Since then a circumstance has presented itself which has engaged me to write to him again.

My letter for the General can in itself serve as he one; but the fear that this last choice might not find favor in Washington prevents me from putting it in your letter. Mister W. Rodney (the Consul of the United States at Havana and the son of the ex-Attorney General) is preparing to go spend 5 months among his friends and his relatives in Delaware, following his annual custom that he has adopted of verifying the duties in a position to be filled by another person. I am convinced that he has lost the hope of being conserved in his position. The reason I do not know. Perhaps it might come from his adhesion to the party philosophy. Although he entered, I have decided to remain on this position to our General-President.

My letter contains some details on this country and on its rapports with the United States. I hope that they will prove that I am rather well qualified in fact and that very surely without flattery one would not be able to make a better choice than the choice of your servant to watch over the interests of our country especially if, as I believe it is the duty of the foreign embassy consuls to observe everything that might interest the government. Without speaking of the evil of Mister Warner and Mister Rodney, it is true that all those have played a very sad role in Havana forming their society with some Yankee merchants and captains of the buildings. Neither the one nor the other has known a word of Spanish other than to drink or to eat. Thanks to following the example of the Spanish and the English agent and the Consul General of France who are very wide spread in instructing themselves on everything about the country, make themselves agreeable and by that make their governments loved. Especially our Consuls will always be held aside and have never sought to profit from the representation for which they were entrusted.

Without doubt the General will communicate to you the letter that I have written to him; in any case, I would be quite at ease that all individuals be informed, such as those in the French news profession, and other organizations that prepare their own comments and opinions political and private. I am stopping here because finally I must not bore you too much. I will dare to beg you for a response of some lines under the cover of John Murdock. *Maison Rouge, who is still here, accords his interests to all your concerns.* Please offer my respectful homages to Madame Livingston and to the beautiful and amiable Cora. Believe me.

Your grateful and devoted servant
Lacarrière Latour

When we received the translation from our colleague, Dr. William Felsher, a retired French professor, we could not have been more pleased. *Maison Rouge, who is still here, accords his interests to all your concerns.* The American translation of Garrigoux's book had conflated *Maison Rouge* or "red house" in French to one word that emerged in English as a surname: *Redhouse.* We realized immediately that our initial search for that surname had been completely unnecessary. Latour had actually written the words *Maison Rouge* in the Princeton letter—and we suspect the same is true in the Fonds Martine Bardon Collection letter. *Maison Rouge,* as we now saw clearly written in French, could be only one person: the man who owned a red house in Galveston—their mutual friend, Jean Laffite. Taken at reasonable face value, we saw this as compelling evidence that Laffite was alive in Havana, Cuba, in April 1829, existing close enough to his old buddy Arsène Latour to be considered "here" with him. Jean Laffite was not so dead after all.[22]

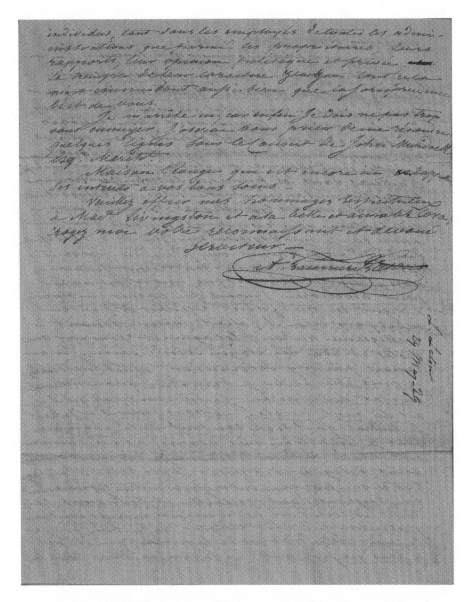

The discovery of the "Maison Rouge" letter was a pivotal discovery in our research. This letter dated May 23, 1829, from Arsène Latour in Havana, Cuba, to Edward Livingston proved that Jean Lafitte was still alive in 1829, several years after historical sources claim his death. Courtesy of Princeton University Library

II

MISSISSIPPI

CHAPTER NINE

THE LAND OF COTTON

The journey that led us into the next chapter of Jean Laffite's life uncovered a story that spans nearly fifty more years beyond the prevailing accounts of his death. The abrupt and unsatisfying conclusion to the known Laffite timeline has been problematic for biographers and historical researchers since the 1820s. If, however, you consider the Laffite tales that had swirled in North Carolina since the late 1830s, then the picture becomes considerably less muddy. In short, we now believe that the Laffite timeline continued through the 1820s in Cuba, following which he made the decision to return to the United States by coming through the back door of the Mississippi Delta and settling for a while around Jackson, Mississippi, before finally arriving in Lincolnton, North Carolina, sometime just prior to 1839. The following chapters will outline in detail how we arrived at that conclusion. As the story unfolds, you will see not only how that was likely accomplished but why.

While rumors had circulated in Lincolnton since the late 1830s that the mysterious Lorenzo Ferrer character who suddenly appeared on the tax rolls in 1839 was possibly the pirate Jean Laffite living under an assumed name, locating the connection between Laffite and Lorenzo Ferrer was a monumental task—one made even more difficult by the fact that we decided early on that all major conclusions drawn in the book must be supported by actual historical documents and not small-town innuendo. We were faced with an intimidating decade-long dark period between the Redhouse letter from 1829 and an 1839 tax document that placed Ferrer in Lincolnton. We had compelling evidence that Laffite was not dead, yet we had no idea where he could have been. Meanwhile in North Carolina, historians had been searching in vain for more than one hundred years to try and discover the origins of Lorenzo Ferrer prior to 1839. They, too, had gone in search of missing years with no success.

We were nagged by the question of how Laffite as Ferrer made it back into the United States, knowing that he would have been recognized had he used the port in New Orleans. For years, the Laffite business model had required Jean and Pierre to know which small Gulf waterways they could access to safely transport their fenced goods. While there were many options to choose from, a passage from Davis's book seems a plausible explanation:

> Most important of all was Bayou Lafourche, a distributary that took high water from the Mississippi from a point thirty miles downriver from Baton Rouge all the way to the Gulf, bypassing New Orleans. It was too narrow for sailing vessels to navigate, and often too shallow in summer drought, but with only a few feet of water in it the light draft pirogues could easily row up and down its entire length. That made it ideal not only for trading with Indians and the more reclusive trappers and hunters in the back-country, but also for smuggling goods past New Orleans to Baton Rouge, or else for evading United States customs inspectors at the Mississippi's mouth by bringing commodities up the Lafourche to the big river, then downstream to New Orleans by the back door.[1]

Laffite could have easily re-entered the country by coming up Bayou Lafourche as far as Baton Rouge, then either engaging regular passage up-river to Natchez or traveling over land. The definitive answer, if ever discovered, will have to surface in future research.

While the exact route of entry remains an open question, there is ample evidence that Lorenzo Ferrer made his first appearance on paper in Mississippi. After almost giving up hope, we found him there, along with an eye-opening body of evidence that pointed as much back toward the life and habits of Jean Laffite as it did forward to the man who later arrived in Lincolnton.

As a preamble to those details, we will deal in this chapter with the state of affairs in Mississippi that brought him back into the country af-ter several years in hiding. The area between present-day Jackson and the Mississippi port town of Natchez includes several historical counties that are integral to our theory. One of those counties is Copiah. Officially named as a county on January 21, 1823, and located in the southwest corner of Mississippi, Copiah County is bordered to the east by the Pearl River Basin, which coincidentally is a river Laffite knew well, as that body of water runs right down into the Mississippi Sound just north of New Orleans. One county over from Copiah County is the roaring Mississippi River, also well known to Laffite. The history of the formation of Copiah County is a bit convoluted because it was created from lands that were temporarily part of other counties. The whole chunk of land was obtained after the United States government took it from the Choctaw in exchange for relocation to land in Arkansas. That deal, known as the Doak's Stand Treaty of October 18, 1820, was negotiated by two men, Thomas Hinds and Andrew Jackson—the same Andrew Jackson who fought with Jean Laffite and his band of Baratarians at the Battle of New Orleans just five years earlier. Officials used part of the Choctaw land to form Hinds County in 1821, and then in 1823, Yazoo and Copiah counties were cut out of that area.[2] By 1824, the county seat of Copiah had been moved from a town called Coar's Springs to Gallatin.[3]

The Doak's Stand Treaty brought rapidly increased trade to the region. Dunbar Rowland's *Mississippi: Contemporary Biography* contextualizes the economic opportunity that was realized by enterprising Americans who took full advantage of the opening of the new lands and thought little about the disenfranchisement of the Indigenous Peoples:

> The treaty of Doak's Stand and the removal of the Indians to the west . . . met with much approval by the people of Mississippi, and everywhere in the older southern states an intense interest was manifested in the new territory open for purchase and population. With its succession of dark, level, prairies, rich valleys and heavily timbered tracts of valuable woods, it held out rare inducements not only to the younger sons of the large planters of the older southern states, but to the wealthy planters of Mississippi.[4]

In the 1820s and 1830s, Copiah County was essentially an open frontier without old families who had resided there for generations. It was a place where a new person could settle into town without suspicion about his past—because everyone was new and getting acquainted in an unfamiliar community. It truly was the perfect place to start a new life and maybe adopt a new identity, if necessary. It is plausible that Jean Laffite's prior knowledge of the region combined with word-of-mouth about a cotton boom (discussed below) may have alerted him to this area as an option—a place where a man could disappear while turning a tidy profit on the vast tracts of fertile farmland that had recently opened up for sale.

LAND SPECULATION

According to the Mississippi Encyclopedia, "By the start of the War of 1812 approximately five hundred thousand acres of public land had been sold in the Mississippi Territory, mainly to planters and speculators."[5] Following the war, the United States saw an increased demand for cotton, which prompted "small farmers, planters, and speculators [to] aggressively [use] both cash and credit to purchase quality Mississippi farmland, and the area's population nearly doubled from 1810 to 1820."[6] With a mass of desirable farmland now on the market due to treaties like Doak's Stand and with an eager community of speculators and farmers rushing the area, Mississippi was all of a sudden a very happening place to be.

Historians have written volumes about the Mississippi cotton boom. It was a remarkable time in American industry—however, one that was tarnished by the horrific reality of slavery. The world wanted cotton, the United States wanted to provide it, and all of this perfectly fertile land could be bought at affordable prices. The catch was that the southern United States could not come close to meeting the demand and making a profit, so plantation owners relied on slave labor to capitalize on the unique economic opportunity. The injustices wrought upon the enslaved people—on whose shoulders this unique economic opportunity for white Mississippi rested—are among the worst cruelties ever endured by the human race. The research process has required us to read the historical documents that lay bare those cruelties, and the impact has been truly felt.

Max Grivno, an associate professor of history at the University of Southern Mississippi, wrote an article called "Antebellum Mississippi" that offers a helpful synopsis of how local speculators and planters worked all parts of the cotton industry to maximize their returns. Grivno explains that "between 1833 and 1837, Mississippi's five land offices sold some seven million acres of public lands, much of it on easy credit."[7] The Mt. Salus land office was a major hub of activity during the years of the Mississippi Cotton Boom. Located near Clinton, Mississippi, it is also the site of the first post office in the area.[8] The facility operated from 1827–1836 and was known as the Jackson office for lands opened in the western part of Mississippi.[9] Grivno continues, "Between 1820 and 1833, Mississippi's cotton production soared from approximately 20 million to 70 million pounds. By 1839, the opening of the Choctaw and Chickasaw lands had catapulted that figure to some 193.2 million pounds, making the state the nation's largest producer of cotton."[10] The only way for such a sudden increase in cotton yield to occur is through the exploitation of slave labor.

THE SLAVE TRAIL OF TEARS

At the time when cotton began its meteoric rise within the Mississippi economy, there were not enough enslaved people to farm the tracts that opened when the US government usurped Native lands and sold them. In other parts of the country, however—places like the Carolinas and Virginia— there was an abundance of slave labor. Slave holders in the mid-Atlantic region realized they could sell their enslaved workers to brokers, who would then transfer them for resale via boat—or more commonly over land—to the Deep South, where prices were at a premium. This journey became known much later as the Slave Trail of Tears.

It is staggering really that many Americans do not know more about this appalling time in history. Even more unbelievable is that many Southerners whose land this Trail of Tears crossed are unaware of the reality enslaved people faced as they were marched in coffles, chained together in lines to prevent their escape. Those who were transported by land walked (oftentimes shackled) for hundreds of miles over the span of several months to slave markets in places like Natchez, Mississippi, and New Orleans. Edward Ball's "Retracing Slavery's Trail of Tears" details the horrors that enslaved men and women faced as they moved south to meet their fates on cotton plantations in states like Alabama and Mississippi:

> The Slave Trail of Tears is the great missing migration—a thousand-mile-long river of people, all of them black, reaching from Virginia to Louisiana. During the 50 years before the Civil War, about a million enslaved people moved from the Upper South—Virginia, Maryland, Kentucky—to the Deep South—Louisiana, Mississippi, Alabama.[11]

Historians tell us the majority of the enslaved people who were moving on this Trail of Tears originated in Virginia.

Surprisingly, at the precise moment in Mississippi when slave trading was at a peak, the sale of enslaved people was prohibited. According to the Mississippi Encyclopedia, "From 1833 through 1845, selling slaves was officially illegal in Mississippi. The Constitutional Convention of 1832 prohibited 'the introduction of slaves into the state as merchandize, or for sale.'"[12] Even so, the illicit trade continued because the financial returns for the risk were massive. The upstanding gentlemen of Southern society had to keep their slave deals relatively quiet. This explains why we conclude several of the prominent figures who will be discussed in later chapters were slave traders, yet we do not find as many legal documents related to their trading as one might expect.

It is difficult to pin down exact statistics regarding the importation of enslaved people in Mississippi during the cotton boom, but historians have pieced together useful estimates. Grivno writes, "During the 1830s, Mississippi's slave population increased by nearly 200 percent, exploding from 65,659 to 195,211."[13] He cites a historian who estimated that more than 100,000 enslaved people were brought into Mississippi during the 1830s alone, a figure that is truly stunning when it is fully considered. The writer for the Mississippi Encyclopedia explains, "In 1820, Mississippi had 33,000 slaves; forty years later, that number had mushroomed to about 437,000, giving the state the country's largest slave population. While new births accounted for much of that increase, the trade in slaves became a crucial part of Mississippians' social and economic life."[14]

The area where Jean Laffite (now calling himself Lorenzo Ferrer) decided to settle in Mississippi—a conglomeration of counties in the southwest close to the Mississippi River—is significant. The counties of Hinds, Copiah, and Madison, where we tracked him for a decade of his life, all played a major role in the cotton boom. Eron Opha Rowland writes in *History of Hinds County Mississippi 1821–1922* that Hinds County especially was a critical cog in the wheel of cotton production in the Magnolia State:

> Hinds County, along with the other counties . . . shared the prosperity that marked the State's financial history during these years. Cotton, the great staple industry, held first place in agricultural products, and about this time Mississippi was largely furnishing the country with cotton for clothing and numerous other purposes. No county in the State was making greater progress in the growth of cotton and other products such as corn, peas, syrup, and great varieties of fruits than Hinds.[15]

Mississippi planters who wanted to purchase enslaved people usually did not have to travel very far to make their transactions. Barnett and Burkett write, "In the decades prior to the American Civil War, market places where enslaved Africans were bought and sold could be found in every town of any size in Mississippi. Natchez was unquestionably the state's most active slave trading city, although substantial slave markets existed at Aberdeen, Crystal Springs, Vicksburg, Woodville, and Jackson."[16] The busiest market at Natchez was known as "the Forks of the Road," as it was located where two active highways intersected.

The traders involved in these sales sometimes worked for large firms in places like New Orleans. Deals from these conglomerates have been tracked to banks large and small all over the country. Even individual men working

on a smaller scale often teamed up to form short-lived partnerships, sometimes acknowledging their illicit trade and other times simply calling themselves "merchants." Still others chose to remain lone wolves and traded as individuals, oftentimes out behind the land office or courthouse or in less than
upstanding locations such as bars. Truth be told, there were a lot of men in
the South operating this way, whether occasionally or regularly. While these
traders are definitely hard to track, it is possible to identify what they were
doing through slave schedules (logs of enslaved people in the United States
produced with the 1850 and 1860 Censuses), tax rolls, and land purchase
records that indicate quick sales. Most notable are the men who showed up
in a county tax roll for one or two years and then skipped town and moved
to the next county over. These traveling traders had to keep moving to prevent the law from catching up to them. As we were soon to find out, this
is the exact pattern of behavior that we found for Lorenzo Ferrer when we
finally exposed his Mississippi secrets.

CHAPTER TEN

NEW BEARINGS

The decade of prosperity in 1830s Mississippi that presented itself to Jean Laffite marked the second time in his adult life that he recognized a rare and remarkable opportunity and took full advantage. The first, of course, was the success of his privateering empire a full century after the Golden Age of Piracy had ended.

With knowledge of the geography, the economy, and the culture that was at work when Laffite arrived in Mississippi, we have set the scene for the reader to better understand the decisions he made in the next phase of his life. We will preface the account of these years with a bit about the research journey that led us to Mississippi in the first place. Knowing that the man calling himself Lorenzo Ferrer had obviously lived fifty-nine years of his life elsewhere before coming to Lincolnton in the late 1830s, we were nonetheless stumped as we pondered the question of where that could have been. We began by digging into ancestry records using every conceivable variant spelling of Lorenzo Ferrer's name to rule out all the possible locations where he could have been prior to arriving in Lincoln County. Previous local researchers had tried, just as we had, to find evidence of Ferrer's origins. Taking him at his word, at least as it was recorded on his tombstone, the reasonable place to begin was Lyon, France. In spite of the fact that the French kept detailed birth and death records in their churches and other institutions that reached back several centuries, we found no records there or anywhere else abroad for Lorenzo Ferrer.

Then turning our focus to the United States, we quickly discovered that there was no early record of Lorenzo Ferrer anywhere in America, either. We checked the 1790 Census and the 1800 Census and found nothing. The same was true for 1810 and 1820. For that span of thirty years, there was no record of anyone by that name in the United States. He was not being born, buying land, getting married, entering into business contracts, suing anybody, making the newspaper, serving in a war, joining a church, or dying. He was not in the United States in any capacity that would have put him on the grid. Logic would then dictate that he must have come in from another country, and yet here is where we found the most convincing evidence of all that his story did not add up. Concerning Ferrer's past, we could not find him entering any United States port, and this was after an exhaustive search of ship records in every harbor of the day.

As far as our research told us, Lorenzo Ferrer appeared out of thin air as a fifty-nine-year-old man in North Carolina in the year 1839. The day we discovered the 1830 Census changed the trajectory of our research. On M19, roll seventy, page 121 of the Copiah County, Mississippi, Census, we found *Lorenzo Farrier* with one enslaved male, three enslaved females, and one free white person.

This discovery set off a flurry of questions in our minds: Was this *our* Lorenzo Ferrer, or another man with the same name? Considering he owned four people and employed a free white person, what land was he working? Where was his house?

To find the answers to these and many other questions, we continued digging into the thread that had produced the hit in Mississippi. We reached out to the Copiah County chancery clerk's office in Hazlehurst, Mississippi, which led us to the treasure trove that is the Mississippi Department of Archives and History digitized records portal. And there came another hit—*L. Ferrer* on the 1831 tax roll in Copiah County, which meant he was an established resident who paid taxes there. He is noted as having $400 in loans and reported employing one white person and owning one enslaved person under the age of sixty. The record indicates he paid $2 in taxes.[1] He was also listed in the 1832 Copiah County tax roll on page nine. He owned two enslaved people and paid $1.25 in taxes. It is interesting to note in these tax rolls that some residents have all the columns filled out with information about township of residence, occupation, etc. Ferrer's columns on these forms all appear largely blank, a fact that we found not coincidental.

With information now beginning to flow, we continued the search on the Copiah County chancery clerk's webpage. Our search there yielded two land patents in Copiah County from the Mt. Salus land office in the years 1833 and 1834. The first document is a land patent granted to *Lorenzo Ferrer* on December 30, 1833 for 120.96 acres in Section 24, Township 2N, Range 2W, in Hazlehurst, Mississippi. The second patent was filed on September 10, 1834 for 40.32 acres, Section 24, Township 2N, Range 2W, also in Hazlehurst. Not knowing anything about nineteenth-century land patents or much about Mississippi (other than the fact that Elvis was born in Tupelo), we knew we needed to visit the area where Ferrer emerged so unexpectedly and see it for ourselves.

ON THE TRAIL IN MISSISSIPPI

That is how we eventually came to find ourselves in Hazlehurst in October 2018 on a mission to learn what could have been happening in Copiah County that made it so attractive for a man we suspected was Jean Laffite. More importantly, however, we were there because the Mississippi trail had not only heated up, it was smoking hot—all thanks to a subsequent discovery that made the trip a top priority. Ferrer was in Copiah County having bought two pieces of land in the same general area, but further research indicated that he never built houses on that land. This, along with the fact that he owned multiple enslaved people at the time of the 1830 Census, led us to hypothesize that he was in the area acting as a slave broker and a land speculator, or possibly doing some land speculating for a quick profit. He had to live somewhere while in Mississippi, and the discovery of the Henry Brewer Collection at the East Texas Research Center in Nacogdoches, Texas, told us where. With the assistance of librarians Joy Pitts and Tina Oswald, who graciously scanned and emailed documents we requested, we were not only able to learn where Ferrer lived in Mississippi, but we also located the missing piece of information that would definitively link *Mississippi's* Lorenzo Ferrer to *Lincolnton's* Lorenzo Ferrer, a pivotal turning point if ever there was one.

LOUISA SPEAKS

Ferrer was involved in several business dealings with a prominent man named Henry Brewer, a Hinds County resident in the early part of the 1800s. The first important document we located was a written deal allowing George Brewer, Henry's son, to "hire a negro girl from Lorenzo Ferrer named Louisa about seventeen years of age."[2] The document goes on to list the ways in which Brewer agrees to take care of Louisa (including the clothes and bedding he will provide for her). According to the agreement, on the "day appointed for her delivery" or return back to Ferrer, Brewer will have met all conditions of the document along with paying $10 to Ferrer.[3] The agreement also includes a clause that Brewer agrees to deliver the said negro girl to Lorenzo Ferrer at any time that he demands her and pay for what time she served. We agree not to transfer her to any other person or persons also not to . . . send her [off] to any other county without Lorenzo Ferrer's consent. We agree to deliver the said negro girl Louisa to Lorenzo Ferrer on his order on the twenty fourth this day of December in 1832 Thomson store where he now [resides] on the route between Galattin and Jackson.[4]

The agreement was signed by George Brewer and J. Thompson on December 27, 1831.

The first detail of importance here is the written proof that Lorenzo Ferrer owned an enslaved girl named Louisa, and in 1831, she was about seventeen years old, making her birthdate approximately 1814. She was loaned out to the Brewer family for one year under some very specific conditions, parameters that gave Ferrer a great deal of control over what happened to her. Considering that the United States made it illegal to import any new enslaved people after 1807, and considering that 1831 was a peak time in the South's cotton boom, it is highly possible (and sickening to contemplate) that Louisa was hired out to Brewer for the purposes of natural reproduction, though that possibility is not supported by any hard evidence. While the first name of an enslaved woman in the 1830s might not seem like such a significant detail, the identity of *this* woman was a critical piece of evidence that united our narrative in a way that few other facts would ultimately do. We recognized this revelation for what it was—the key that definitively connected the man in Mississippi named Lorenzo Ferrer with the man of the same name in North Carolina. Almost every account of Ferrer in Lincolnton is accompanied by the mention of his octoroon slave (and presumed mistress) named Louisa. While it is feasible that there were two men of the same name (albeit both of them, for some odd reason, with completely invisible past lives) living in the southern United States at around the same time, the likelihood that *both of them* were attached to an enslaved girl named Louisa, whose age in Mississippi comported with her later age in North Carolina, stretched the credibility of that notion to the breaking point. In fact, mixed in with our satisfaction at having uncovered a very important piece of research was the sense of poetic justice that one whose life had been lived in bondage and irrelevance was now able to speak across the centuries from her grave and shine a light on the truth.

Also revealing in this document is the place where Lorenzo Ferrer lived at least for a time in Mississippi: Thompson's store. We searched diligently for any information we could find about a Thompson's store on the road between Gallatin (near current Highway 28 west of Hazlehurst) and Jackson.

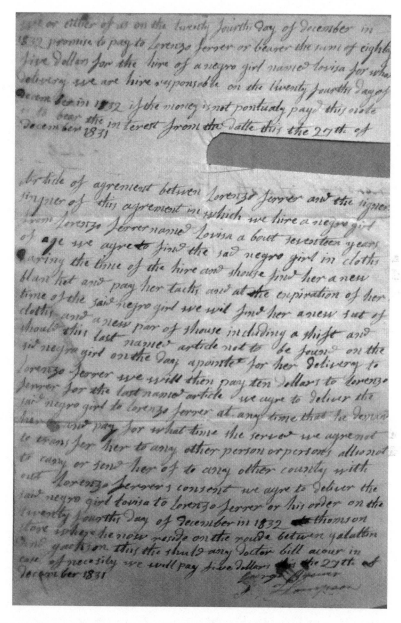

The "Louisa" document, as it came to be known during our research adventure, was the link that definitively connected Lorenzo Ferrer in Mississippi to Lorenzo Ferrer in North Carolina. The fact that her age in 1831 corresponded to her age in Lincolnton years later made it clear that these two Lorenzo Ferrers were the same man. *Courtesy of the East Texas Research Center, Ralph W. Steen Library at Stephen F. Austin State University, Nacogdoches, Texas*

We even consulted several local historians and sources in regional libraries with only a precious few nuggets of information as a result, but we considered even the smallest piece of the unfolding puzzle important.

Copiah County resident Paul Cartwright told us that Thompson's store was on Highway 28 past Gallatin at the corner of Browns Wells Road. He said the Jesse Thompson family lived near Sweetwater Church in far southwestern Copiah County, which is close to Highway 28.[5] Dunbar Rowland's *Mississippi: Contemporary Biography* provides some additional valuable insight into the Thompson family:

> John H. Thompson was a son of Jesse and Margaret (Harvey) Thompson, who came to Mississippi in the territorial epoch, removing hither from Hancock [C]ounty, Ga. He resided in Copiah [C]ounty from early childhood until within a few years prior to his death and was one of the influential and honored citizens of that section of the State, having been a zealous member of the Methodist church and having been prominent in political affairs, representing his county in the State legislature in 1846 and 1858 . . . Jesse Thompson was a soldier in the War of 1812, having served under General Jackson in the battle of New Orleans, as a member of the Mississippi troops.[6]

It is extraordinarily coincidental that sixteen years after the Battle of New Orleans, a man named Lorenzo Ferrer would find himself living in a frontier region in the house of a man named Jesse Thompson, who also served in the Battle of New Orleans, a battle greatly facilitated by Jean Laffite. Note, too that *J. Thompson* was a witness to the Ferrer/Brewer agreement involving Louisa.

A few other details are available about Thompson's store. We were able to locate an advertisement on the third page of the January 22, 1840, edition of Natchez's *Weekly Courier and Journal* that announces a lost item "somewhere on the road between Natchez and Paynes or Thompson's Store, Jefferson County."[7] Jefferson County is actually to the west of Copiah, so it is possible this announcement could have been about a different Thompson's store in a neighboring county. Copiah County's National Historic Register application references the development of Gallatin and mentions that a "brick courthouse was erected in 1825 at a cost of $1200 by one of Jesse Thompson's slaves, who was a skilled carpenter but whose name is unknown."[8] Similarly, an uncatalogued book in the Copiah County library in Hazlehurst called *WPA History Copiah County Ante-bellum Days 1823* also confirms that Jesse Thompson's enslaved worker built the courthouse along with the halfway house, the first brick house to be constructed in Copiah County, sometime between 1823 and 1824.[9]

Returning briefly to the Brewer collection, one other document also makes reference to a Ferrer transaction involving a girl (possibly Louisa). In Box A-11, B1, Folder 6, there is a ledger titled "George Brewer to Jes." The paper is broken off, so the complete name is not known, but because Folder 6 is labeled "Account of George Brewer with Jesse Alford for Supplies," and because every other item in that folder concerned Brewer's dealings with Alford, we can safely assume the "Jes" when completed reads "Jesse Alford." In a December 9, 1833, entry in that ledger, there is a notation for "1 DO Ferrer–girl 12/11.50."[10] We are not quite sure what this means, considering that the expense is noted a full year after Brewer was supposed to have returned Louisa to Ferrer, if indeed Louisa was the "Ferrer girl" in question, but given what you are about to read, the name of Jesse Alford in connection with Lorenzo Ferrer becomes crystal clear.

This brings our Mississippi timeline to 1832. If he was Jean Laffite in disguise, a full two or three years had elapsed with no exposure, and a newly minted and perhaps more confident Lorenzo Ferrer found himself at a juncture which was about to change his life in a very big way.

WEDDING BELLS

It appears that sometime between 1832 and 1834, Lorenzo Ferrer made a move north to the neighboring county of Hinds. While searching through the resources in the local history room of the Hazlehurst library, we found Clara Wright Forrest's book, *Hinds County, Mississippi Marriage Records, 1823–1848,* which contained a January 1834 notation for a marriage between *Lorenzo Ferror* and Nancy Alford, with Jesse Alford listed under the column for the bondsman who gave consent for the woman to marry.[11]

It is important to understand why a bondsman was used. The marriage bond was essentially an announcement that a man intended to marry a woman. The bond required that the prospective groom go to the local courthouse with a bondsman (sometimes the father or other relative of the bride or a family friend) to create an official document for the engagement. The bond was the set amount the groom would have to pay if at some point before the marriage a reason was discovered that would prevent it from taking place.[12] At the time of the courthouse visit, there was no transaction of money between parties. The bond only had to be paid if the planned marriage fell through. In 2012 Judy G. Russell wrote an interesting piece for *The Legal Genealogist* that provides further clarification about why stating this intention to marry was so significant. Russell cites the history in the United States of "banns" or announcements of public marriages being required so that the people in a town would have an opportunity to speak before the wedding or forever hold their peace. When marriages took place between couples who were not from the same communities, however, it became necessary to come up with a new strategy for notifying the public of the impending nuptials. Russell writes, "What that bond actually was, then, was a form of guarantee that there wasn't any legal bar to the marriage. Enforcing the guarantee was a pledge by the groom and a bondsman . . . to pay a sum of money, usually to the Governor of the State . . . if and only if it actually turned out that there was some reason the marriage wasn't legal."[13] Our brief research into marriage bonds during the 1830s revealed that they were much more common in the South than in other parts of the country.

After discovering this notation in the Hinds County marriage index, we headed to Jackson, where we thought marriage bonds were housed, only to be told that the old Hinds County records are actually kept in the original courthouse in the town of Raymond, just to the west of Jackson. Once there, we settled into a side room with the big red marriage ledger, which is called "Marriage Record 1832 1837 Hinds County," and began scanning

The Raymond courthouse in the picture housed the undigitized marriage records that blew Lorenzo Ferrer's attempt to conceal his comings and goings in Mississippi.

each page of the book. The ledger was not indexed—a fitting "gift" it seemed to us, after the circuitous route we had traveled to find it. Nevertheless, we dove into the enjoyable task of locating a needle in a haystack. By tag-teaming the ledger book and each scanning a side—a speed-reading technique we had perfected in rural courthouses all over the South in the preceding months—we found the needle.

The marriage licenses for Hinds County during the 1830s were set up as a blank set of three separate declarations. The three were entered into the record book together as a unit and then filled out individually as each of the following happened. The first section was the longest and most detailed, as it outlined the bond posted by the groom and a witness, declared to the governor of the state the groom's intention of marrying the named bride, and posted the promise of money if for whatever reason the marriage did not happen. In that event, the groom and witness were promising to be held liable for whatever amount is stated. You can see from the marriage bond that *Lorenzo Ferrer* and "Jefs" Alford (a common clerk's shorthand for "Jesse") entered into a marriage bond agreement for $200 and promised that "marriage is shortly intended to be celebrated between the abound Lorenzo Ferrer and Nancy Alford." In examining other marriage bonds of the day in this region for comparison, we noted that $200 was a hefty sum.

The middle section of the marriage document was left blank until the actual marriage took place. This part authorized the minister or justice of the peace to perform the marriage. Usually, but not always, this middle section got filled out on the same day as the top section. You can often tell that blank spaces were left by the clerk for future use because sometimes the empty area was way too large for the information that was later entered. The date on this section of the marriage bond for Lorenzo Ferrer and Nancy Alford was January 17, 1834.

The last section of the marriage bond is the actual declaration by the minister or justice of the peace that he did perform the marriage on the date noted in the declaration. Again, very often this date was the same as the bond declaration, meaning that the couple went to the courthouse, posted the bond, and got married right then. In the case of Lorenzo Ferrer and Nancy Alford, their marriage was officiated on January 22, 1834, by the minister Elisha Lott. They waited five days after their marriage bond was entered to perform the wedding ceremony. Also important to note is that Nancy was young when she wed (sixteen or seventeen), but not unusually so considering the time period. He, on the other hand, was around fifty-four, which makes for a very strange match.

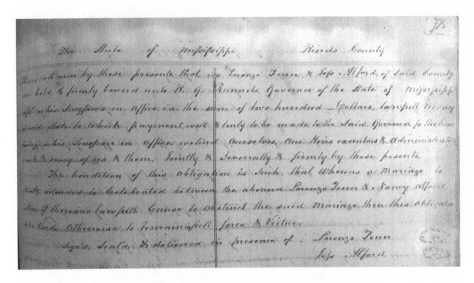

The January 1834 notations for the marriage of Lorenzo Ferror and Nancy Alford were found in the red Hinds County Marriages book in the Raymond courthouse.

There is a separate smaller ledger book in the same room of the Raymond courthouse as the marriage index. The second ledger is only marked in pencil on the first page as "Index to Marriage Bond." It provides a listing of the names and amounts of the bonds. Notation number 298 is for "Ferror Lorenzo to Nancy Alford," serving as further proof that the bond was finalized.

Several historical clues exist that tell us how Lorenzo Ferrer may have met Nancy Alford. In an online document called "Mississippi 'Alford' Federal Land Records" published by the Alford American Family Association, Jesse Alford is listed. The document states: "Note that over a period of about 11 years, he was involved with eight different land transactions that totaled about 640 acres."[14] These eight land purchases were all made at the Mt. Salus land office beginning in 1829—the same office where Lorenzo Ferrer was documented as purchasing land.

We know too from several documents in the Henry Brewer Family Papers that Jesse Alford did regular business from 1833–1837 with Henry and George Brewer. Remember George Brewer is the man who Ferrer allowed to borrow Louisa. In addition to the ledger sheet mentioning the "Ferrer girl" that we have previously noted, these documents also include:

- a receipt from Henry Brewer to Alford in 1833 for $22.81

- a receipt from George Brewer to Alford on July 22, 1833, for two dozen plates, cups, saucers, and a wash pan

- a receipt from Henry Brewer to Alford on January 11, 1834, "to the credit of his note which I hold in favor of George Brewer" (a receipt that is dated six days prior to the marriage of Lorenzo Ferrer to Alford's daughter)

- a $600 receipt on October 19, 1837, for a wagon and four horses (signed by Jesse Alford)

- a $1000 receipt on August 5, 1837, indicating Jesse Alford bought from George Brewer "a negro woman named Maria which negro I warrant sound in body and mind and a slave for life"[15]

These receipts tell the story of the Brewers likely being merchants and maybe even slave traders, which would cast further doubt over their intentions for Louisa when she was in George Brewer's possession for that year. This evidence also supports the notion that Lorenzo Ferrer likely became connected with the Brewers through his future father-in-law or perhaps connected with Alford through some prior dealing with the Brewers.

Following his marriage to Nancy, we found evidence that Ferrer stayed in the area—at least for a while. He appears on page nine of the 1834 Hinds County tax roll as *Lorenzo Ferrow*, claiming eighty acres of land at a value of $160. He is documented as having $400 loaned to him, and he paid one white poll tax and owned one enslaved person (likely Louisa). She would have been around twenty years old at this time—just three years older than Ferrer's wife. He paid $2.40 in taxes. The column for "Situation of" the land denotes where it was located. Many of the entries in the list are for towns like Clinton, Raymond, Pearl River, and White Oak. They are not filled in for every resident, but *Lorenzo Ferrow* is noted as living in "Rhodes Cr" or Rhodes Creek. Any additional information that historians in this area of Mississippi can provide by following this lead would be greatly appreciated.

Several other documents give us insight into what was happening with Ferrer during his Mississippi years. In November 1834, just ten months after his marriage, he and Nancy sold 160 acres in Copiah County to Martin W. Eagan for $700.[16] These 160 acres were in the same area where Ferrer purchased acreage via land grant (120 acres in December 1833 and forty acres in September 1834—for a total of 160 acres). Note as well that the forty acres were purchased just two months before the sale to Eagan was finalized, making Ferrer look very much like a land speculator flipping properties.

A Stunning Twist

However, here is where Lorenzo Ferrer's timeline in Mississippi takes a turn that seems to demonstrate the transient—if not secretive—nature of his dealings while there. A man who came to town and did business with prominent men such as Jesse Alford and the Brewers should have left a trail beyond a few land deeds and business transactions. We conducted a thorough search of any records we could find on the ground in multiple counties in Mississippi. We looked at literally every digitized document available for all Mississippi counties through the Mississippi Department of Archives and History—and then we drove to that facility and spent a day researching their physical holdings. Through several newspaper databases we found no trace of Lorenzo Ferrer or any variant spellings in Mississippi. We checked church records hoping he and Nancy found a congregation. We called all the Freemason lodges in the area to see if he had joined one of them, and every search came up empty. We paid special attention to Hazlehurst Lodge #25 in Copiah County. He was not on their charter in 1836. Our conclusion is that Lorenzo Ferrer wanted to fly under the radar in Mississippi. To our knowledge, he never owned a house there. He stayed out of public affairs and out of the newspapers. He was not an active citizen in any of these communities where he showed up. This is especially peculiar, given the fact that this area had just been opened up for American settlement. Every historical account of early settlers (which was not a large group of people and was thoroughly covered in most accounts we ran across) bears no mention of his name. He was, in a word, incognito.

At this point in our research, yet another plot twist presented itself. We happened upon a curious document in the tax records of Madison County, Mississippi, just to the north of Jackson. This is the county where the Henderson brothers from Lincoln County, North Carolina, had recently settled. In the Madison County seat of Canton, records in the chancery clerk's office show a *Lorenzo D. Farrow* on the 1834 tax roll. He was not there in 1833 or in any previous year. He is listed by himself, paying only one white poll tax. He is there again in 1835 on page nine as *L. D. Farror.* The first and most obvious question—where was Nancy?—would not remain a question for very long, but before we arrived there, we did find evidence that he had simply pulled up stakes and taken up the same game in another county. We located a land grant for thirty-nine acres purchased in the Mt. Salus land office on September 30, 1835. Then another hit came our way: *L. D. Farror* on the Madison County tax roll in 1836, page seven. No information was given other than what appears to be one white poll tax paid. The addition of the "D" as a middle initial was and still is curious. Was it perhaps the construct of a man who was trying (yet again) to reinvent himself? After these hits, he was gone from Mississippi altogether, which indicates he was the same Lorenzo Ferrer who had been doing business in neighboring counties to the south, and that Madison was apparently the last stop on his way to a completely new area of the country.

Before we leave Mississippi, though, a nagging loose end needs to be explored. We discovered a deed in the Madison County chancery clerk's office dated June 6, 1834 in which *L. D. Farrar and his wife Mary* deeded to William Walker and William Anthony land in Town No. 11 Range No. 3E near Love's Creek for $2,000. Her seal is indicated as "Mary" by the clerk. However, we believe there is a distinct possibility that the clerk could have misunderstood her name. There is a reasonable chance this was Nancy Alford Ferrer. By this date, Ferrer had been married to her for six months. The possibility also exists that Ferrer was living a double life in Madison County with a different wife. This document is the only reference to Mary that we found, and we searched marriage records all over Mississippi. There is simply no documentation to prove a second marriage.

And what of Nancy Alford Ferrer? Did she move to Madison County with her husband? Did they set up a house there? More information was needed about the Alford family, so we decided to focus attention on the life of Jesse Alford, Nancy's father. We certainly did not expect to find what came next. We were able to locate a notation in an online document called "Probable Descendants of Ferrell and Phebe Alford" on the Alford Association's genealogical portal, where we learned Jesse Alford was born to them in 1797.[17] Then came this revelation: "From MISSISSIPPI COURT RECORDS FROM THE FILES OF THE HIGH COURT OF ERRORS AND APPEALS, 1799–1859, compiled by Mary Louise Flowers Hendrix, 1999: Heirs of Jesse Alford, deceased: 1838, Hinds Co. MS—Nancy (wife of J. Brewer Munger) *1ˢᵗ husband was Lorenzo Ferror.*"[18]

Just to be sure we could believe what we were reading, we cross-checked with the print version of Hendrix's book to confirm. We already knew that *Ferror* was the way Lorenzo Ferrer's last name was spelled on the marriage bond to Nancy because we had seen the original in the Raymond courthouse. That part squared. What this meant, then, was that by the time Nancy's father, Jesse Alford, died in 1838, *Nancy was already married to someone else—a man named J. Brewer Mounger.*

We began working backwards feverishly, consulting all of the sources that had led us to the proof of Lorenzo Ferrer and Nancy Alford's marriage. We were back in North Carolina at the time, so running over to the Raymond courthouse to get the red marriage ledger was not an immediate option. Using what sources we could access at home, we immediately ran into a problem. We found John Brewer Mounger easily enough, and he definitely married a woman named Nancy in Hinds County in 1836. Numerous print sources and online genealogy tools established that unequivocally. Our issue was that they all referred to her as *Nancy Ferris.*

Could Hendrix have made a mistake in her recording of Nancy's maiden name? That seemed logical, and that is when we zeroed in on a common thread that ran through every genealogical site we consulted about the Mounger family: *no one doing research about the Mounger/Ferris union could find any information about Nancy Ferris's family.*

We were confident that we knew the reason why, but it required a trip to Mississippi to confirm. It would be several months before we could get back to the Raymond courthouse, but when we did, the answer came quickly. There in the red book was the triple-layered notation for the marriage between John Brewer Mounger and Nancy *Ferrer.* Reading the original handwritten entry, it was clear to us that one genealogist misread *Nancy Ferrer* as *Nancy Ferris* in the original marriage bond in Raymond. That mistake was then repeated by numerous other researchers, several of whom have commented in their family histories that the family of Nancy Ferris was impossible to locate. The reason, of course, is that her real name was *Nancy Alford Ferrer.* We are happy to be able to clear up this mystery for any Mounger family researchers who would like to now follow the trail back through the Alford family line. Ironically for us, the notation of Nancy's marriage to Lorenzo Ferrer is listed beside the entry of her marriage to John Mounger in the same index book. Months before, when we originally discovered Lorenzo Ferrer's marriage to Nancy Alford, we were looking at the same page with Nancy Ferrer's second marriage and did not realize it.

The unexpected discovery of this marriage just two years after she married Ferrer presented itself as a glaring new wrinkle and set off a new line of inquiry and a swirl of questions. How does a marriage dissolve with no record of divorce or annulment and with both spouses still alive? (We double checked Mississippi death records to make sure Ferrer had not died and another equally mysterious Ferrer emerged from the vapor to take his place. The answer, of course, was no. Ferrer—our Ferrer—was alive and well.) And even more confounding for us—how did all of this happen within the same community where the first marriage took place? At a maximum, we know that the Ferrer marriage could have lasted two years, but a much shorter union is within the realm of possibility. They were together at least for the sale of the 160 acres of land in November 1834, which should put aside any notion of annulment on grounds of failure to consummate. Indeed, we spent two weeks in Mississippi trying to find a record of divorce or annulment, even contacting the closest living Mounger descendant, George M. Mounger of Calhoun City, Mississippi, to see if there were any family stories circulating about Nancy's first marriage. While we learned some very interesting things when we met with Mounger and Rose Diamond of the Calhoun County Historical Society in their Bullard Street headquarters in Pittsboro, Mississippi, they were not able to provide any insight into the mystery.[19]

What we do know is that Lorenzo Ferrer, with Louisa in tow, soon appeared in North Carolina minus Nancy. Absent that, and absent any divorce records, annulment records, death certificates, or other documentation, we can only speculate. The reader is welcome to consider any one of these theories, all of which are plausible, and some of which could point, yet again, to Ferrer's previous life as Jean Laffite:

- The vast difference between their ages could indicate that Lorenzo and Nancy Ferrer's marriage was simply a business deal between Ferrer and Jesse Alford. Though Nancy was very young and was Alford's first-born, we have no way of determining Alford's scruples or sentimentality (or Ferrer's, for that matter). And if a simple business deal, then all parties may have mutually agreed to a collective case of marital amnesia once the need for the union no longer existed.

- Perhaps there was abuse of such magnitude that it dictated a dissolution of the marriage. Relationships and residencies being as fluid and as tenuous as they were in that area and that time could have seen Alford suggesting to Ferrer that he simply move along and never come back, in exchange for which Nancy's freedom would never be challenged.

- Infidelity is most certainly a possibility. Lorenzo Ferrer, as we will soon see, remained with Louisa until her death in North Carolina at the young age of forty, and we already know that Louisa was with him before he even married Nancy. Perhaps Nancy Ferrer discovered that her husband's relationship with the beautiful enslaved girl was much more than met the eye. We have found court records from this period of time in other states that indicate infidelity was a common ground cited for divorce, but, again, in an effort to wipe the slate clean, perhaps Ferrer, after being caught and confronted, agreed to move on in exchange for no fanfare, and perhaps Nancy was happy to comply.

- There is also the distinct possibility that one or more of these parties discovered that Lorenzo Ferrer was not who he claimed to be. This could hold true in more than one way. It is possible the Alford family, including Nancy, knew Ferrer's true identity and had no problem keeping that secret. In that case, an external force, such as someone else identifying him as Laffite and threatening exposure, could have precipitated an end to the charade and a quick exit by Ferrer (and Louisa). Another possibility is that the Alford family did not know Ferrer's true identity and only discovered it after the marriage—at which point they made their own threats of exposure if Ferrer did not agree to immediately take Louisa and get out.

- A final possibility is that Nancy Ferrer could simply have opened her eyes one morning to discover that she had been abandoned. In that case, abandonment could have come because Ferrer was tired of being married, was struggling to keep up appearances, or had discovered some other compelling reason why he needed to evacuate.

In any of these cases, what is clear is that Nancy Alford Ferrer Mounger's marriage to her second husband, John, was long, fruitful, happy, and blessed with eleven children, the first of which arrived in 1837. We have included as much information as we have been able to gather on the rest of Nancy's story in the Chapter Ten appendix. Hopefully it will be helpful to historians and Mounger family researchers alike.

THE COTTON CRASH

Simultaneous to the dissolution of Ferrer's marriage and his exit, the Mississippi economy got the shakes. As history tells us, when that rare convergence of factors actually happens and people in a specific moment in time are able to capitalize financially in an extraordinary way, it usually does not last long, whether that is a cotton boom, a gold rush, or even a lottery win. The historians who composed Copiah County's application for the National Register of Historic Places pointed out one of the infrastructure weaknesses that made the foundation of the Mississippi cotton boom so tenuous:

> The new territory had the potential to export tens of thousands of bales of cotton, but the rivers and roads in the state were inadequate trade arteries. Planters and farmers were attempting to transport their produce over inferior roads and rivers that were barely navigable. The Pearl River, one of the state's major waterways, was only navigable during the flush season, which at best was six months per year, and cotton shipped by this route was often severely damaged when rolled up and down muddy banks and exposed to rain and numerous delays.[20]

In a nutshell, Mississippi was not especially prepared to support such a vast industry. It was, in essence, a house of cards that had to fall—and it deserved to, considering the fact that it was built on the foundation of slavery and the theft of Native lands. As well, the price of cotton was not stable, so any fluctuation caused a major ripple in the larger pool.

Perhaps the greatest reason the cotton boom was doomed to fail was the fact that the Mississippi land sale system simply could not handle the lengths that speculators and those who were extending them credit would go to in order to make a profit. The whole process became very corrupt, with banks allowing individuals to overextend themselves and speculators moving land between parties in unregulated ways. In 1836, President Jackson issued an executive order that tried to get a handle on the situation, but which instead essentially imploded the system. Jackson's "Specie Circular" required that public lands like those taken from the Native Peoples in Mississippi be purchased only with *actual money*—gold and silver. (Specie is hard currency with an intrinsic value [like coins made of precious metals] rather than a note drafted by a bank or a government.) At that point, the speculator's shell game—which was largely built on agreements rather than actual money changing hands—was toast. What followed was the Panic of 1837, a series of events that pushed the United States into a recession until the mid-1840s and ruined the fortunes of many of the speculators who were in Mississippi betting on cotton prices remaining high. The dominoes then tumbled. Cotton prices began to fall. The selling price for enslaved people bottomed out. The government made it more difficult for individuals to turn a profit on flipping land. The banks became less willing to push their limits in the way that they had been, especially in a climate where some banks had failed due to the overexposure caused by imprudent lending. Simultaneously, the industries of land speculating and slave trading evaporated. At that point, the cotton explosion in Mississippi came to an end, and our friend Lorenzo Ferrer, now an aging man of fifty-seven years, needed a new place to call home.

The conclusion of Lorenzo Ferrer's time in Mississippi brought us back around to the Redhouse letter from Latour to Livingston on April 4, 1829: "Redhouse has been striving here to recover [some money due for work . . . he will visit you in Washington] . . . he wants to talk with you about assets he may be able to recover in France."[21]

If Jean Laffite was broke in 1829, living in Havana with or at least near Latour while he waited for Livingston to help him retrieve assets that had somehow been squirreled away in France, word of easy money in Mississippi would have been welcome news. The letter suggests Laffite was planning to make a trip to Washington to visit Livingston, who at the time was transitioning from his role as a US representative from Louisiana to that of a US senator in Congress. It is very possible that Jean Laffite had to go to Mississippi to earn some money while Livingston worked on his behalf. This would explain why *Lorenzo Ferrer* had to take out a loan to buy land and why he never bought a house or put down roots in Mississippi. Perhaps he was living at Jesse Thompson's store because he had no other choice. And regardless of residence, the paper trail of Ferrer in Mississippi shows that Laffite arrived and promptly began doing what he knew best—brokering enslaved people and making money under the table.

We have no proof that Laffite ever made the trip to Washington to see Livingston. We did find one more compelling nugget in Princeton that tugged at us though. The Edward Livingston Papers include a small gray journal with a blue and red marbled design on the jacket. It covers the years 1834–1836. From 1833–1835, Livingston served as the American ambassador to France. We discovered a notation in the notebook on August 9, 1834, in Livingston's notoriously bad, scribbled handwriting.[22] The reader is certainly free to disagree with our interpretation of the handwriting, which we see as "Laffite . . . (claim holding him in Paris)." If this is indeed a notation referring to Jean Laffite, it would appear that more than five years had elapsed without resolution to his called-in favor, which could indicate that he was potentially in dire financial straits. This may be explanation enough for why an aging pirate with an alias was skipping in and out of land offices in the state of Mississippi in the 1830s trying to piece together a living.

It would be great if Edward Livingston had better handwriting, but alas, we had to read the Edward Livingston Papers at Princeton University despite his horrid penmanship. This notation from August 9, 1834, in his notebook appears to reference "Laffite" and a "claim holding him in Paris." Courtesy of Princeton University Library

CHAPTER ELEVEN

KEEPING UP WITH THE HENDERSONS

Circling back to our last hit on Lorenzo Ferrer, we had him on the Madison County, Mississippi, tax roll in 1836, far north of where he lived when he was married to Nancy. It is here that we pick up the tale of the Henderson brothers from Lincolnton, North Carolina. These men were engaged in the same buying and selling habits as Ferrer and in the same locations in Mississippi at the exact moment in time when Ferrer appears on the Madison County tax rolls. Still, that extraordinary coincidence did not reveal itself until we were well into our search of Ferrer's activities in Mississippi. Almost from the beginning of the Mississippi discoveries, we had been searching for any reference that could shed light on how and why Ferrer would have chosen Lincolnton, North Carolina, as a new home. Unless he had simply thrown a dart at a map, there must have been a reason, some connection that was as yet undiscovered. And then we realized it had been right under our noses all along.

Woodside, a lovely 1798 federal-style dwelling in Lincolnton, was built by Major Lawson Henderson, a very wealthy landowner of more than two thousand acres. Henderson and his wife, Elizabeth, had thirteen children, ten of them boys. At various times, Major Henderson also served as sheriff of Lincoln County and as Lincoln County clerk of court, both at the county and superior court levels. It is no small wonder that a good number of his sons later showed the same talent for advocacy, forcefulness, leadership, and business in their own lives. During the course of the rest of this book, you will come to see that nine of the Henderson sons, plus one grandson and the husband of a granddaughter, connect either directly or indirectly to Ferrer, as does their family seat, Woodside.

While many of the Henderson sons were successful, the most prominent of all the siblings was James Pinckney, first governor of Texas. In one of those "aha" moments that are fondly looked back on by researchers everywhere,

Built in 1798, Woodside is one of Lincoln County's
most treasured historic homes.

one day we thought to ask ourselves how James P. Henderson made his
way from North Carolina to Texas, and in so doing, we found the key that
unlocked the mystery of how Ferrer had landed in Lincolnton. We discovered that Henderson did not go directly from North Carolina to Texas, but
that he had first settled briefly in (drumroll, please) the Madison County,
Mississippi, town of Canton. Almost immediately, the puzzle pieces fell into
place. Following this revelation, we began searching the Mississippi archives
for any evidence of Henderson's stay there—only to discover that he was not
the only one in his family to have moved to Canton. The same tax rolls that
had shone a bright light on Ferrer's presence in Madison County now gave
evidence that Lawson F. Henderson, older brother of James, had arrived in
1833. Not only that, younger brother George W. Henderson quickly followed. Even though the Henderson and Ferrer timeline in Mississippi only
overlapped for a couple of years, we knew that in a small and sparsely populated area such as Madison County, chances were good that these men had
become friends.

In fact, the untold portion of Jean Laffite's later life as Lorenzo Ferrer cannot be accurately recounted without acknowledging the repeated connections that we eventually found, across multiple states and five decades, to this very influential family. Time and again during our research, their names emerged in Census records, tax rolls, abstracts of deeds, and even the minutes of Masonic lodge meetings, all in connection with Ferrer's various places of residence, his business and social dealings, and even his last will and testament. In fact, the trail of documentation laid down by this family was so central to our understanding of Laffite's story that without it, the tale may not have been fully possible to tell.

Local historians will no doubt appreciate the Henderson family data that we gathered in the course of this writing, and for that reason, we are providing complete genealogical and historic information on each family member in the Chapter Eleven appendix.

For the purposes of completing the Mississippi timeline and making the transition into North Carolina, we will focus on the three brothers who likely first made the acquaintance of Ferrer in Madison County.

1. **Lawson Franklin Henderson**, 1806–1858, left Lincoln County and relocated to Canton, Mississippi, county seat of Madison County, sometime during the 1830s. Once there, he formed a business partnership with his brother, James Pinckney Henderson, who briefly established a law practice in Canton around 1835. Legal documents show land deals involving the two brothers and also transactions shown as Henderson & Henderson beginning in the mid-1830s in the Canton area and continuing on for years. He was married to Ann Dunavant and died in New Orleans in 1858. His will became part of a well-documented Mississippi Supreme Court case.

2. **James Pinckney Henderson**, 1808–1858, was educated in Lincoln County and studied law at the University of North Carolina at Chapel Hill. He briefly set up a law practice in North Carolina after passing the bar in 1829. According to *The Writings of Sam Houston 1813–1863* in a section called "On the death of James Pinckney Henderson, June 5, 1858," Henderson's health began to suffer (some have speculated it was tuberculosis) sometime between 1830 and 1834, during which time he made a trip to Cuba in an attempt to regain his strength.[1] Following this trip, Henderson set up a law practice in Canton. We confirmed with Darin Panel at Freemason Lodge #28 in Canton, Mississippi, that James Pinckney Henderson was a member of that lodge in his brief time in Canton.[2] Henderson's law practice was right on the main square where the now vacant Canton courthouse stands.

He quickly distinguished himself as an ardent and passionate advocate for the cause of Texas independence from Mexico, gaining notoriety for delivering rousing public speeches designed to enlist local militia willing to travel to the Texas territory and assist in the fight. *The New Handbook of Texas* reports he arrived in the Lone Star State on June 3, 1836, where he received his commission from Provisional President David G. Burnet as a brigadier general in the conflict.[3] His charge was to travel to recruit additional forces for the cause. Henderson naturally came back to North Carolina to find recruits, which were placed under the command of John B. Harry. In fact, Harry's original muster rolls are available for study today at the Dolph Briscoe Center for American History in Austin. (We scoured them just in case, but Lorenzo Ferrer's name is not on them.) Yet by the time Henderson arrived in Texas with his recruits, the Mexicans had already surrendered at the Battle of San Jacinto, so Henderson's soldiers never saw combat. Henderson remained in Texas and eventually became the first governor of the new state in 1845. Prior to that, he served as the Republic of Texas's ambassador to England and France (where he met and married Frances Cox), and before his death he served as a US senator from Texas. When not functioning in these capacities, Henderson tended to a successful law practice in Nacogdoches and then later in San Augustine, Texas. In an ironic twist, we discovered that the profiles for Jean Laffite and James Pinckney Henderson appear back-to-back in John Warner Barber and Henry Howe's massive two-volume set *Our Whole Country, or the Past and Present of the United States, Historical and Descriptive* published in 1861.[4] The edition consists of thousands of pages, so it is quite the cosmic joke that these two appear in tandem in such a large work.

3.   **George William Henderson,** 1814–1850, traveled to Madison County, Mississippi, and lived there, working as a merchant. George died in Springfield, Livingston Parish, Louisiana, in 1850, the same year that he was shown in the Madison County Census. He married Amanda M. Moore in 1835.[5]

While these three Henderson men formed the bulk of the Madison County business activity that we discovered, it is worth noting that two or three more of the brothers eventually came to reside in Canton, as well as several other Lincoln County, North Carolina, residents of note. Their names were Hugh L. Henderson, Walter C. Henderson, Wallace Henderson, and George W. Motz.

In addition to James Pinckney Henderson, another Henderson brother showed up in Cuba, providing an additional odd angle to this story. Most people who know the general details of Laffite's exploits associate him with New Orleans and Galveston. However, our story has deep roots in Cuba, that sunny island ninety miles south of Key West, Florida. Not surprisingly, the Henderson boys put down a few roots in Havana as well. Wallace Alexander Henderson, the first of the fourteen children, died on April 24, 1823, at the age of twenty-three in Havana. Once Henderson caught pulmonary consumption around 1822, he moved to the favorable Cuban climate for rest and recuperation. Upon his death in Cuba, Henderson family members could have been summoned to the island. At the time, Havana was a small town. We have already established that Jean Laffite was in the hands of Cuban officials twice in 1822, making his hysterical hospital escape in February 1822. The Cuban overlap of Laffite and Wallace Alexander Henderson offers an unlikely but still plausible opportunity for Ferrer to have connected with the Henderson family even earlier than the mid-1830s in Mississippi.

One final Henderson family member is worth noting here for his potential connection to Laffite in New Orleans: Lieutenant Colonel James Henderson. He was born on July 5, 1775, in Lincoln County, though some genealogy sources list his birth in Gaston County, which borders Lincoln County to the south. He was the son of James L. Henderson Sr. and Violet Henderson and the brother of Major Lawson H. Henderson. He was, therefore, the uncle of all the Henderson children we have listed here and in the appendices. He married Margaret Dickson in 1796. Notably, Henderson County, Tennessee, which sits in the western part of that state, was named for him in 1821 to commemorate his death on December 28, 1814, in a skirmish with the British that preceded the famous Battle of New Orleans by eleven days. Henderson ranked as a Lieutenant Colonel in the Tennessee State Militia.

Elbert L. Watson's *Tennessee at the Battle of New Orleans* describes the encounter with the British that sealed Henderson's fate. In late 1814, the British, unwilling to relent, began pouring thousands more soldiers into the area around New Orleans. Watson writes that by December 24, General Andrew Jackson and other commanders realized the British were not going to retreat, and plans were made to address the situation. Watson claims

> On the evening of December 27, the British rushed a strong force forward, causing Jackson's advance guard to fall back under heavy cannon, rocket,

and musket fire. [British Major General Sir Edward] Pakenham staged a reconnaissance in force the next day and before it was called off the British were able to install a sizable force behind a fence oblique to the American line. [American Major General William] Carroll instructed Colonel James Henderson and a detachment of 200 men to sweep along a wooded area, make a turn to the right toward the river and thus cut off the Redcoats.[6]

Alexander Walker in *The Life of Andrew Jackson* offers even more detail about the miscalculation of Henderson's unit:

> Col. Henderson, with two hundred Tennesseeans [*sic*], [was ordered] to steal through the swamp, gain the rear of Rennie's [British] party and then oblique to the right so as to cut them off from the main body. It was a rash adventure, such as General Jackson would not have sanctioned had he been present in that part of the line. But the Tennesseeans were impatient to take part in the fight, and could with difficulty be kept within the lines. Henderson's movement might have succeeded, if he had not advanced too far to the right, and thus brought his men under the heavy fire of a strong body of the British who were posted behind a fence nearly concealed by the trees and weeds. The Colonel, a gallant and promising officer, and five men were killed by this fire, several were wounded, and the others seeing the object of the movement defeated retired behind the lines.[7]

Watson concludes that the "slant to the right" was just wide enough to take Henderson and his men outside the reach of their protective cover.[8] This mistake led to tragedy for the Henderson family.

We searched extensively for documented proof that Jean Laffite and Henderson may have crossed paths during the skirmishes leading up to the Battle of New Orleans with no luck. It is unclear when Henderson actually got to the area with his men from Tennessee. Nonetheless, a Lincolnton Henderson dying in a precursor battle to a conflict history has proven Jean Laffite played a significant role in is reason enough to take note, especially considering that we can outline the strong and solidly documented presence of the Henderson brothers (and sister) in Mississippi, Louisiana (including New Orleans), Texas, and North Carolina. These time frames and locations directly correspond to the activities of Laffite both before and after he re-entered the United States under his new identity as Lorenzo Ferrer. What is more, you will see a continued connection to this family after Ferrer arrives to take up residence in their hometown of Lincolnton. The sum of these connections, then, moves the Henderson/Laffite/Ferrer relationship beyond the circumstantial and into the realm of established fact.

We cannot conclude this chapter without making mention of another coincidence. Edward Livingston was the American ambassador to France from 1833 to 1835. Following Livingston's turn as ambassador, one James Pinckney Henderson—representing the Republic of Texas—served as minister to England and France. Laffite had money in France that he wanted to get back, and he was known associates with Edward Livingston. Lorenzo Ferrer was in tight with the Henderson clan from Mississippi and North Carolina, men who also had ties to France. And all of these men were Freemasons.

As the 1830s dawned, most of the members of Jean Laffite's posse were dying. These were not just the men he commanded in his glory days in Barataria and Galveston but the men who had run interference for him for years before— the kind of gang a renegade needed to keep himself off the gallows. History tells us that pirates—even the most capable ones—get caught and pay the ultimate price. Laffite, as perhaps the last pirate way beyond the reach of the Golden Age of Piracy, operated in a world that was shrinking in on him. International governments in his usual haunts were becoming increasingly adept at managing their borders and preventing pirates from gaining strongholds. Likewise, their naval forces were becoming much better at controlling their waters. American legislation had made the importation of enslaved people (one of Laffite's main sources of income) illegal and punishable by death, and he had pretty much burned his ability to operate anywhere in the Gulf because he was so well-known. The only way he persisted and kept his head for as long as he did was because he still had connections to powerful men like Edward Livingston and Arsène Latour. With Livingston's death in 1836 and Latour's in 1837, Laffite, even in his newly invented persona as Lorenzo Ferrer, needed a new backup crew, and we argue he chose the rich, powerful, and very connected Hendersons.

Regarding the extensive activity of the Hendersons that we uncovered in Madison County, we encourage the reader to explore the Chapter Eleven Appendix, which provides a detailed and fully sourced guide to everything that we were able to find. While the deals outlined in that appendix appear to be mostly related to land speculation and promissory note underwriting, we had a strong suspicion that the Hendersons were also slave traders like Ferrer. Our suspicions were confirmed when then Lincoln County Historical Director Jason Harpe forwarded a newspaper clipping from the December 1, 1854, edition of the *Western Democrat*.[9] It certainly appears that Slade, Henderson and Company in Lincolnton were in the business of trafficking human beings.

To recap, we have documented many members of the very large Henderson family conducting business in the exact area of Mississippi where

Thirteen Likely Negroes for Sale.

11 **STOUT FELLOWS,** ONE WOMAN AND A little girl, also six mules. Said property will be sold at public auction, in Lincolnton, on Wednesday the 20th December, 1854, on a credit of 8 months with interest from date. Notes payable at the Bank of Cape Fear Branch at Salisbury.

SLADE, HENDERSON & CO.

November 28, 1854.   1050—3tw.

Advertisements like this one from the December 1, 1854, Western Democrat *indicate that the Henderson men of Lincoln County were an active part of the slave trade.*

Jean Laffite chose to begin his new chapter as Lorenzo Ferrer. This happens at the exact time in Laffite's life when the last of his supporting wing men had died. Then Ferrer makes a precise and fortuitous exit from Mississippi just ahead of the tidal wave that destroyed the 1830s cotton boom, only to arrive shortly thereafter in the Henderson family seat of Lincolnton (with enough money that he never again worked).

We are convinced Ferrer came to Lincolnton *because of the Hendersons* and that he remained there as a man of means, doing business with them, socializing with them, and increasing his own coffers, largely hidden away from history while the memory of Jean Laffite faded from view in the waters of the Gulf. Had it not been for the quiet voice of an octoroon woman named Louisa, whose presence with him in both Mississippi and North Carolina confirmed his identity, he may have always remained simply a local legend whose origins were impossible to determine. Indeed, one of the most daunting elements of our research stemmed from the likelihood that Lorenzo Ferrer was quite happy to live in relative obscurity, safe in the belief that he had severed ties with his past life and had left no paper trail. Discovering proof and truth under those circumstances is a difficult task by any measure. As it stands, however, Louisa bridged the gap between Cuba in the 1820s and the North Carolina town in 1839 that he finally called home.

And no one will be surprised to learn in the coming pages that even at his death thirty-six years later, the Hendersons were still by his side.

III

NORTH CAROLINA

CHAPTER TWELVE

A PIRATE COMES TO LINCOLNTON

On November 22, 1970, the *Gastonia Gazette*, a hometown paper from Lincoln County's neighbor Gaston County, included an article by Jay Hampton called "Lincoln County Rich in History." Hampton wrote,

> After the war of 1812, after the pirate LaFitte was pardoned by President James Madison for his help in the fight against the British, a swashbuckling Frenchman arrived in Lincolnton with a trunk of gold. Some people thought the man, who called himself Lorenzo Ferrer, was the notorious LaFitte. The grave carries the name Ferrer. But the legend says it was LaFitte. But that was long ago—too long ago for fact.[1]

This prevailing belief—that the myriad of local stories could be nothing more than fantasy—was the attitude we first experienced when beginning to poke around in the nooks and crannies of Lincoln County where true answers might actually reside.

> *You can't mean the pirate.*
> *That's just an old wives' tale.*
> *Our records don't go back that far.*
> *There's no truth to those old rumors anyway.*
> *So-and-so wrote an article about that in 1950. She found everything there*
> *was to know about it.*

To a couple of stubborn southern girls like us, these dismissive comments were all the more reason for us to push forward. Fiction and fact are first cousins on their daddy's side, and we knew enough to recognize that local stories are rarely born completely in a vacuum. Our task required us to collect all of the evidence, rescue it from its compartmentalization in individual sources, and lay it out side by side to see what kind of collective conversation it created. This had to happen before any of it could be accepted or discounted. After just a few months of research, it became abundantly clear that the local effort to learn about Lorenzo Ferrer had been plagued by several critical limitations. First, the historians who did the most thorough work on Ferrer conducted it in the days of the card catalog—before records were digitized and online databases existed. Resources like access to a research library and unlimited interlibrary loans were also not available. The furthest even the most ambitious of previous historians traveled for answers was the state archives in Raleigh. As well, none of them were Jean Laffite scholars, so they were operating with a fundamental lack of understanding about his personality, characteristics, habits, experiences, connections, aptitudes, weaknesses, and tendencies. Without this macro view of the full evidence, no complete Laffite/Ferrer investigation could occur.

THE LINCOLNTON CONNECTION

The final document identified with the name *L. D. Farror* in Mississippi was the 1836 tax roll in Madison County. From that point forward, there is no evidence we could put our hands on to suggest that he ever went back, and every man with a similar name who does appear in some form in that state is definitely too young to be him. Just as inexplicably as he had appeared, he was gone.

But then . . .

In the year 1839, a man named *Loranzo Ferrer*, aged fifty-five, appeared on the Hedrick's Company tax roll in Lincoln County, North Carolina, a moderately sized county northwest of Charlotte. Lincolnton, with a current population of about 10,000 people, is the county seat.

Upon discovering this 1839 reference, we began to work backwards in Lincoln County to see if there were any earlier mentions of Ferrer. In the state archives, we consulted a list of Lincolnton residents from 1836–1837, and Mr. Ferrer was not included. We also checked the 1836 and 1837 Lincoln County tax rolls with no hits. We were ultimately unable to locate any North Carolina documents prior to 1839 that included Ferrer.

The Charles R. Jonas Library on West Main Street in Lincolnton houses the best collection of local print sources of the three main county libraries. Within that collection is a book called *Lincoln County Heritage, 1997*, which contains an entry that asserts Ferrer "is first mentioned as a guest at a local

Hedrick's Tax List, 1839

hunting lodge, frequented by wealthy statesmen and financiers. He arrived later with his enslaved octoroon housekeeper/mistress, Louisa, and took up residence in Lincolnton. They were often seen riding down main street in his hack, the Frenchman and his lady. She was described as a striking beauty."[2] This was the same Louisa that Ferrer had with him in Mississippi. She was "about seventeen" in the George Brewer document in 1831, which matches her age at death (forty) in the year 1858 in Lincolnton. Finding her name associated with Lorenzo Ferrer in Mississippi was the critical piece of evidence that allowed us to know this was the same Lorenzo Ferrer who showed up in Lincolnton. Even though Louisa was one of several hundred thousand enslaved women in the United States who never had a voice, simply with the presence of her name on that document, she managed to speak up and identify Ferrer for us. It is worthy of note that few references to Ferrer's life in Lincolnton ever went without mention of Louisa, and we are pleased that she got the last word from the grave.

Lincoln County Heritage, 1997 is the only source that notes Ferrer at the hunting lodge or the fact that he came to town alone before bringing Louisa. If true, this begs the question of where she was in the interim. It could be that she had been rented out again as she had been in Mississippi in the early 1830s. A word of caution is necessary here, too, because local historians who were part of the publication of the *Lincoln County Heritage* volume reveal it was not curated for accuracy—anyone could submit anything for inclusion.

A LINCOLNTON TIMETABLE

With the 1839 tax roll as our gateway, we began compiling all the documentation we could find. By charting a timeline of every primary document mentioning Ferrer in Lincoln County, we were able to see a stark difference between his behavior in Mississippi and his new life in the Old North State. In Lincolnton, he *immediately* weaved himself into the fabric of society by making a wide variety of friends, joining a church congregation, attending public events, entering into business deals, paying taxes, talking more freely with the Census man, offering public toasts, joining a local Freemason lodge and at least one committee, participating in activities that put him in the local papers, and—most tellingly—providing limited details about his past. Like Jean Laffite, he was identified by locals as a Frenchman (likely due to his accent). Victor Fair's *The Hills of Home* even claims (but with no supporting documentation) that Ferrer was "a soldier in the French Army under Napoleon."[3] The difference in Ferrer's behavior in Mississippi versus North Carolina may also be attributed to the difference in atmosphere. Lincolnton in the 1830s was, according to local historian Gaither Schrum, "a lawless frontier town" that was home to "a bunch of hell-raisers."[4] Schrum surmises that Ferrer would not "have been bored to death. I bet they drank more whiskey than water."[5] Schrum says at the time, "[s]ecluded Lincolnton had few homes and no rail system."[6] Add to this the fact that the Henderson family made Lincolnton their home base. In essence, Lorenzo Ferrer had found a comfortable, cloistered place with a network of friends to protect him. As a result, he blossomed in Lincoln County and inserted himself into almost every facet of the community.

For the benefit of future historical research, we have compiled an organized outline by decade of all the documents we were able to locate that demonstrate Ferrer's activities in Lincoln County for the remainder of his life. Every piece of information that we have found, including citations for each record, appears in the Chapter Twelve appendix. This data will be of especially keen interest to Lincoln County historians, as it details every shred of primary material available. Below we offer a summary of this information.

1840S:

During his first decade in North Carolina, Ferrer quickly became a resident of record, showing up in the 1840 Census. Because he did not declare any other members of his household in this Census, it could support the notion that he first came to Lincolnton without Louisa. Additionally, the first recorded business deal for Ferrer in Lincolnton involved, not surprisingly, one of the Hendersons. Ferrer entered into a joint indenture involving the affairs of Dr. Samuel Simpson—a transaction which in modern-day terms would be considered a private loan.[7] Another participant in this loan was Lawson Henderson, son of Lincolnton resident Charles C. Henderson and nephew of the Henderson brothers who had relocated to Canton, Mississippi. Ferrer also put down roots during the 1840s, purchasing several pieces of property within the Lincolnton city limits.

Subsequent records for the 1840s show that he added enslaved people to his household as well as properties, but perhaps the most striking aspect of Ferrer's first decade in his new hometown was his willingness to become publicly involved in matters of civic affairs.

In November of 1844, *L. Ferrer* signed a petition that was submitted to the General Assembly of North Carolina in protest of neighboring Catawba County being formed out of lands taken from Lincoln County.[8] The signatures around Ferrer's—names like C. C. Henderson (whose signature immediately follows Ferrer's on the document, indicat-

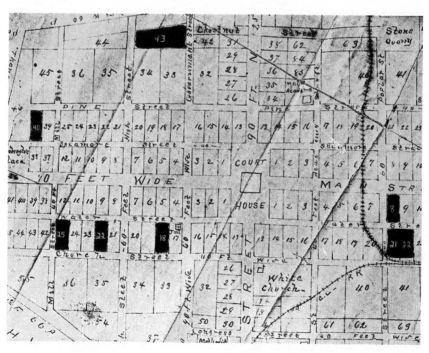

This Sanborn map of downtown Lincolnton in Lorenzo Ferrer's day highlights in black the pieces of property he owned.

ing they could have been standing side by side at the signing), Vardry McBee, Jacob A. Ramseur, Andrew Motz, and D. W. Schenck—suggest the document was likely displayed at a public gathering of the town's most important figures.

Then in 1847 and 1848, Ferrer's participation is noted in two separate and very public events. The first, an 1847 Independence Day celebration in town, was covered by the *Lincoln Courier* on July 7, 1847. Ferrer offered the following toast: "Honor to the brave and honorable citizens, who have not only taken up arms against the atrocities perpetrated by the sanguinary Mexican savages; but whom, like Romans, in the midst of carnage have preferred death to disgrace."[9] It was an eloquent speech and a testament to Ferrer's intelligence and breadth of vocabulary, not to mention his opinions on the Mexican-American War involving the state of Texas and Lincolnton's James Pinckney Henderson, whose recent election as the first governor of the new state had placed him squarely in the middle of that conflict.

Likewise, the 1848 Independence Day celebration on the courthouse lawn focused on the same war and the matter of how to honor local troops who had participated. A motion was made to assemble a committee that would be tasked with making those decisions, and "L. Ferrer, Esq." was listed as a member of that committee.[10]

Taken as a whole, Ferrer's actions after arriving in Lincolnton provide an interesting contrast to his behavior in Mississippi where, still seemingly with the remnants of a renegade's past nipping at his heels, he took care not to be seen or remembered in any significant way, and indeed seemed to work very hard at not staying in one place for very long, much less putting down any roots. We attribute evidence of this newfound confidence and security to the theory that he felt increasingly safe due to two major factors: First, Lincolnton's location is far removed from those in the Gulf region who might possibly recognize him; and second, of course, is his friendship with the powerful Henderson family.

1850s:

The protection of a new location and a powerful set of friends notwithstanding, the 1850s proved rather tumultuous for Lorenzo Ferrer. His presence in town continued to be documented on tax rolls and Census records, and we found evidence that he still bought and sold property, made loans, and even sold an enslaved man named Ephraim in the year 1853 to C. C. Henderson for $1000.[11]

Beyond that, however, he became increasingly involved in local conflict, even ending the decade with a lawsuit against a few fellow residents that found its way to the North Carolina Supreme Court. Much of this drama connected either directly or indirectly to Ferrer's membership in the local Masonic lodge, a group that was chartered in 1852 with Ferrer noted in the lodge records as an early founding member. We have devoted an entire later chapter to this segment of Ferrer's time in Lincolnton which will delve into the 1850s in detail, but suffice it to say that the second decade of Lorenzo Ferrer's life in North Carolina was not as tranquil as the first. It also appears that some of Jean Laffite's old tendencies and characteristics, while having been shoved into a corner for a spell, may have reasserted themselves during this time.

An interesting public mention of Ferrer in the 1850s provides a bit of insight as well. The January 19, 1858, edition of the *Western Democrat* described a political meeting held at the Lincoln County Court House on January 12. The purpose was to talk about representation from the county at the upcoming Democratic convention to appoint a candidate for governor. Those in attendance were looking for one hundred names to nominate as delegates. The name "L. Ferrer" is included under a list of men "appointed under the 1st resolution."[12] In the late 1820s, a wave of antagonism about the supposed elitism of Freemasonry brought about the formation of the Anti-Masonic Party. It fizzled a decade later, but many of its members transitioned over to the Whig party, a wing of which absolutely loathed Andrew Jackson and his dedication to the tenets of the Brotherhood. In the years that followed this anti-Masonic movement, even state elections became battlegrounds. It is reasonable to assume that Ferrer's support of Democratic candidates may have been connected to his desire to counter attacks brought about by politicians whose suspicion of Freemasonry colored their positions.

One other notable occurrence during the 1850s involved the death of Louisa, Ferrer's octoroon mistress, who died on November 29, 1858, and was buried in St. Luke's Episcopal Cemetery the next day.

1860s:

By the 1860s, Ferrer was eighty years of age, a period of life which naturally entails slowing down—both physically and socially. Having exited the Masonic lodge in 1858, and with most all of the local drama and intrigue seemingly behind him, the Ferrer record becomes sparse, indicating that he settled in to enjoy his remaining days in relative peace and quiet. Had it not been for the Civil War, it is indeed possible that not much else would have been heard of this man. As it stands, though, two accounts involving Ferrer during the 1860s survive—one of them very familiar to most local Lincoln County residents, and the other not so well known. Both of them, however, are instructive and intriguing for anyone who believes, as we do, that this man truly was Jean Laffite.

Wallace Reinhardt was one of Lorenzo Ferrer's best friends. His story, as it relates to Ferrer, is detailed in Chapter Thirteen. One of those stories involves the single account of Lorenzo Ferrer in Lincolnton that seems to have been mentioned in every news article or historic essay ever written about him. For the purposes of the 1860s timeline, we point it out here in summary. Reinhardt related to friends that on the eve of the arrival of the Union Army in Lincoln County in 1865, Ferrer summoned him and asked for assistance. He was concerned about his chests of valuables—gold coins, jewels, and other items—that might fall prey to theft if they were discovered by Union troops. With the help of Reinhardt and several others, the chests, which Reinhardt reported to be very heavy and filled to overflowing, were moved by wagon from Ferrer's house to safekeeping in the basement vault of the Lincoln County Courthouse, which was only a few blocks away. Following the securing of the chests, Reinhardt says that Ferrer opened one of them, scooped out a handful of gold coins, and paid Reinhardt with those coins for his kind service. Henceforth, that story alone has become part of the permanent Ferrer-as-Laffite canon in local folklore. And while no record exists of what happened to those chests during the occupation or after the war, it is noteworthy that Reinhardt was later named the executor of Ferrer's will and also the recipient of Ferrer's main residence, along with the contents of that house and everything on the property.

The second story, not widely known, involves an alleged altercation between Ferrer and some of the Union troops on the streets of Lincolnton. It is found in an article in the *Lincoln County News* from July 1, 1915, called "Some Reminiscences of the Confederate War." The article harkens back to a shooting that occurred at the county jail, which was right beside Ferrer's house. The article explains:

> [A]n old gentleman, named Ferrer, a very nice clean dressy man, I rather think he was a Frenchman, anyway, he lived next to the jail, and came out to see what was going on, as shooting in the street was something exciting. One of the soldiers asked him 'what time it was,' and when Mr. Ferrer got his nice gold watch out, the Yankee said, 'that is a nice watch,' and took it apparently to look at it. He said, 'it will just fit in my pocket,' and so he did pocket it. Then another soldier proposed to trade boots and he

made Mr. Ferrer pull his boots off and the soldier gave him in exchange his old cavalry boots, and told him he would give him his spurs to boot. Mr. Ferrer protested and said, 'Why, you would not make a gentleman pull his boots off in the street.' Another Yankee tried to make one of the negroes who was with them, take Mr. Ferrer's silk beaver hat and give him an old greasy army cap in exchange, to the negro's credit, he said a beaver hat would not look well on him as long as his mule was scary. Mr. Ferrer was so disgusted that he left the old cavalry boots in the streets and went home and he would never talk about it as it made him mad ever afterwards to refer to it.[13]

If true, this would have happened in April 1865, which is when the Yankees were in the vicinity of Lincolnton near the close of the Civil War. Lorenzo Ferrer would have been at or near eighty-five years of age. A younger man with more to lose might have pushed the issue further, but one in his mid-eighties would likely have responded just as Ferrer did and would certainly have been as disgusted, both at the behavior of the soldiers and also at the handicap of his own advanced years. Note the reference to the "fine silk beaver hat," which is not inconsistent with eyewitness accounts of Jean Laffite's similar fondness for fine otter-skin caps.

While thinly supported, these accounts from eyewitnesses who knew Ferrer are nonetheless compelling and should at the very least be taken into consideration as part of the narrative. In actuality, they contain details that inadvertently reference the life of Jean Laffite, even though the ones recounting them were not aware they were supplying such details.

1870s:

Following the end of the war, and now at the age of ninety, Ferrer was approaching the final days of his life. Reportedly bedridden during these latter years, he was under the care of a housekeeper named Eliza, whose presence in his life is documented both in public records and also in a curious letter that was reportedly written by Ferrer and later recounted in print by local historian Victor Fair, who was the grandson of Wallace Reinhardt.

Fair reports in his account that "in his late years, [Ferrer] was bedridden, and was waited on by his negro woman."[14] There are two indications that Ferrer's opinion of Eliza was less than stellar. Even though his estate was considerable by the standards of the day, and even though he left detailed sums of money and property to many friends, or descendants of earlier friends, he left nothing to Eliza in his will. The eyebrow-raising passage in the Ferrer letter (recipient unknown) states it pretty clearly: "the negro hussy that stays with me is stealing all my money."[15] We have never seen this letter, but Fair clearly did or else he would not be able to quote it directly. It may be that Ferrer was suspicious of Eliza but was too old to care for himself and needed her. She may have been stealing from him, and just as likely, he could have been delusional in his advanced age.

The last evidence of Ferrer's dealings in Lincolnton during these years consists of one final land transaction, which was basically a donation (for the sum of $1) of a tract of land three miles north of Lincolnton to the Episcopal Diocese of North Carolina for the purpose of building St. Paul's Church.[16] Following that, he wrote his last will and testament on May 1, 1873.[17] There were two witnesses. One was a man named Thomas Wells. The other, Robert Sowers, had recently been married to Theodora Henderson, a daughter of one of the original Henderson brothers—Charles Cotesworth Henderson.

Chapter Thirteen

A Pirate Finds a Port

With his mistress Louisa by his side, the man known as Lorenzo Ferrer made the decision that Lincolnton would be his permanent home. If his early years in town were a test to see how he would blend in with the people and the rhythm of North Carolina life, his determination to remain there until his death indicated that Lincolnton had apparently passed the test. The pirate had found a safe port.

Louisa and Vatinius

The most important relationship of Ferrer's life in Lincolnton was with his mistress, Louisa. In the lower graveyard of St. Luke's Episcopal Cemetery at 315 N. Cedar Street in Lincolnton is a modest but lovely tombstone commemorating her life. Her tomb marker reads as follows:

> To the memory of Louisa, born in Richmond, VA. Died November 29, 1858. Aged 40 years. The deceased was amiable, kind and pious. She was in life respected and in death lamented by all who knew her. The marble monument will crumble and decay, but the virtues of the deceased will live forever. This token to the memory of the deceased is erected by her master L. Ferrier.

Strangely, her last name is misspelled as *Ferrier* on the tombstone, even though Lorenzo Ferrer was the one who made arrangements for her funeral. What is actually known for sure about Louisa from historical documents is quite limited. The old ledgers kept in the church office of St. Luke's indicate Louisa was part of the congregation at least as early as 1856. There is an entry showing that she sponsored the baptism for Maria Elizabeth, a "coloured" girl who was the daughter of Hannah Guion, on July 30, 1856.

Bishop Atkinson was the clergyman performing the baptism. *Louisa Ferrier* is listed (along with a boy named Vatinius, who will be discussed later) as a communicant of the congregation in 1856. *Ferrier* is listed as "owner" for the pair. The *Lincoln County Heritage, 1997* book also reports about Lorenzo Ferrer and Louisa's participation in the church:

> He owned property in several locations in the town and county, including the property he gave for the St. Paul's Episcopal Church, 3 miles north of Lincolnton. He became friends with the McBees and others at St. Luke's Episcopal Church where they worshipped. Louisa sponsored several young people of mixed blood at the church, who excelled in education and religion, one being a co-founder of Livingston College. Louisa died young and was placed in the graveyard at the foot of his chosen grave site.[1]

In another list of communicants in the same ledger mentioned above, Louisa and Vatinius are both documented on individual lines as "a slave of Mr. Ferrier." Finally, Louisa's burial in 1858 is catalogued in the church ledger on November 30 (the day after her death). She is listed as a "servant of L. Farrier" aged "about 40 years."

Jason Harpe Restoring Louisa Monument. Courtesy of Mary Whisonant

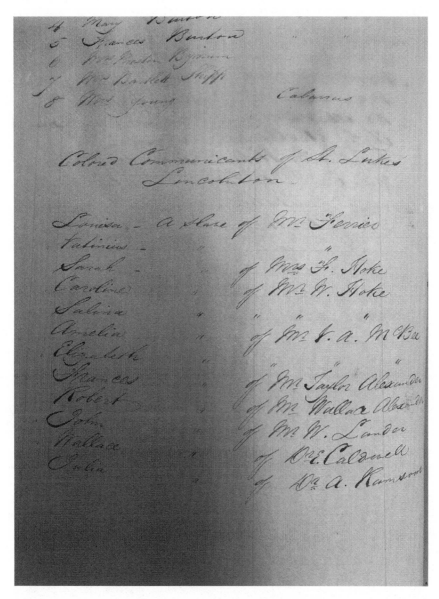

St. Luke's List of Louisa and Vatinius

By all other accounts, however, Louisa was in Lincolnton with Lorenzo Ferrer long before she showed up in the St. Luke's archives in 1856. (Note: the church was not established until 1842.)

Almost all of the local sources written after the death of Lorenzo Ferrer mention Louisa in some capacity, including the books, newsletters, and loose documents that populate the Lincoln County history shelf at the Charles R. Jonas Library. The local writer with the most to say about Ferrer's life in Lincolnton was Gladys Childs. Copies of several of her essays, composed on a typewriter and mimeographed, appear in folders throughout various Lincoln County archival depositories, including at St. Luke's and at the Lincoln County Historical Association. Childs writes in "Lincolnton's Pirate: Lorendzo Ferrer" that "Lafitte was a man of intelligence, much ability, a good navigator, and a fine organizer. At the time [of his New Orleans days], he commanded a fleet of more than a hundred ships. Lorendzo Ferrer, having the same attributes, came to Lincolnton from New Orleans, bringing with him a beautiful octoroon girl who served him as his house-keeper. Louisa lies buried about a hundred yards in the back of her Master's table monument in St. Luke's Episcopal churchyard."[2] It is interesting that numerous local reports suggest Ferrer came *from New Orleans*, which probably indicates that is what he told the people in town, though we know he was in Mississippi before coming to Lincolnton. This story may have been used by Ferrer to cover for the fact that he was living with an octoroon, a custom that was extraordinarily popular and socially accepted at the time in New Orleans. The fundamental truth, though, is that he previously was in New Orleans as Jean Laffite for many years. Robert Williams also discusses Louisa's presence in Lincolnton in *People Worth Meeting and Stories Worth Repeating*, a collection of tales and folklore relating to North Carolina, claiming Ferrer "took up residence with a quadroon woman (a person with one-fourth African blood; that is, a person with one black grandparent) named Louisa."[3] Scotti Cohn, writing in "The Stranger from New Orleans" chapter of the book *It Happened in North Carolina: Remarkable Events That Shaped History*, characterized Louisa as "a strikingly attractive young woman of African descent."[4] Remember Laffite was always in the company of a beautiful mixed-race woman.

Throughout the middle part of the twentieth century to the present, newspaper articles about Ferrer have appeared every few years in local papers like the *Lincoln Times-News* or the regional *Charlotte Observer*. Occasionally, a newspaper very far removed from Lincolnton will run a piece that chronicles the Ferrer/Laffite mystery—sometimes with a story that is picked up for syndication and published in multiple national papers. Judy Ausley wrote a 1996 article for the Alexandria *Daily Town Talk* in which she mentioned Louisa: "Many historians also have told the tale that Ferrer arrived in early Lincolnton accompanied by his black mistress. She was called Louisa and is buried in what is called the 'old black cemetery' at the church. . . . The location of her grave is about 100 yards directly behind Ferrer's grave."[5] These newspaper stories very rarely add any new details to the known story of Ferrer, and most of the time it is evident that the out-of-town writers leaned heavily on what local writers had already published and simply paraphrased.

The question then becomes whether Louisa lived with Ferrer as a well-treated servant or as a poorly treated enslaved woman; as a willing lover or as a forced sexual partner. Relying as we are on historical documents to draw conclusions, only the George Brewer document from Mississippi loaning Louisa out for a year gives us any indication of what her situation with Ferrer might have been. The talk around Lincolnton about this issue has always centered on a boy named Vatinius, with many people suggesting he was the son of Lorenzo Ferrer and Louisa. Robert Williams writes, "The couple [Ferrer and Louisa] who 'lived on the square like a true married pair' as Kipling put it, had a son believed to have been named Vatinius."[6] Childs's "Lincolnton's Pirate" also claims "Lorendzo had a son by the octoroon, Louisa. The boy disappeared about the time of Ferrer's death in 1875, but was reported to have returned to Lincolnton in 1895."[7] Ausley asserts, "They [Ferrer and Louisa] had a son together, according to church history."[8] However, there is no evidence to indicate that Vatinius was Ferrer's son, and there is nothing in the St. Luke's church record to suggest he was anything other than Ferrer's forced servant. There is no proof even that Vatinius was Louisa's son.

The most insidious rumor that regularly circulates about Ferrer in Lincolnton is that he injured Vatinius one day when the boy enraged him. Local historian Therne Dellinger relays the tale in a typed document called "Ferrer or Lafitte" housed in a folder in the archives of the Lincoln County Historical Association. Dellinger writes Ferrer and Louisa "had a son who resembled the father so much that he burned the boy's face in the coals of a fire. It is said that this child disappeared about the time of Ferrer's death but returned in 1895."[9] Fair tells a similar story:

> Ferrer had a son by the New Orleans octoroon woman he brought here with him. This boy looked so much like him that the Frenchman could not bear to look at him. So, one day, so the story goes, he grabbed the little fellow and shoved his face down on some hot coals in the fireplace and so

disfigured his countenance that he no longer resembled his father. After the old man was very kind to the boy. This boy disappeared about the time of Ferrer's death, but it is recalled by some that he returned to Lincolnton some twenty years after Ferrer died and visited around here for some time. Nothing has been heard of him since that time.[10]

This story is echoed in a 1988 newspaper article written by Jim Mathews, who takes the story a step further based on a personal interview he conducted with Gaither Schrum. Schrum said, "It is rumored that Ferrer beat Louisa to death. . . . Here's another instance of his cruelty. She gave birth to Ferrer's son, Vatinius. Ferrer, the story goes, hated his son so much that he grabbed him and shoved him face-down onto some hot coals in the fireplace and disfigured him so that he no longer resembled his father."[11] There is no telling what may have compelled Ferrer to do such a thing—if he really ever did it—and no other sources we have uncovered suggest that Ferrer ever killed Louisa. In fact, by all other accounts, Ferrer was completely devoted to her and was even willing to risk his reputation in town by living openly with his lover outside the bounds of marriage—a situation that would have been tolerated in New Orleans but likely viewed with suspicion in Lincoln County in the middle part of the 1800s. He also paid for a costly tombstone for Louisa and according to many in Lincolnton insisted that she be buried close to him once he died. The story did catch our eye in light of passing comments made about Jean Laffite by his contemporaries or those writing shortly after his death. Bancroft cites a source who knew Laffite, and in describing his eye, he explained, "as he grew animated in conversation, [it] would flash in a way which impressed me with a notion that 'Il Capitano' might be, when roused, a very 'ugly customer.'"[12] Whether these tales are true or not, they still make the rounds in Lincoln County.

One extraordinarily compelling twist in the Vatinius storyline is that Ferrer mentioned him in his will. Two years before his death in May 1873, Ferrer composed his will, a document that will be scrutinized line by line in Chapter Seventeen. In the list of people to whom he left various sums of money, Ferrer wrote, "I will and bestow to my former slave Vatinius Sextius, to him and to him only one hundred dollars."[13] First, this is the only reference we were able to locate that mentions that Vatinius had a middle name, and an unusual one at that. It was not uncommon for slave holders in the South to assign classical names to the people they enslaved. If Vatinius Sextius was born into bondage with Ferrer, the name selection is a fascinating one. Roman figure Marcus Tullius Cicero had acquaintances named both Vatinius and Sextius. In the accounts of Cicero's time (106 BC to 43 BC), we learn that Quintus Sextius was on trial, and Vatinius appeared as a witness against him. This enraged Cicero, who in the last days of the Republic launched into an oratory (called "The Interrogation") against Publius Vatinius, who he said was a villain. Caesar liked Vatinius and was trying to help him gain political power. The name Vatinius Sextius then represents two opposing forces within the same person. This name could be considered metaphorically significant if Vatinius Sextius Ferrer was the son of Ferrer and Louisa, and thus of mixed blood. Such a name would be further evidence of Ferrer's sophistication and the nature of his education. We do know from the probate records of Ferrer's will that Vatinius never appeared to collect his $100. It is also noteworthy that Ferrer's will contained no other gifts to anyone described by him as a "former slave." If Vatinius was not freed from slavery by Ferrer beforehand, he would have been liberated by the passage of the Thirteenth Amendment in January 1865.

We were also struck by a passage in an article called "Thirty-Five Years Age" that appeared in the *Weekly Lincoln Progress* on February 7, 1880. The writer takes an imaginary walk through town and reminisces about the changes that have taken place over the last few years: "In the rear of this lot, on Water Street, lived Lorenzo Ferrer, a curious old Frenchman, who idolized the memory of Julius Caesar, and scattered in the community seeds of infidelity that have born fruit in many minds. He has gone and 'left no continuance.'"[14] This article was published five years after Ferrer's death, and there is only one way to interpret the phrase "scattered in the community seeds of infidelity." There was a sour taste associated with Ferrer's memory. The Julius Caesar reference is also compelling considering that it was composed by a local writer with obvious knowledge of Ferrer's character and personality. It would not be a stretch to conclude that Ferrer, the Julius Caesar fan, was responsible for Vatinius's most unusual name. While a name cannot prove paternity, it does suggest that Ferrer may have owned Vatinius from birth. The name also comports with what we know of Jean Laffite's familiarity with classical writing and language.

The next step in searching for Vatinius's history was to peruse the slave schedules pertaining to the time he was alive. Interestingly, Ferrer was listed in the 1850 Census in Lincoln County at the age of fifty-seven owning $800 in real estate with a birthplace in France. However, there were no enslaved people on record for him in the 1850 Lincoln County slave schedule. Louisa then died in 1858. The 1860 Lincoln County slave schedule listed a sixteen-year-old enslaved male belonging to *L. Ferrier* who could have been Vatinius, though there is no proof of that. Also documented was a twenty-five-year-old enslaved female. In the 1870 Census, *Lorenzo Ferrier* was noted as having only a forty-six-year-old black female domestic servant named Eliza. His place of birth was listed as Lyon, France, and he was eighty-seven years old. Notice his age jumped from the 1850 Census to the 1870 Census by thirty years. Eliza's place of birth was listed as North Carolina, and her age was forty-six.

Our conclusion about Vatinius Ferrer is that he may have been Ferrer's son, but there is no documented proof of him being anything other than Ferrer's forced servant, as the will and the St. Luke's records confirm.

Two more details from Louisa's tombstone are tremendously important. First, no birth date or even year is given. It would not be unusual for a woman born into slavery in the early 1800s to be unaware of her birthdate. Enslaved children were commonly sold away from their parents with their ages estimated. Indeed, the first mention of Louisa in our research, the 1831 legal document between Ferrer and Brewer, gives her age as "about 17."[15] The more significant detail, however, is that Louisa's grave marker says she was born in Richmond, Virginia. Back in Chapter Nine, we explained the Slave Trail of Tears that ran from Atlantic Seaboard states—namely Virginia—down to Mississippi and Louisiana, with slave market stops all along the way. It is possible that Louisa was part of this brutal forced migration. Because of the way her beauty is described in local sources, because of the likelihood that she was rented out as a concubine and may have lived as Ferrer's mistress, and because of the great age difference between Ferrer and Louisa, she could have been what was known in the slave trade as a "fancy girl," a young female who was forced to work as a sexual servant. Most of these young women of mixed blood were selected because of their light complexions and their exceptional beauty. While Robert Williams speculates that Laffite/Ferrer may have met Louisa in Charleston, there is no way to know that, and no documentation that places Ferrer in Charleston exists. The much more likely scenario is that he bought her in Mississippi. There were known markets along the Slave Trail of Tears route in Raymond, Crystal Springs, and Natchez. Since we do have documented evidence of Ferrer in Mississippi, indeed in Raymond specifically, it makes much more sense that Louisa may have been purchased there, having come down from Virginia. This also lines up with the birthplace of Richmond which is listed on her tombstone.

THE MISSING YEARS

At first glance, it appears that there is a significant gap of years between the last evidence of Lorenzo Ferrer in Mississippi on the Madison County tax roll in 1836 and the first evidence of Lorenzo Ferrer in North Carolina on the Lincoln County tax roll in 1839, but a very close look explains that there could feasibly have been no gap at all. Once we began looking at a timeline of possible exits from Mississippi and possible entries to North Carolina, we understood how this could have unfolded. Assume for the sake of argument that Ferrer stayed in Mississippi for almost a full year past the compilation of the 1836 tax roll—exiting perhaps only a few weeks before the 1837 tax roll would have been taken. And along those same lines, assume he just missed the 1838 tax roll in Lincoln County by a few weeks, meaning that by the time he showed up on the 1839 list in North Carolina, he could have already been there for nearly a year. Following that scenario, the time-frame between his two known residencies would narrow considerably. It is possible Ferrer left Mississippi in late 1837 and arrived in North Carolina in early 1838. If you choose to subscribe to the one account that claims he came here first as a hotel guest before leaving town and returning with Louisa, this theory makes even more sense. As a hotel guest, even on an extended visit, Ferrer would not have been considered a taxable resident in Lincoln County, and given the slow nature of extended travel in those days, a trip back down to Mississippi or elsewhere to retrieve Louisa could have taken weeks if not months.

MORE LINCOLNTON TIDBITS

Still intrigued by the possibility that records of an early hunting lodge or hotel might reveal Ferrer's name on a guest register, we consulted with area experts about which hotels were in existence during that time. Three possibilities were mentioned: the Catawba Springs Hotel, the Eudy Hotel, and the inn at Woodside Plantation.

A hotel and spa was developed around some natural springs in Lincoln County sometime after the Revolutionary War. The springs were first named "Reed's Springs" after Captain John Reed, and the area was demarcated on maps in the 1790s.[16] Numerous references to the hotel, the springs, and the people who visited can be found in contemporary newspapers. The original guest register from 1838–1854 is housed at Davidson College, but pictures of each page are available in the photographic archive of the Lincoln County

Historical Association. We viewed the ledger, and while we found all sorts of interesting entries that warrant further inquiry, Ferrer's name was not among them.

Very little information about the Eudy Hotel is available. We learned in a February 7, 1880, *Lincoln Progress* article that it was "owned and kept by Capt. Wm. Slade. He was a negro trader in those days, and often took fifty to sixty negroes at a time to Alabama for sale."[17] We were unable to locate a guest register to prove if Ferrer stayed at the Eudy Hotel, however.

Woodside Plantation in Lincolnton could be the house where Ferrer visited. Ann Dellinger explained in a personal interview that the only description of a "hunting lodge visited by wealthy statesmen and financiers" that she ever heard of in Lincoln County is connected to Woodside.[18] Built in 1798 by Daddy Lawson Henderson, it was designated on the National Register of Historic Places in 1973 and stands today as one of Lincoln County's many great architectural treasures.

Yet for the people of Lincolnton, Lorenzo Ferrer's name will forever be associated with Woodside not because he may have used it as a hunting lodge but because of an alleged murder that took place in the upstairs bedroom in the year 1859. The first written record that we uncovered concerning this alleged murder came in a *Lincoln Times-News* article dated October 16, 1998, called "Plantation opens its doors for 200th birthday." The staff writer, Mary-Kathryn Craft, wrote that "French-born pirate Jean Lafitte is said to have lived in Lincolnton under an assumed name in the 19th century."[19] Sue Ramseur, former owner of Woodside with her husband Jack, is then credited in paraphrase as explaining, "Legend says that Lafitte, who was acting as Woodside's watchman for several days while the Richardson family was out of town, killed another pirate on the plantation's grounds because the enemy had discovered Lafitte's true identity and traveled to Lincolnton to kill him."[20] Ramseur then adds as a direct quote, "[Lafitte] chopped him up and cremated him in that fireplace."[21] A second article in the *Lincoln Times-News* on October 24, 2003, by Diane Turbyfill called "History of Haunts" quotes Myra Ramseur, Jack and Sue Ramseur's daughter-in-law. Turbyfill wrote, "During the 19th Century, Jean Lafitte, also known as Lorenzo Ferrer, came to work at Woodside Plantation. Ferrer met and killed an enemy who legend says was burned in an upstairs fireplace. Rumors say the victim still roams the estate."[22]

Of all the various tales connected to Lorenzo Ferrer, we viewed this one with a great deal of skepticism, but not because we doubted the word of Sue Ramseur. Both of us knew Sue and Jack personally. Affectionately known to everyone in town as "Miss Sue," she taught generations of children in kindergarten, specializing in music. Likewise, Jack, a distant cousin of ours, was not only a highly regarded local citizen who was active in civic, cultural, and religious pursuits, but he was very well known for his versatile abilities as a wood carver and musician. We knew that such a tall tale could not have originated whole-cloth with either of them, and it turns out we were correct.

We first searched for any other mention of this murder story by checking back through early newspaper articles and library archives, hoping to discover the origin. With no luck, we then turned to our friend Rick Ramseur, who shed a great deal of light on our questions.

Rick Ramseur's interest in our project was there from the beginning, and while we had carried on numerous discussions with him about the various aspects of the Henderson family (who owned Woodside before the Ramseurs, and whose connections with Ferrer were already unfolding in our research), we had never thought to ask him about the origins of the Ferrer murder tale.

"Oh, that's interesting you should ask," he said, when we finally did get around to posing the question. "I hadn't thought of that in years. My parents first heard that story from Gaither Schrum. I remember my dad saying that Gaither called him one day and asked if he would mind going upstairs to check the hearth in the master bedroom for blood stains. Then, of course, the story unfolded from there."[23] Ramseur does not remember hearing his dad, Jack, say where Schrum got the story. But we do know that Schrum was not prone to exaggeration. In fact, he was a tireless researcher who had devoted a great deal of time trying to uncover the truth behind the Ferrer rumors. Schrum was also quoted about the Woodside incident in the 1990 *Charlotte Observer* article cited earlier. In that piece, Schrum relayed that Ferrer was said to have "killed a fellow pirate who found him while he was a watchman at Woodside."[24] The likelihood that this story was born in the mind of Schrum was as remote as the chances of either of the Ramseurs making it up. Therefore, we elected to proceed as if the nucleus of the tale began with fact. And our research on this topic continues. While we are still working to discover the source, we can say that we do believe the Ramseurs took the story seriously enough to repeat it. As for Rick Ramseur, he views the entire notion of Ferrer, this portion of it included, with a realistic, open, and hopeful mind. If it turns out to be true, he will be delighted to add another interesting detail to the ongoing story of Woodside Plantation.

With the matter of origin at least now bearing some credibility, we returned to our initial skepticism, which, as we have said, had nothing to do with Sue and Jack Ramseur but very much to do with details.

Did this story comport with what we knew of either Jean Laffite or Lorenzo Ferrer so far? In terms of Ferrer—possibly. There were elusive tales of his treatment of Vatinius, as well as whispers that he may have physically abused Louisa. Other than that, we had uncovered no evidence of physical violence by Ferrer. (An altercation we will explore in an upcoming chapter between Ferrer and a man named Peter Stuart Ney will be interesting to compare considering this context though.) What, then, of Laffite? The written record was of course more extensive, but given that, we still found little evidence that Jean Laffite was prone to physical violence. Obviously, in order to hold sway over such a large and varied assemblage of men as the Baratarians, Laffite would have needed at least the capability of holding his own in a fight. The prospects of him having led such an unruly crew without that capacity was slim to none. On more than one documented occasion (the calming of tensions during the British visit to Barataria being one, and the management of wild egos and hot tempers while he ruled Galveston being another), we know Laffite successfully navigated some very dicey interpersonal waters in his day. Men in a state of turmoil do not automatically or easily simmer down at the request of one who they do not believe can best them in a fight. Of all the men who ruled various bands of pirates and privateers in those days, Jean Laffite was perhaps the master of that art. As to the matter of whether Lorenzo Ferrer would have been capable of this act, then, the answer was "probably so," with the acknowledgement that throughout his life, he seemed most successful at resolving conflict by virtue of his wits and not his fists. But what of his age in the year 1859? Ferrer would have been seventy-nine years old, an undeniable fact no matter how one slices the bread. The only way he could have successfully defended himself would have been with a gun—and this could easily have been the case. Woodside is also secluded enough that no neighbors would have heard a gunshot.

Past all of this, we were still left with glaring questions, motive being at the top of that list. It could only have been one of two things—robbery or personal grudge of some sort—unless we wanted to consider it a bit of both. But either way, what other clues did the story hold? For starters, if the murder had been self-defense, then why no public mention? Why not get in touch with the authorities, who were barely a mile away, and tell them what happened? We have searched sheriff's records, court records, and newspaper accounts from that time period with no success. We even contacted two sitting Lincoln County sheriffs at different points in our research to see if they had records we were not aware of, but none exist. Furthermore, why chop up the body and burn it in the fireplace? There were certainly undertakers in those days. The answer to all of these things seems to point to the fact that Ferrer knew his attacker, that he had good reason for secretly disposing of the body, and that the attacker was not a local individual or else his "disappearance" would have soon been the subject of speculation and a manhunt. It must also be pointed out that a man must have lived a colorful past life in order for enemies to still be stalking him in old age.

After many months of consideration, combing through all sorts of research and thinking about the story from every angle, we decided that *if* the story was true, there was only one plausible scenario. The man who would have attacked Lorenzo Ferrer at Woodside was likely an enemy who had traveled some distance to confront him. Whether the bad blood was many decades old or recent, we cannot say. Was someone sent to kill him? Or did someone come looking on his own? We may never know if any of this is true, and if true, we may never be able to determine the exact facts.

We will leave this subject with a reminder about a man we previously introduced to you—William Mitchell, a former contemporary of Laffite who roamed the waters of the Gulf at the same time and even worked for the Laffites in the process. He was also a sadistic killer, capable of excessive cruelty. His death was erroneously reported (if not even celebrated) more than once. And his final fate was never known. The last word of him came from the Caribbean around 1841. Add to this his very recognizable countenance. He was a man with a disfigured face and only one eye. Is it conceivable that Mitchell, still alive and well in 1859, could have nursed some kind of a decades-old grudge against Laffite and managed to find his way to his intended target in Lincolnton? We have no firm opinion yet, but you are free to form your own.

MILTON, NC

And as if the plot needed another twist, let us tell you what we know of another house named Woodside, and of the town and county where it resides. This story, too, carries legends connected to Lorenzo Ferrer, although we want to say up front that the story we have uncovered only comes from one obscure source and so closely tracks with the tale we have just told you about Woodside in Lincolnton as to make it almost certainly suspect. Still, we will put it out here just by way of full disclosure.

Caswell County, North Carolina, sits on the Virginia border. The county seat is Yanceyville, but one of the oldest towns is Milton. In the time of Ferrer, it was home to many prominent families of the planter class, one of which was the Dodson family. Two Dodson sisters married men from Lincoln County and moved to Lincolnton. Fanny Dodson married Andrew Motz, who left her a widow after his sudden death in Lincolnton at a young age in 1851. It was officially ruled an accidental drowning, but suspicion arose at the time that he may have been murdered. Andrew Motz was a business partner of Elisha Barrett—the same man whose crooked dealings caused ripples of scandal and financial ruin in Lincolnton that will be discussed in Chapter Fourteen. One of the men who suffered complete loss of everything he owned at the hands of Barrett was Jacob Abel Ramseur. His wife, Lucy Dodson, was a sister of Fanny Motz. Before the trouble which ruined the lives of both Lucy and her husband, Jacob, they produced a son named Stephen Dodson Ramseur. Born in 1837, Stephen Ramseur graduated from West Point and went on to become one of two decorated Civil War generals from Lincolnton. Just before the war, however, Stephen Ramseur took a bride from Caswell County named Ellen Richardson. The Richardson family home, named Woodside, was built in 1838 on the edge of town and still stands today. During visits to his Dodson grandparents in Milton, as well as during his courtship of Ellen and after their marriage, Stephen Ramseur spent a great deal of time at Woodside, which also served as an inn for the community. While all of these details seem a little convoluted, they are necessary to serve as the backdrop of the story about Ferrer and Caswell County that we uncovered.

On the Caswell County Genealogy page, we ran across a post that placed Lorenzo Ferrer in Milton. It said, "It appears that a person named Lorenzo Ferrer (or Ferrier) spent some time in Milton, Caswell County, North Carolina during the early-to-mid 1800s. He may have been a guest (or boarded) at the 'Woodside' House in Milton. Ferrer is from Lincolnton, Lincoln County, North Carolina."[25] Local legend also reports that Ferrer deposited a great deal of money in the Milton branch of the State Bank of North Carolina. During his time there, Ferrer is reported to have murdered a man in the upstairs bedroom at Woodside and disposed of his body by burning it in the fireplace. There is also the tale of a young woman named Malvina whose ghost frequently appears on the stairs at Woodside (in both Milton and Lincolnton). The story went on to say that Lorenzo Ferrer is believed to have been Jean Laffite, living there under an assumed name, and the person writing the account was requesting any further information that anyone could provide. Apparently, the Milton bank suffered a devastating fire some time during the late 1800s that destroyed most of its records.

We can fairly easily assume that the tale of the upstairs murder, as well as the account of Malvina's ghost, has somehow made its way across the state to

Woodside in Milton

land in some of the local folklore of Milton, especially given all of the travel back and forth in those days between Ramseur and Dodson relatives and the existence of a house named Woodside in Lincolnton that was frequented by Lorenzo Ferrer as a guest. So, for the sake of clarity, let us set these portions of the story aside.

That leaves us with the matter of money in the bank, and the fact that so many names connected with Lorenzo Ferrer and Lincoln County (not to mention Madison County, Mississippi) are also connected to Milton. We cannot entirely throw out the notion that Ferrer did visit this town, quite possibly did deposit money in the bank, and likely did have friends there, given his obvious friendship with the same families here in Lincolnton. What to make of it past that point, we cannot say—except that this is part of the story that we believe needs much further scrutiny.

THE "PIRATE'S HOUSE"

Biographical accounts of dead historical figures are by nature more difficult than the same type of narrative concerning a living subject. The lives of those long deceased must be pieced together using eyewitness accounts, original correspondence, and legal and historical documents, taking the sum of the information collected and turning it into a story easily absorbed and understood. Our task in telling the true story of Lorenzo Ferrer came with that inherent difficulty and then some. Most historical figures worthy of a biography left an abundant paper trail. Many of them hoped to be remembered and took great care, as did most of those who knew them, to preserve their letters and other papers so that future historians would have a clearly lit runway to understanding their life. Lorenzo Ferrer bore no such hopes. If anything, he worked very hard at not being remembered. What we were able to find in the course of researching this book was hard-fought and hard-won, made even more difficult by an understandable overlay of local legends and tall tales that had grown up around the truth of this man. Every fact that we discovered had to be put through the research equivalent of a fine mesh strainer, subject to questions of where the tale first originated and whether it lined up factually and plausibly with the established timeline and documentation. The lore in Lincolnton surrounding "the pirate's house" serves as a great example of this process.

Recorded deeds between 1839 and Ferrer's death in 1875 reveal a good number of land transactions between Ferrer and local citizens. Likewise, his last will and testament conveys certain parcels and houses to intended recipients. Ferrer owned multiple properties and lived in a house in the southwest quadrant of Lincolnton on a parcel known as lot eighteen. That house and the land that went with it was left to Ferrer's close friend Wallace Reinhardt, who was also the co-executor of his estate.

As clear as that record was, it would have made perfect sense that the old house located on that parcel of land in Lincolnton, was, in fact, the one owned and occupied by Lorenzo Ferrer. The house was recently demolished, and the land is owned by Lincoln County, but for a few brief years, the house served as the office of the Lincoln County Historical Coordinator. During that time period, which also corresponded with a renewed surge of interest in the mystery of Ferrer as Jean Laffite, the house began to be commonly referred to as "the pirate's house."

All well and good—and why not?—except for the fact that it was not the pirate's house, or anyone else's house during the mid-nineteenth century. The truth of the matter is that the house did not even exist at that point in time. Ann Dellinger, a long-standing member of the Lincoln County Historical Association, took it upon herself in a 2006 Reader's Forum column for the *Lincoln Times-News* to set the record straight. In her thoughtfully composed column, Dellinger wrote the following: "Ferrer, a Frenchman, appeared in Lincolnton in 1839. He purchased an old house on Lot 18 Southwest in 1846 and resided there until his death in 1875 at age 96. He is buried in St.

Luke's Episcopal cemetery. While he did reside on West Water Street, the house in which he lived was demolished over 100 years ago."[26] The house that sits on the lot now was built by Robert S. Reinhardt in 1906 according to Dellinger.[27]

Therefore, what seemed like an intriguing piece of physical evidence connected to Lorenzo Ferrer, a place that could be pointed out as "the pirate's house" for tourists and interested locals, was in reality nothing more than a cautionary tale outlining the dangers of blindly following conventional wisdom without taking a deeper look. Thus was the road we traveled on the way to separating fact from fiction.

FERRER'S OTHER RELATIONSHIPS

Another one of the missteps in local reporting about Ferrer after his death is that he lived in seclusion and did not have very many friends. Many of the twentieth-century sources published about Ferrer in Lincoln County were highly derivative of each other, so multiple sources reporting the erroneous claim that Ferrer was a recluse can be thus explained. For more than thirty years in Lincolnton, Ferrer put himself out there into the public sphere in a big way. Perhaps what these writers were trying to articulate was that Ferrer was *secretive* about his past life, which is very different from being *reclusive*. Cohn writes that Ferrer was "of French descent and very wealthy, yet there was much [the people in Lincolnton] could not discern. For example, he seemed not to be of any particular profession, and his family background was not known. He never offered an explanation for how he came by his money."[28] Similarly, Robert Williams points out that the Frenchman "told no one much about his background, but his actions suggested mystery."[29] Childs concurs, writing that Ferrer lived "under a cloud of mystery" and left behind "nothing to identify him other than a six legged table top monument."[30] Considering Laffite's profession before he was Ferrer, what was he supposed to do? Come inland and open a bakery? Preach the gospel? No, he went back to what he knew: backdoor business.

This state of affairs leads us to a few important observations that seem to reveal a lot about Lorenzo Ferrer's character. First, it is remarkable that the people who knew him and suspected he might be a famous pirate were much more interested in his *identity* than they were in any possible location of a treasure (though a treasure story is coming). These folks were intrigued by him, and what they talked about related to him as a person whose presence in Lincolnton did not make sense instead of as a pirate whose treasure they wanted to find. This is one of the characteristics of the Lorenzo Ferrer narrative that makes it so different from stories told in other towns by people who claim Laffite may have visited. The treasure stories in those locations dominate, and little or no attention is paid to the person who may have but likely did not deposit riches there.

Secondly, for a man with as many business associates, political acquaintances, church friends, and Masonic brothers as Lorenzo Ferrer had, it boggles the mind that he left behind <u>no record of correspondence</u>. Save for the few signatures that we have uncovered, we have yet to put our hands on a single letter written by him, any correspondence sent to him, or any letters that even mention him, and we have searched correspondence records of many families that we know had dealings with him. Absolutely nothing remains.

Given all of this evidence, it is difficult to argue that Ferrer was not trying to keep his true identity under wraps. If there was a crack in his armor, though, it came through a close friendship he had with a man named Wallace Reinhardt.

WALLACE REINHARDT

Born in 1819, Wallace Reinhardt was roughly twenty years old when Lorenzo Ferrer came to Lincolnton in 1839. Reinhardt did not die until 1907, so he was a witness to Ferrer's entire life in Lincoln County. By all accounts, he was Ferrer's best friend. Childs reports Ferrer "did have one intimate friend, Wallace Reinhardt, grandfather of the late Lincolnton Postmaster V.N. Fair and his sisters Frances and Mary Irving. Reinhardt firmly believed his friend Ferrer was the notorious Ex-pirate Jean Lafitte. . . . Wallace Reinhardt based his knowledge on various remarks made by the Frenchman during their friendship."[31] Victor Fair himself, Reinhardt's grandson, revealed, "There was one citizen of Lincolnton who came to know this man Ferrer quite well. He was Wallace M. Reinhardt. In his many conversations with Ferrer there were many things the Frenchman said which led to the firm belief that he was an ex-pirate."[32]

Beyond his relationship with Reinhardt, Ferrer also fostered other friendships in town, including with many families at St. Luke's. He also apparently let down his guard a bit with the children in town. According to Robert Williams, Ferrer "had a liking for children, and he loved to tell them stories about piracy. . . . Ferrer would come to town and sit at the Court Square, and the boys, who called him The Pirate, looked forward to his daily visits."[33]

Ferrer's fellow Lincolntonians held suspicions about his connection to Jean Laffite for a number of other reasons as well.

- Jean Laffite and Lorenzo Ferrer were born within the same time range:1778–1782. Ferrer's gravestone—which he commissioned before his death—claimed a birth in France in 1780. France is where most scholars suspect Laffite was born, especially because the pirate himself claimed it on an official port document.

- Local historian Gaither Schrum suggested Ferrer's wealth was a definite tip-off—beyond the fact that he never worked a day in his life in Lincolnton. Schrum said "after the Civil War, when everyone else was broke and the economy was in such a bad state, Ferrer was living wealthy. He hadn't invested in Confederate money. So his wealth had to be in gold, which wouldn't have lost any value."[34]

- Ferrer came to town with what was clearly a captain's inkwell (more about that in Chapter Nineteen), and he was often described by citizens in town as a seafaring man. Like Laffite, Ferrer was reported to be highly intelligent and a strong leader. This is supported by his leadership role in the Lincolnton Freemason lodge and his participation in Lincolnton's political affairs.

Further, there are many connections we have not yet made that should be added to the discussion.

- *Ferrer* is actually a surname tied to the occupation of blacksmithing. Remember Jean Laffite used a blacksmithing shop as a front business in New Orleans. Ferrer's selection of this alias could have been a homage to his past "profession," which was also a ruse. As well, the name *Lorenzo Ferrer* calls to mind the name Lorenzo Ferrer Maldonado, a Spanish explorer who claimed to have first navigated the Northwest Passage in the fourteenth century. This alias could have been the wink and nod of a fellow seagoing man.

- Davis says Laffite "impressed people as an easy and genial conversationalist, and liked to tell stories of his experiences, no doubt with embellishments."[35] Bancroft writes Laffite was "evidently educated and gifted with no common talent for conversation."[36] These descriptions mirror the way the people in Lincolnton described Ferrer's willingness to talk to local children. Fair also describes Ferrer as "a bachelor and somewhat eccentric, but educated and warm-hearted."[37] Parallels can also be drawn with Ferrer's excellent July Fourth toast in 1847 and the eloquent language that he included in composing his will.

As the many document discoveries outlined in this chapter prove, Lorenzo Ferrer was a suspicious character from the moment he stepped foot on Main Street in Lincolnton. Those who had secret hunches that there was more to his story than he was telling did not have to look far for similarities that made them suspect Jean Laffite was not dead and was instead quietly living out his final days in anonymity and solitude. What we discovered next, however, revealed a side of Lorenzo Ferrer that *nobody* in modern-day Lincoln County knew existed.

CHAPTER FOURTEEN

SEEDS OF INFIDELITY

American history, as it pertains to this story, was heavily influenced by the Freemasons, a fraternal order whose origins can be traced back to the early part of the eighteenth century. The reach of this group extended across national boundaries, even oceans, and was evident from the highest levels of government all the way down to the man on the street. Across a young and growing nation, local Masonic lodges were a part of nearly every town from the large seaports to the small rural communities. Lincolnton in Ferrer's day (which was at the junction of two major trade routes, one of them east/west and the other north/south) landed somewhere between those two classifications. It was by no means urban, but it was also not completely rural. Predictably, a Masonic lodge was formed. And, yes, Jean Laffite, now flying under the radar as Lorenzo Ferrer, was right in the thick of it. Before we tell the story of Ferrer and his tenure at Lincoln Lodge 137, however, the story of what transpired in the community at large during the early formative years of the lodge needs to be told. Those events, which destroyed lives, fortunes, and families, eventually found their way inside the doors of Lodge 137, leaving a trail of broken relationships in their wake and ensnaring Ferrer in the process. They were set in motion by one man. His name was Elisha S. Barrett.

An article from the *Weekly Lincoln Progress* in February 7, 1880, referenced in the last chapter mentioned the "seeds of infidelity" scattered by Ferrer.[1] To what degree the negative memories were connected to Elisha Barrett (who at the time of the article's publication was now also long gone) is hard to say, but recorded facts of the day show the two men participating in joint loans. Toward the end, their paths converged in the Masonic lodge that they both helped to organize. There is also the additional matter of the time in 1858 when Ferrer hauled Barrett before the North Carolina Supreme Court, but we're getting ahead of ourselves.

Barrett was born in New York and arrives in our story by virtue of his marriage to a Lincolnton girl named Mary Ann Hoyle. Her wealthy parents were Eli Hoyle and Cynthia Ramseur Hoyle. This marriage placed Barrett squarely at the intersection of at least three very prominent families, a circumstance that he promptly used and abused—the results of which would haunt the town and those affected families for years to come. The three families were Ramseur, Motz, and Dodson—introduced to you in the previous chapter in the section about Woodside Plantation via their connections to Ferrer in Milton.

THE SUSPICIOUS DEATH OF ANDREW MOTZ

The first sign of trouble showed up one night in March 1851 when Andrew Motz fell (or was pushed) off a bridge and drowned. Elisha Barrett was his business partner. The two men had formed Motz, Barrett & Company and were operating a cotton mill on Clark's Creek at the edge of town. The land for the mill had been purchased from William Slade, whose grist mill sat adjacent to the cotton mill. (This is the same William Slade mentioned earlier as the owner of the Eudy Hotel. He was also a known slave trader.) There were conditions attached to the sale of that land to Motz and Barrett, outlined here in an excerpt from *Lincoln County, North Carolina* by Jason Harpe. Alongside images of both mills, Harpe writes:

> On December 4, 1848, Andrew Motz of the firm of Motz, Barrett & Company, proprietors of the Ivy Shoals [Elm Grove, Laurel Hill] Cotton Mill on the South Fork River at Clark's Creek, purchased from William Slade a tract of land containing 2 acres with a special right-of-way over the lands of Slade for $300. In this transaction, Slade stipulates that Motz is forbidden from building or establishing a gristmill or sawmill on the property opposite Slade's mill, for which Motz owns. On the night of March 7, 1851 [one year after having built a cotton mill on that property with his partner, Elisha Barrett] Andrew Motz drowned while crossing the bridge at Slade's Mill on his way home.[2]

Motz's body was not immediately recovered. During the interim, the reaction of the community was a mixture of grief, shock, and suspicion, all of which made its way into local newspaper accounts of the tragedy. Viewed collectively, they recounted that Motz had left the cotton factory about eight o'clock p.m. on a stormy Friday night, apprehensive about venturing out but concerned that his family would worry if he did not come home. The accounts give no indication of who he voiced these concerns to, but obviously there were people still at the mill to whom he conveyed these words.

Standing between Motz and the town was a bridge across Clark's Creek that had no railings, though at least one newspaper account made mention of the fact that the bridge was broad. Being on his regular route to and from the mill, the bridge was also familiar to Motz. The weather outside was described as heavy rain with high winds. The level of Clark's Creek was way above normal that night, and the water was swift. Motz, wearing a hat and cape and carrying an umbrella, left the mill and never made it home. An immediate search began, though it would be a week before his body was found.

In the meantime, speculation was rampant about Motz's fate. Even after the discovery of his hat and cape downriver from the bridge, indicating the likelihood of drowning, there was discussion about whether he fell off the bridge or had met with foul play and was pushed into the water. Instrumental in that search were the members of the local Oddfellows Lodge, of which Motz was a very active and pivotal member. Newspaper accounts reveal that the Oddfellows were tireless and relentless, even going to the trouble of constructing a specially designed boat that would better search the waters of the river. All of this, combined with nearly unbearable grief at the loss of a young father, husband, friend, business associate, and valued member of the community, prompted the *Raleigh Register* to reprint a *Lincoln Courier* article, which claimed the death was "a most painful event, and the most serious that has ever occurred in our community."[3] In another account from the *Salisbury Watchman* (reprinted by the *Weekly Standard* in Raleigh), it was noted that Motz's business partner was out of town on the night in question: "Mr. Barrett, his partner in business, was on a visit to Milton at the time of this sad event."[4] However, immediately below that article there appears the following paragraph bearing the headline "Mysterious":

> A gentleman from Lincolnton arrived here on Monday night last about eight o'clock, on his way to Milton. He stated that a difficulty had lately arisen in that Town between Mr. Andrew Motz, and a Mr. Moony. That threats had been made by the latter against the life of Mr. Motz; and that both were now missing. The last time they were seen, each, from opposite directions, were going towards a bridge which spans the river; and that the hat and coat of Mr. Motz had subsequently been found in the river below. The gentleman who brought this news was going to Milton on business in some way connected with the affair.[5]

We could find no other mention of the disappearance of or the ensuing search for the man cited as Mr. Moony in this report and no other indication of anyone by that name ever being investigated in connection with Motz's death. The investigation that did ensue, once his body was recovered, determined that he died by drowning. The official report of Motz's death was published in the *Carolina Republican* on April 3, 1851:

> A Jury of Inquest was empannelled on Sunday last, on the river bank, about one mile south-west of the Town of Lincolnton, in Lincoln County, to inquire into the cause or causes of the death of ANDREW MOTZ, his body being there found. On examination, and due deliberation, no marks of violence being found, the Jury returned a Verdict: 'That Andrew Motz, on the night of the 7th of March, 1851, about the hour of 8 o'clock, left the house near the Factory of Motz, Barrett & Co. on his way homeward by way of the Bridge, at the mill of Capt. Slade; the night being dark and stormy, and that by causes to this Jury unknown, he got into the water at or near the bridge and met his death by drowning. W.H. MICHAL, Coroner'.[6]

Whatever the circumstance surrounding the death of Andrew Motz, one thing is clear: his widow, Fanny Dodson Motz, suffered painfully at the hands of his former partner in the years following. While we will further elaborate on the depth of that pain in the coming pages, we continue with the story of Barrett's troubles in Lincolnton, as only a few months later, he served as a founding member of Lincoln Lodge 137 in another connection that would eventually blow up in the community's face.

Forward from the summer of 1851, Barrett appears to have wasted no time in his efforts to make money. In addition to his ongoing pursuits at the cotton mill, he also appears to have become an agent for a company specializing in the recovery of those running away from slavery. Though Barrett was among many slaveholders in Lincolnton, his practice of buying and selling enslaved people was worthy of mention in a letter written by Stephen Dodson Ramseur, first cousin of Barrett's wife, Mary Ann. Writing to his sister from Davidson College in October of 1853, Ramseur asks, "Have you seen cousin Mary Ann . . . lately? Is Mr. Barrett still buying negroes? I do sincerely hope that he may soon see the wickedness of such a course."[7] This would not be the last mention that Ramseur made of Elisha Barrett, but it was by far the most charitable.

Throughout the mid-1850s, Barrett's diverse efforts at earning a living increasingly included borrowing money in sizeable amounts, much of it from local citizens. Sadly, it appears that one man in town made the grave mistake of overexposing himself financially on Barrett's behalf by signing as security for the large bulk of Barrett's loans. That man was Jacob A. Ramseur,

whose sister, Cynthia, was Barrett's mother-in-law. Also remember that
Fanny Motz, Andrew Motz's widow, was Lucy Ramseur's sister, and therefore Jacob Ramseur's sister-in-law.

Ramseur by all accounts was a decent and honorable man whose mer-
cantile business on the northwest square in Lincolnton was successful and
solid, providing him and his family of nine children with a comfortable
home and abundant holdings. Arguably their most accomplished child was
the aforementioned Stephen Dodson Ramseur. Following Davidson, he was
accepted into West Point and graduated with honors before resigning his
commission in order to join the ranks of the Confederacy as a general. His
life and accomplishments have been well-chronicled by historians and biographers alike, but we mention him here by way of his involvement in the
scandals caused by Barrett. By the time Ramseur's father, Jacob, realized the
depth of his financial exposure where Barrett was concerned, it was too late.
Two footnotes from *The Bravest of the Brave* give the sobering details:

> Jacob Ramseur had thirty debts filed against him in late 1857 and 1858
> totaling more than $24,000 in judgements and court expenses and cost-
> ing him his mercantile business. [This according to Fieri Facias, Lincoln
> County Civil Action Papers, 1857–1859, NCOAH.] The social impact
> of his financial obligations, involving six co-defendants and twenty-five
> creditors [one of whom was Lorenzo Ferrer] must have been devastating in
> a county of 6,000 white inhabitants, 496 living in Lincolnton, with many
> families interrelated.[8]

Kundahl also reports Barrett was tangled up in thirty-two lawsuits for
a combined total of $30,000, a staggering figure in the 1850s.[9] Barrett de-
faulted on most of the loans he asked Jacob Ramseur to underwrite. The
result for Ramseur was total financial ruin, coupled with devastating humiliation before his friends in the community. The most crushing blow of all,
however, was the death of Lucy Ramseur, who succumbed as a result of the
strain in November 1859.

Even before Lucy's death, her son, Stephen, spoke of the matter while
attending West Point in an 1857 letter to his best friend, David Schenck.
As it pertained to Elisha Barrett and the harm that Barrett had inflicted on a
good and decent family, Ramseur spared no punches. He wrote:

> I do not grieve for myself. Oh! no. But the thought that those who are ten
> thousand times dearer to me than Life itself may suffer in this selfish world
> continually oppresses me. The knowledge that they have been robbed of
> all earthly goods by the damning treatchery [sic] of a miserable Yankee, a

villain, a liar, a fiend of Hell . . . too overcomes me. I try not to think of the author of all this. It will never do for me to meet him, for if I do I shall certainly crush him to atoms.[10]

The same volume of correspondence sheds further light on the matter of Fanny Dodson Motz, Ramseur's "Aunt Fanny," who was left to raise her three children after the death of her husband, Andrew. While we do not see specifics, it is clear from the following excerpts that Fanny Motz was still struggling to recover from the same sort of treatment at the hands of Barrett. Her strife continued for more than ten years as she tried (in vain) to gain acceptance to West Point for her son, George. In that attempt, Fanny Motz reached out to the highest post in the land, the office of the president of the United States. In a series of 1859 letters addressed to President James Buchanan written by various prominent North Carolinians (including one that she composed herself), the matter of Barrett's misdeeds came to light yet again, and in very unflattering terms. Kundhal writes, "These letters and Fanny's spoke of her penury as a helpless widow who had been cheated by a scoundrel."[11] As part of this effort, Stephen Ramseur joined the cause by writing his own letter to the president from his post at West Point. Yet again, Ramseur spared no expense in his efforts to portray the shameful character and actions of Barrett. In speaking of his aunt and her hope of providing a good West Point education for her son, Ramseur wrote, in part:

> Death took from her embrace the husband of her bosom, and left her with three little children, mourning and desolate. Col. Motz was accidentally drowned in March 1851. Since then, his widow has been robbed of all of her property by the villainy of Col. M's partner, who continued the business after his death. Her home with all of its endearing associations was publicly sold to pay the debts of this false-hearted man.[12]

Suffice it to say that while no one placed blame for Andrew Motz's death at the feet of Elisha Barrett, and while Barrett may have been successfully able to talk his way past any social or financial misgivings toward him in the wake of that tragedy (especially as evidenced by his ongoing ability to "raise money" from members of the same family), it is clear that he was an opportunistic predator whose ability to talk a good game far outshone his ability to manage money, much less make any on his own.

We mentioned earlier that Lorenzo Ferrer was one of the creditors whose finances became entangled in this mess. While it appears that Ferrer's exposure was minimal as compared to the tens of thousands owed, we do have clear evidence that he stayed on top of the matter all the way to the North Carolina Supreme Court. The case of *Ferrer v. Barrett* appears in the public record of cases heard by the Western North Carolina division of the state Supreme Court in Morganton, North Carolina in 1859.[13] Our discovery of the case made it evident that the dispute was a residual of the vast Barrett scandal that had unfolded during the latter part of the 1850s. The language, however, was so encumbered with legal terminology that we decided to turn it over to our friend, Alton Reeder, who is a local attorney. Reeder graciously digested the court's ruling and provided the following analysis of what happened—thoughtfully phrased so that two non-legal minds could get it straight. The reader is welcome to follow along:

Summary of <u>Ferrer v. Barrett</u>, 57 NC 455 (1859)

Barrett owed money to a number of people under the terms of multiple notes and bonds.

Ramseur was the surety for these debts of Barrett. He had at some previous time signed something that put him on the hook for these debts if Barrett failed to pay them.

We are not told how much Barrett owed to his various creditors, but we are told that the total amount for which Ramseur was bound as surety for the debts of Barrett did not exceed $10,000.

Ramseur got worried that Barrett wouldn't pay his debts and asked Barrett for a counter-security and indemnity. He wanted someone to hold him harmless and reimburse him in the event that he ended up having to pay Barrett's debts.

In response to Ramseur's request for a counter-security, Barrett, Briggs, Henderson, and Hoyle executed a penal bond to Ramseur. They promised to pay $20,000 to Ramseur in the event that Barrett defaulted and Ramseur had to pay Barrett's debts. The penal bond contained a condition that if Barrett paid off the debts for which Ramseur was bound as surety, then Barrett, Briggs, Henderson, and Hoyle would have no obligation to pay Ramseur.

One of the debts for which Ramseur was bound as surety for Barrett was a $509.80 debt to Ferrer from a bond dated January 17, 1856. Both Ramseur and Mosteller were sureties for that particular bond. They had signed something saying they would pay the debt if Barrett did not.

Barrett defaulted on the debt to Ferrer, and Ferrer sued Barrett, Ramseur, and Mosteller and got a judgment against them for the payment of money damages. By the time Ferrer got the judgment in April of 1858, Barrett, Ramseur, and Mosteller had all become insolvent. Ferrer could not enforce the judgment and recover money from any of them because they had no assets.

Ferrer, Ramseur, and Mosteller filed an action in equity against Barrett, Briggs, Henderson, and Hoyle. In this action in equity (this "bill"), Ferrer, Ramseur, and Mosteller were seeking a declaration that if Barrett paid the debt to Ferrer, then Ramseur and Mosteller would have no further obligation as sureties for Barrett's debt to Ferrer. They were also seeking a declaration that if Barrett failed to pay Ferrer, then Briggs, Henderson, and Hoyle would have to pay the debt owed to Ferrer.

Barrett, Briggs, Henderson, and Hoyle filed a motion to dismiss, claiming that Ramseur was not entitled to the relief requested because he had not yet suffered a loss by paying out money for Barrett's unpaid debts. They said that until he actually paid out money as surety for Barrett's unpaid debts he was not entitled to bring any action based on the penal bond given to him as counter-security.

The court said that while the fact that Ramseur had not yet suffered a loss would have made him unable to bring an action at law (a lawsuit for money damages), it did not make him unable to bring an action in equity. In a court of equity (where you are seeking a remedy other than money damages), a surety can bring an action against the principal (Barrett) and the people who executed the penal bond as soon as the principal's debt becomes due.

The court ruled in favor of Ferrer, Ramseur, and Mosteller and denied the motion to dismiss.

Granting the motion to dismiss would have resolved the case in favor of Barrett, Briggs, Henderson, and Hoyle without the necessity of having a trial. The North Carolina Supreme Court did not do that. Instead, they denied the motion to dismiss and sent the case to the Court of Equity for a trial. The judicial opinion pertains only to the motion to dismiss and how the Supreme Court ruled on the motion. It does not tell us whether the parties later settled the case in the Court of Equity or whether they actually had a trial, so we do not know from this opinion how the case ended.

We followed up in North Carolina court records to try and determine if Ferrer actually did take the matter to the Court of Equity, and while we strongly suspect that he did (knowing what we do of Laffite and his money), we have not found that record.

A MASONIC TRAIL

Against the backdrop of who Elisha Barrett was and the extent to which he had the ability to insert himself into the fabric (and pocketbooks) of Lincolnton, we return to the year 1851 and the formation of Lincoln Lodge 137. Of course, the matter of the lodge would not have come into play at all, save for our curiosity about Lorenzo Ferrer's behavior and the degree to which it mirrored the behavior and actions of Jean Laffite. Because of the strong Masonic history associated with Laffite, the obvious question was clear.

From the start, we wondered how a man as well-known and notorious as Jean Laffite could have managed re-entry into the United States under a new name to live safely hidden for the next forty-six years without being exposed. On its face, that seemed unlikely, and it may in fact have been an ongoing reason through the years why earlier historians trying to research Ferrer were reluctant to buy into the "Jean Laffite living under an assumed name" theory. Famous pirates, after all, hardly blend in. Word leaks out. People talk. That is exactly what happened with Ferrer. Tongues did wag, almost from the day he arrived in Lincoln County, and they still wag, a full 145 years later. That fact notwithstanding, we did have a healthy dose of "what are the chances?" as we considered the likelihood that Ferrer's legend was actually true. As often as Laffite and the Freemasons had already intersected in our research, it was a natural impulse to investigate whether Ferrer was a practicing Mason in Lincoln County. Evidence of that would provide yet another solid parallel between the life of Laffite and the life of Ferrer.

The first most obvious stop was local. If Lorenzo Ferrer was a Mason, we supposed, then there must be a record of that fact somewhere in Lincolnton. We found that not only was Ferrer a Lincolnton Freemason, he was one of the earliest founding members of the local lodge, Lincoln Lodge 137. Much more about that in a bit. The next logical area of inquiry was to look at the men who were known associates and contemporaries—both during the years of Jean Laffite's tenure in the Gulf and later during his time here as Ferrer. Again, we were heartened—so much so that with every subsequent discovery, we became more convinced that whatever story it was we were uncovering was intertwined with the Masons from start to finish. As it turns out, almost all the men involved in this story were known Masons. That list of names includes Pierre Laffite, Barthélémy Lafon, Dominique You, Edward Livingston, Arsène Latour, Andrew Jackson, James Madison, William C. C. Claiborne, Texas Governor and US Senator James Pinckney

Lincoln Lodge 137

Henderson, and, of course, Marshal Michel Ney (aka Peter Stuart Ney)—not to mention the scores of unnamed Baratarians that we discussed in a previous chapter who worked under the Laffites during the height of their power in the Gulf. Even Napoleon Bonaparte himself was at the very least considered a close friend of the organization.

As easy as the task was of documenting Lorenzo Ferrer as a Mason in Lincolnton, the matter of documenting Jean Laffite as a Mason was an entirely other row to hoe. Various writers have speculated, based on the fact that he was surrounded by Masons on all sides—at Barataria, in high government and social circles, and even within his own family—that Laffite himself must have been a member. And while discovering documentation of this fact in early Masonic records from Louisiana (the most likely location) proved daunting, we did uncover a 2020 publication from the Grand Lodge of Louisiana that gave an account of Laffite holding Masonic communications with Andrew Jackson just prior to the Battle of New Orleans.[14] However, Poll, writing for a Texas Freemasonry publication, reveals, "there is no record of Masonic membership of either of the Lafitte brothers."[15] This supports what we were told by officials in the Grand Lodge of Louisiana. The conclusion drawn here does not have to be that Jean Laffite was not a Freemason, because we suspect that he was. Nevertheless, there is no paper trail to prove it.

Having no experience with Freemasonry, its history, its rules of conduct, or its conditions for membership, we quickly turned to two longtime friends for help.

Jason Harpe, who at the time was the director of the Lincoln County Historical Association, gave us early insight and also specific information related to Ferrer in the local lodge, drawn directly from documents in the archives of his office. Harpe had already been working alongside us in his capacity as a local historian with extensive knowledge of Ferrer and of the various documents concerning him that existed in local files. He immediately furnished us with a copy of Ferrer's petition for lodge membership and encouraged us to get in touch with the local Freemasons, knowing that additional information existed within their internal files.

Following up on that information and encouragement, we contacted Brent Turner, another old friend and current member and past Master of Lincoln Lodge 137, whose gracious and enthusiastic support enabled us to get a clear picture of Freemasonry. His knowledge has proven itself time and again to be extremely informative.

One of our first questions for Turner was this: How does one become a member of a local Masonic lodge? As we found out, there are two ways. One can apply to join a local lodge as a non-Mason, which involves a formal application, followed by a certain sequence of steps, at the end of which one is voted on and admitted into the fold. Alternatively, one can petition to join a local lodge as an *existing Mason transferring in from another lodge*, which requires proof using certain secret methods known only to those already a Mason, plus the ability to prove he is a Mason in good standing in a recognized lodge along with the testimony of approval from two other existing Masons within the lodge that he is asking to join. One of those Masons "recommends" the applicant to the group and the other "vouches for" that applicant, at which point a vote is taken and membership is complete.

Knowing that as an existing Mason, Jean Laffite (even under a new name) had given petition for membership in the Lincoln Lodge as a *transfer*, we were encouraged when Turner confirmed that process. Had Ferrer applied for membership as a new Mason, this story might have taken a different turn, but the application clearly showed that Lorenzo Ferrer claimed *he was an existing Mason seeking to transfer in.* It is important to note here that we contacted both local and statewide Masonic organizations (including archival repositories) to see if Lorenzo Ferrer had been a Mason in either

Mississippi or Louisiana, and we have concluded that he was not. Mississippi in 1830 is the first hit on Lorenzo Ferrer in the United States, and he was not a documented Freemason, though some of the lodge secretaries admit that there has been record loss over the years, especially due to fire and water damage. Yet Ferrer came to Lincolnton and knew the intricacies of Masonry well enough to gain entry.

The petition itself, as you can see from the photo below, is hand-written and faded. It appears to bear the handwriting of more than one person. Based on the use of two different capital "L's," it also appears that the person who signed the petition (presumably Ferrer himself) used an entirely different form of capital "L" than the person who filled in the blank on the petition that states the name of Ferrer's former lodge. The name appears to say "Liore," a variant spelling of the "Loire" region in France.[16]

Ferrer was citing earlier membership in a French Masonic lodge, and that being the case, we should have been able to get verification of that from old French Masonic records in very short order. It came as no surprise to us, though, that no such verification could be found. And we did try. If some-

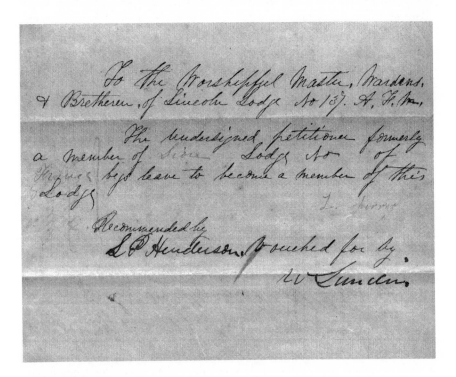

Ferrer Lincolnton Lodge Petition

one in France with the capacity to help is reading, please consider this our official S.O.S. signal for archival assistance.

The possibility also exists, as we pointed out in an earlier chapter, that *Jean Laffite* was not the pirate's original first name. If that is true, his actual first identity has never been discovered. It is possible that his real name is part of the archives of a French lodge he could have joined as a young man.

The lodge petition appeared consistent with what we would have expected Jean Laffite to say and do—cite a false lodge in an effort to divert attention away from his true (even if unofficial) membership in the Louisiana Masons. Bearing that in mind, we took a closer look at the petition. It states simply "Loire, France," with no lodge number provided—even though a space was left on the form for Ferrer to include that information. Understandably, with Ferrer having lived in the United States for a minimum of thirty-three years, and now a man of seventy-two, his memory could have been fuzzy. However, his memory was apparently clear enough to enable him to recite the various secret words and codes necessary to prove his status as a Mason. How does one manage to remember intricate words and phrases and yet fail to remember the name and number of one's former lodge? That, to our mind, was slightly akin to failing to remember one's own name. This omission is especially suspect because our experience with Freemasons in multiple states revealed to us how important the lodge numbering system is to its members. The Brothers know their lodge numbers. With this document we are left with what looks like an out-and-out lie on Ferrer's part—in other words, an attempt to disguise the real source of his Masonic credentials. Ferrer, after all, could not exactly apply to Lincoln Lodge 137 with the words "Well, I became a Mason in Louisiana, but they knew me as Jean Laffite, so don't bother to check with that lodge because Jean Laffite is supposed to be dead." Indeed, by the time of Ferrer's lodge petition in Lincolnton, he was already several decades into a charade that was holding up quite well, so a reluctance to rock that boat would be completely understandable. Having said that, we do believe there is a strong chance at least some of his lodge Brothers knew who he was. As you will see in a few moments when we get into the timeline of the Lincolnton lodge, one of them (not surprisingly, one of the Hendersons) vouched for his authenticity—an act which in itself may have been a demonstration of ongoing protection.

In fact, we do not discount the likelihood that Masonic connections were instrumental in Laffite's rise to power as a privateer, his various escapes from impending imprisonment and even death, his ability to hide in Cuba, and most especially his ability to re-enter the United States through the back door of the Mississippi River as another man. Early in our discussions with Turner, we understood that Masons the world over take care of their own, willing and able to assist a fellow Brother without hesitation. Given the various geopolitical forces at odds with each other, especially during the colonization of the Caribbean Islands and the Gulf Coast, the common thread of Masonic bonds may have been one of the only differentiators in an otherwise uncertain environment. This not only tracked with Marshal Ney's story of his flight from France but also pointed a convincing light toward the various circumstances of Jean Laffite's life that ultimately carried him through that upheaval to his final years here in North Carolina.

Lincoln Lodge 137

Whatever the circumstance that resulted in Ferrer's admission to Lincoln Lodge 137, we do have a solid record of what transpired over the following years due to the astute record keeping of its members. These documents not only provide clues about the personality and abilities of Ferrer (traits which square with the personality and abilities of Jean Laffite), but they also open a window onto the local Barrett scandal that had far-reaching ramifications in Lincolnton and beyond.

In the fall of 2018, we were graciously granted access to the archives of Lincoln Lodge 137. This required a vote among the Brotherhood to approve our access. With Brent Turner and Joey Mathis (both past Masters) in attendance, we were allowed to review the very earliest record books, dating all the way back to the formation of the lodge in 1851. These records included membership rosters, meeting minutes, and other transactional documents. Taken as a whole, they formed a fascinating picture.

We were able to reconstruct a timeline of events that provides a new perspective on Ferrer's life, his relationships with other prominent citizens, the talents that he displayed in his interactions with them, and, not insignificantly, the disputes that he ultimately became involved in as well.

Lincoln Lodge 137 was formally organized on June 20, 1851, with forty-five founding members. Ferrer's name appears as one of the founders, number twenty-eight on the list. However, his petition for admission was not voted on until February 6, 1852. A line item listing all the early members written at the time provides copious details on how each member joined, including particulars on when and where he was initiated, passed, and raised. The line item pertaining to Lorenzo Ferrer, however, simply shows "Lincolnton, NC" with the notation "joined by card" and is dated February 7, 1852. That petition,

Ferrer on Lodge 137 Founders' List

as previously shown, was immediately accepted. According to the minutes of that meeting (actual date being February 6, 1852), Ferrer was recommended as a member by Lawson P. Henderson, who was the son of Charles Cotesworth Henderson and the nephew of James Pinckney Henderson, Lawson Franklin Henderson, and the other Henderson brothers.

Once Lincolnton Lodge 137 was formed, it became a hub of business networking. Records from the Abstract of Deeds for Lincoln County during the 1840s and beyond show that C. C. Henderson, Lorenzo Ferrer, and others (who would become future Masonic Brothers of Ferrer's in 1852) were involved in numerous financial ventures as participants if not full partners. These transactions included joint loans made to local individuals. One such loan, massive for the day in terms of the monetary amount and also in the number of participants who contributed to the loan, involved money given to Dr. Samuel P. Simpson, who apparently found it necessary to mortgage nearly everything he owned. Ferrer and C. C. Henderson are both listed as contributors in this transaction.[17]

These events and personal connections, as they led up to the formation of the lodge in 1852, provide a backdrop of the strong connection between Lorenzo Ferrer and the Henderson family. It stretched all the way back into the 1830s land transactions in Mississippi, where both Ferrer and the Hendersons appear on the tax rolls during the same year and where both made land purchases out of the same Mt. Salus land office, all the way forward to the early years of Ferrer's arrival in Lincoln County and his involvement with C. C. Henderson and his various offspring once he came.

Small wonder, then, that the man who stepped up to the plate in 1852 and recommended Ferrer for membership in the fledgling Masonic lodge was Lawson P. Henderson, C. C. Henderson's son.

The other man who stood as guarantee for Ferrer's admission to the lodge was local lawyer William Lander. Lander's reputation as an able litigator extended well beyond the boundaries of Lincoln County. William J. Yates writing for the *Charlotte Democrat* during Lander's life asserted, "As an honest and conscientious public man William Lander has no superior. Unimpeachable in his private and public life, industrious and energetic, he merits the confidence of the people."[18] Adding to Lander's stellar reputation is the fact that he also achieved prominence in Masonic circles as well. Lander served as Master of Lincoln Lodge 137 in 1852 and 1853, eventually rising to the level of Senior Grand Warden of the North Carolina Grand Lodge in 1867.[19]

With two such rock-solid recommendations for membership, it is no surprise that Ferrer was admitted to the lodge without delay. These recommendations also speak to the fact that by the time the 1850s arrived, Ferrer, who had now lived in Lincolnton for more than a decade, had established for himself a well-connected and very wealthy network of friends and associates. This same pattern of behavior was a hallmark of Jean Laffite and his dealings in New Orleans and the Gulf.

Not long after Ferrer's acceptance into the Masonic ranks, he was elected treasurer. The first notation of this comes during the meeting minutes from November 5, 1852, and subsequent notations continue right up until the time of Ferrer's departure from the lodge in 1858. As best as we can determine, the post of treasurer is the only appointed post that Ferrer ever held, though the meeting minutes show him sitting in various chairs in a *pro tempore* capacity on occasions. Those same minutes show him being elected for several committees appointed to investigate potential members, matters of disciplinary actions, legal questions, and collections of lodge dues from members who were in arrears. Between the archives of the lodge and also via the body of historic lodge documents donated to the Lincoln County Historical Association, we found evidence of receipts and reports on various lodge matters being undersigned by Ferrer.

The following is a brief timeline of Ferrer's Masonic activity in the lodge, taken from the original ledger detailing the minutes of each meeting:

- Ferrer signs the by-laws in the opening of the ledger.

- He appears twice in the original record book before his acceptance actually shows up in the minutes of the meeting on February 6, 1852.

- From February 19, 1852, through June 9, 1852, his regular attendance at meetings is noted.

- The August 6, 1852, meeting shows him in the leadership role of junior deacon.

- From August 7, 1852, through October 19, 1852, his consistent attendance at meetings is noted.

- On November 5, 1852, he is shown as treasurer for the first time.

- Regular attendance is evident throughout 1853 up until August 5, following which he is absent for the remainder of that year.

- Regular attendance is solid through 1854, during which time he serves as treasurer and also sporadically as junior and senior deacon.

- Following the January 5, 1855, meeting, Ferrer is absent from the lodge for six months.

- He shows up again on July 10, 1855, designated as treasurer, and attends four more meetings until the end of the year.

- Another big absence occurs in the first portion of 1856, as Ferrer is not present until April 22, 1856, showing up in the meeting minutes as treasurer.

- He attends faithfully throughout the remainder of 1856.

- He is absent again in January and February 1857. He picks up his duties as treasurer in March 1857, attending meetings throughout the rest of the spring and summer.

- He misses three months of 1857, from early September until early December, before showing up as treasurer on December 4, 1857.

- His participation is regular beginning in 1858, leading up to a pivotal meeting in April that indicates increased scrutiny on the lodge finances.

- The April 2, 1858, meeting minutes go into great detail about members in arrears of their dues and feature the report of a recent audit of the books.

- On April 20, 1858, Ferrer attends the meeting, shown as treasurer.

- The May 7, 1858, meeting minutes indicate charges brought against Elisha Barrett, with subsequent charges being brought in June and discussion of Barrett's guilt or innocence continuing toward a vote until October of that same year.

- From May until October 2, 1858, Ferrer attends four more meetings, being shown as treasurer.

- October 2, 1858, is the last meeting that was attended by Ferrer in any capacity. At that meeting, he is shown as treasurer.

- On October 19, 1858, a petition to join the lodge is received from non-Mason Caleb Motz.

- One day later, on October 20, Motz is accepted for membership. In that same meeting, the lodge votes to make a loan to Motz in the amount of money "currently being held by the treasurer." At that same meeting, L. P. Henderson is shown in attendance as treasurer.

- The very last mention of Ferrer appears on January 2, 1859, during which a full financial report is given by a committee comprised of W. J. Hoke, J. T. Alexander, and L. P. Henderson, detailing money that is due to Ferrer. He had apparently requested to be paid for his service (perhaps as loan officer for private loans) and had also requested to be paid interest (also presumably for certain loans). The lodge votes at this meeting to grant the requests.

CONFLICT AND RESOLUTION

As you can see from this timeline, it should come as no great shock that a group of men, no matter how lofty their goals or oaths of allegiance, should find themselves at odds with each other from time to time, and such was the case with this lodge. Beginning in November of 1856, there were rumblings of financial misgivings that made their way into the records of the lodge. On November 15, 1856, a special Tuesday night meeting was called for the express purpose of authorizing a loan of $120. Ferrer was treasurer at the time. The loan note was signed by Lawson P. Henderson as principal with Elisha Barrett and J. T. Alexander as security.

Eight months later, in July of 1857, more extensive financial unrest was revealed in the meeting minutes. At another specially called meeting, the Brothers adopted a motion to make legal inquiries of a local lawyer to determine if the lodge was on firm footing to loan money or somehow placing itself in jeopardy of being sued for such activity. Three men were appointed to a committee to carry out this task and report back: Barrett, Ferrer, and Alexander. At the very next meeting, the committee came back to report that the lodge was, indeed, permitted to loan money out of its account as long as the loan was properly documented with a signed note. There is no indication in the minutes of either of these meetings, or in any of the meetings prior to this, about what precipitated the worry in the first place.

In April of 1858, financial matters surfaced again, this time in what appears to be the results of a recent audit of the lodge books, brought before the body in the form of a report from this same finance committee—Barrett, Ferrer, and Alexander. The report contained a list of everyone who was in arrears on their dues, plus an account of the various loans that had been made. Curiously, the loans were to Elisha Barrett himself and one other man in amounts totaling $240. During this meeting, the membership directed the lodge secretary to try and force all those in arrears on their dues to pay them and to force notes on those who refused.

While these details may seem inconsequential, they illustrate what appears to be growing financial discord among the members with Elisha Barrett at the center of the fray.

Concurrent with this situation at the lodge, we have already seen that Barrett had managed by the year 1858 to create a trail of bad deals and financial misdeeds in the community at large. And this puts it mildly.

Against this backdrop, we come to May 1858, roughly one month after the curious April lodge meeting during which a lot of financial laundry was apparently aired. It is fair to say that what happened in May far eclipsed any spats over audits or unpaid dues. But it could very well have been the tornado that resulted from those early rumblings of thunder.

At that meeting in early May, J. A. Richardson made the charge that reports had reached the lodge of Elisha Barrett acting with un-Masonic conduct toward various members of the community, and Richardson further stated that Barrett had also acted with un-Masonic conduct toward him. In the world of Freemasons, this is the ultimate claim against another Brother. The Lincolnton Masons who read these passages with us for the first time were flabbergasted by the severity of the situation.

The following June, Richardson again brought a charge against Barrett, this time charging that Barrett had deceived him by forfeiting on a loan and preventing him from collecting money that was due him. (Richardson and

his wife had just taken up residence at Woodside Plantation, by the way—
the same Woodside where Ferrer allegedly murdered an intruder a year later
in 1859 while house-sitting for the Richardsons.)

After these charges were brought, the minutes reflect several subsequent
meetings during which the matter of voting on Barrett's guilt or innocence
was postponed. The meeting on October 2, 1858, is the last gathering of
the Freemasons that Lorenzo Ferrer ever attended. The collective evidence
suggests that this correlates with the scandal involving Barrett. We see several
meaningful things in the minutes of the next meeting, held on October 19,
1858:

- In that meeting, L. P. Henderson is shown as treasurer. We see no
  evidence that Ferrer had been voted out as treasurer. Neither do we
  see that Henderson is sitting in the treasurer's chair as a temporary
  measure. This indicates to us that Ferrer was no longer serving in that
  post, for whatever reason.

- Also in that meeting, a local man named Caleb Motz is presented for
  membership. It appears he is bringing petition as a non-Mason.

- The bulk of the meeting is taken up with what is described as lengthy
  debate on the matter of Elisha Barrett and his guilt or innocence
  as they pertain to the charges brought earlier in the year by J. P.
  Richardson.

- By a vote of nine to three, Barrett is found not guilty.

In an even more telling read of the records, two more meetings were held in
very short order—one on October 20 and another on October 22. Though
the minutes seem to be jumbled a bit, the evidence shows the following:

- Roughly one day after bringing petition as a non-Mason, Caleb Motz
  is admitted for membership.

- In the same meeting, the members vote to make what is worded as a
  "loan" to Motz in the amount of *whatever is being held by the treasurer*.

- There is no mention in any of the three meetings—October 19,
  October 20, or October 22—of Lorenzo Ferrer.

The Freemasons who studied these records with us noted it is unheard of for
a new Mason to petition for membership and then be admitted a day later.
New members petitioning a lodge for the first time have to memorize and

then be able to recite verbatim voluminous passages of Masonic doctrine. Most petitioners spend months preparing. The fact that Motz was admitted immediately is highly suspicious.

There is no mention of Lorenzo Ferrer ever again in the records of Lincoln Lodge 137, with the exception of a very lengthy entry at the start of the New Year in 1859, roughly two months after all of this transpired. In the January 2, 1859, meeting, a long and detailed report was presented to the membership by a finance committee consisting of W. J. Hoke, J. T. Alexander, and L. P. Henderson. Remember Henderson is the same man who recommended Ferrer for lodge membership at its inception in 1852. Henderson's father and his uncles were likely the men who paved the way for Ferrer's arrival in town just prior to 1839. In the report, the three men appear to be offering a final accounting of the money as it stood when Ferrer exited the lodge. Additionally, they make the request that Ferrer be reimbursed a small monetary amount as payment for his services and that he also be paid some interest due him. Whether this recommendation is being brought at their request or at Ferrer's, we are unclear. However, given what we know of Jean Laffite and his tendency to be a proverbial dog-with-a-bone when someone else was holding money that was rightfully his, our guess is that a very angry old Frenchman was demanding that he be paid every penny due him after years of diligent service. Whatever the case, the record shows that the membership voted to pay the man.

Barely a month after the October meeting which turned out to be his last, Ferrer's mistress Louisa passed away at the young age of forty. It is entirely possible that Louisa was gravely ill, which would have explained Ferrer's absence at the volatile October meeting, but it is much more likely that the matter of Barrett's innocence or guilt could also have kept Ferrer away from the lodge on that night.

On December 2, 1859, a notation appeared in the lodge minutes that Barrett had demitted out of the lodge. This is a formal process whereby a Brother leaves a lodge in good standing and pays a years' dues in advance. Demitting greatly facilitates a future re-entry into the lodge with nothing more than a vote required.

As for Ferrer's exit, he simply disappeared from view, rendering a much different picture. There is no record of him submitting a demit request, as Barrett did. There is also no mention of Ferrer being subject to discipline or expulsion by the lodge. There is simply a notation in the financial records of the lodge indicating "withdrawn by letter." Each member was accorded a ledger sheet that gave the full record of his payment of dues from the day he entered the lodge until the day he left. As expected, Ferrer's ledger sheet began in 1852 and ran right up until October 1858. Clearly visible at the end of the payment entries are the words "Withdrawn by letter."

Leaving a Masonic lodge in this manner is distinctly different from requesting to demit. To withdraw by letter implies that a member has decided to renounce his membership in the Freemasons altogether. Ferrer was by this time one year shy of his eightieth birthday, so it is highly possible that his advanced age, or perhaps lingering grief over the loss of a much younger Louisa (who, by all rights, should have survived to care for him in his old age) were contributing factors to his exit. Men of that age are not immune to making errors in computation and record-keeping, a completely understandable possibility in this case that would imply no ill will or accusation of wrongdoing. Also, the odd and seemingly turbulent circumstances in the months leading up to his exit may have at the very least caused such a strain and had such a demoralizing effect on Ferrer that he simply lost heart. A third, but unlikely, notion is that he was forced to leave as a result of those same circumstances. We use the word "unlikely" because there is no further record in the lodge minutes to give us an explanation for his exit—and those notations would most certainly have been made had there been an issue of scandal. As Turner explained to us, and as we saw for ourselves from reading through years of meeting minutes, the Masons were not shy about calling out a Brother who had been deemed unworthy in any regard. There

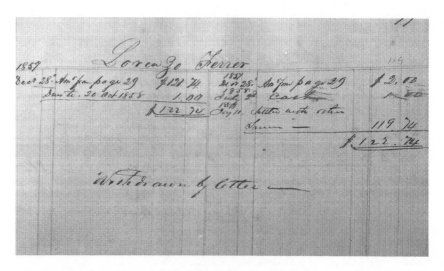

Ferrer Withdrawn by Letter

was even a formal process of expulsion, following which an entry was made in the records of the local lodge, and in many cases, a broadly distributed notice was sent to other lodges in an effort to prevent the expelled Mason from attempting membership elsewhere. And yet, pertaining to the matter of Lorenzo Ferrer, not another word was said. After taking all of the above into consideration, we are of the opinion that Lorenzo Ferrer left the lodge of his own free will in a state of anger. He was already embroiled in a legal conflict with Elisha Barrett, one that involved default on a loan for which Ferrer was a co-signer. Additionally, the current situation in town that involved Barrett's dishonesty was reaching out to harm a lot of prominent men. Ferrer served as treasurer on and off since the beginning of the lodge. Then he endured the years from 1856–1858 with some form of controversy surrounding the lodge finances and Barrett's involvement in those transactions (possibly even being stripped of his position as treasurer in the process). He watched the behavior of Barrett ultimately go unpunished (whether rightly or wrongly) by a vote of nine to three. Due to all of this, we believe that Lorenzo Ferrer simply got mad and quit.

ECHOES OF LAFFITE

To put it charitably, seeds of infidelity were indeed scattered in Lincolnton during the years that Lorenzo Ferrer lived here. And, as seeds are wont to do, they had apparently taken root and sprouted by the time the *Weekly Lincoln Progress* made that observation in 1880, five years after Ferrer's death. By way of illustrating the hot-house climate in which the local scandals flourished, it is useful to understand how money was loaned and (sometimes, but sometimes not) repaid during those years. There were banks, yes. But much of the lending was accomplished via private loans from wealthy citizens or groups of citizens. Time and again, our research uncovered records of what looked like massive loans to local individuals, very often granted by a collective group of men. One might say that these loans made with pooled resources were the precursors to modern-day private equity loans. Many of them were duly drawn up and notarized in legal documents that found their way into the public records, which is where we found them. Tracing their progress and eventual outcome, however, proved nearly impossible. Often, the only way to connect those dots was when notice of a scandal became evident in some other forum such as the minutes of lodge meetings, in a lawsuit which alleged non-payment of debt, or, sadly, in some form of bankruptcy notice that showed a property owner signing over rights to everything he owned to his creditors. Such was the obvious case of Jacob A. Ramseur.

The involvement of Lorenzo Ferrer in such loans is outlined in Chapter Twelve and its corresponding appendix, giving the dates and circumstances of his participation and also the names of others involved. These represent only the ones we were able to uncover. If there were others, perhaps never entered into public records, we cannot know—but a safe guess is that others did exist.

As we bring this chapter to a close, you may wonder, as we did, about the true nature of the relationship between Ferrer and Barrett. After considerable thought, we arrived at a couple of useful conclusions.

If we are to believe the accounts of Jean Laffite and his dealings on the Gulf Coast during the first part of the nineteenth century, then there is abundant evidence that he was an opportunist at best and a thieving scoundrel at worst. Men of such dubious talent can spot one of their own kind in very short order. The record is clear that Laffite's modus operandi in any new situation was to first observe and evaluate, following which he rarely took on a task that he was not already convinced he could successfully accomplish. That is not to say he never rolled the dice (the famous gamble with a certain British military officer comes to mind), but for the most part, Laffite never entered a fight without having a decent picture of the outcome. We also know that he was tenacious when it came to money and had no scruples about whether that money was earned honestly or not.

By comparison, in his later life as Lorenzo Ferrer, the talent and the tendencies remained. This is clear on many counts, not the least of which is the fact that Ferrer sustained nearly a forty-year residency in Lincolnton without the benefit of holding down a job of any sort. Knowing this, we believe that he likely had Elisha Barrett sized up and categorized from the get-go. Having done so, we think that the opportunist in Ferrer did not especially care that Barrett was who he was, as long as Ferrer believed there was opportunity to make a dollar in the process. By that same token, however, we also think Ferrer never took his eye off the ball and would not (and did not) hesitate to turn adversarial toward Barrett if the need arose.

Finally, we address the matter of the lodge scandal and how it seemingly blew up in Lorenzo Ferrer's face, making the observation that times had changed greatly from his early days as Jean Laffite and that the free-wheeling Gulf Coast of the early 1800s was a far cry from small-town North Carolina of the 1850s, a place where everyone not only knew each other's business but most all were cousins of some sort (and still are to this day, truth be told). Careless and self-serving attempts to feather one's own nest, regardless of the legality, were not as easily passed off as they once were for an old privateer who had made a career of living by his wits.

Given Ferrer's exit from the lodge, with no further reference to the Masons evident in the record of his life here, we are left to conclude that the memory of Ferrer in Lincolnton and those "seeds of infidelity" may very well have had their roots in the wide-reaching trouble involving Barrett, Ramseur, and others, and, by extension a very large chunk of the small population of the town. And this is just one scandal that happened to break the surface and go public. Given what we now know of a man whose life had been marked by the presence of double-dealing, it is almost certain that there was a lingering bad taste in Lincolnton whenever Ferrer's name was mentioned.

Barrett moved away from Lincolnton, settling with his wife in Sedalia, Missouri, where he reinvented himself and was buried with full Masonic honors. While it is possible that Missouri was far enough removed from North Carolina that any disparaging word about Barrett's past dealings may not have reached the Show Me State, for whatever reason, that past did not affect his standing as a Mason when he died.

For Ferrer's part, we show no record of him ever returning to Freemasonry, and when he died sixteen years after leaving the lodge, there were understandably no Masonic rites associated with his burial. Also telling, his death was not mentioned anywhere in the Lincoln Lodge 137 ledger—either in the minutes or in the chart of member pathways in and out of the lodge in the back of the book. This is a very odd circumstance.

Regardless of the ending of Laffite's/Ferrer's Masonic journey, however, the beginning and the middle show just how critically important that journey was. Those connections likely enabled him to build a financial empire, come to the aid of the United States in a way that may very well have saved the Mississippi River from falling into the hands of the British, slip through the snare of a pursuing government bent on destroying him, find safe haven in Cuba, and ultimately build a new life after having successfully faked his own death. Given all of this, it is fair to say that Freemasonry saved the life of this man many times over.

In light of this, you will not be surprised to discover in the final moments of this book that there was yet one more secret regarding Laffite and Ferrer that was being held by the Freemasons of Lincoln Lodge 137. Some might call it a smoking gun.

Chapter Fifteen

Les Deux Français

What are the chances? The nineteenth-century arrival of a mysterious Frenchman in a remote place such as Lincolnton, well inland from the coastal port cities that usually boasted such international residents, was enough to make heads turn. History records that the sudden appearance of Lorenzo Ferrer in 1839 did just that. In an odd quirk of circumstance, fate gifted Lincoln County with not one mysterious Frenchman but two—each bearing his own version of intrigue and each leaving such an impression that written accounts of their time here were prolific. The answer to our opening rhetorical question is that the odds of this happening in such a sparsely populated place in the early 1800s were somewhere in the neighborhood of a snowball's chance in hell. And yet, that is exactly what happened.

As soon as we realized this curious wealth of mysterious riches, we immediately wondered if the two men, who for all intents and purposes shared nothing more than a nationality, were here during the same time and, if so, were ever known to have crossed paths. One would at least think that they could have, and probably should have. So did they? And if so, what happened?

Peter Stuart Ney arrived in the port of Charleston, South Carolina, on January 29, 1816, and laid low for several years while training to be a teacher.[1] Other than that, not much is known about his first years in the United States.

Through the 1820s, 1830s, and 1840s, he bounced around and taught at numerous schools in the southeastern United States, including in Cheraw and Darlington in South Carolina and in many North Carolina counties in the Piedmont, including Iredell, Cabarrus, Rowan, Davie, and Lincoln. Census searches for 1790, 1800, and 1810 contain no Peter Ney, so the historical documents back up the claim that he was a new arrival to the country in 1816.

Ney became a noted, much-revered, and even feared school teacher to many students in the upper regions of South Carolina and the area of North Carolina centering around the Catawba and Yadkin Rivers, sometimes boarding in the homes of the families whose sons and daughters he taught and seemingly satisfied with the meager salary he earned. Among his students were several young men from Lincoln County such as Vardry McBee and Wallace Reinhardt, who a few years later would become a close friend and confidant of Lorenzo Ferrer's. All of his students who ever went on record described him as a glorious teacher, a well-educated man gifted with unbelievable aptitude and worldly knowledge.

Even so, in all the places Ney worked, there was a common suspicion among those he knew that he was not who he claimed to be. After all, he was perfectly capable of succeeding in any line of work, yet he chose a very low-key existence and a job that was frankly beneath him. While sober, Ney rebuffed the questions and speculation. On the rare occasions when he was drunk, however, he told a markedly different story: *he was Marshal Michel Ney of France, the famed general of the French Revolution, christened by Napoleon Bonaparte himself as "the Bravest of the Brave," the man who was said to have died by firing squad on December 7, 1815, roughly a month before Peter Stuart Ney arrived by boat in Charleston.*

After Napoleon's defeat at Waterloo in June 1815, Ney was arrested and sentenced to death for treason in December. Murat claims that when he was arrested "in the department of the Lot on August 3, 1816, he was not going to Switzerland, as it appeared from his passport, but to the United States, via Bordeaux."[2]

A variety of compelling sources published since then have revealed fascinating arguments to prove his death sentence was never actually carried out. We, along with many other scholars, believe that the reasons listed below cast doubt over his execution and open the possibility that the firing squad scene was a farce designed to make the world think Marshal Ney was dead.

- The "bullet marks on the wall where Ney had stood were all to the left and right of Ney. Another rumor held that something like an animal bladder had been found at the execution scene and that the bladder had held a bright red fluid, such as a dye."[3] Some sources say the sack was a pig bladder.

- Many of the witnesses who saw the execution said it did not look real.

- Several sources reveal the firing squad consisted of Ney's former men—all of whom loved him deeply—and the place where the execution was to take place was changed several times.

- After the "execution," it was reported that Ney fled with "two companions to Bordeaux and took passage in a vessel sailing for the United States. His companions, Pasqual Luciani and Count Charles Lefebvre-Desnouettes, left the ship at Philadelphia, but Ney continued on to Charleston, South Carolina"[4]—the port where Peter Stuart Ney came into the United States. It is said he made it out of France dressed as a peasant in a farmer's cart.[5] Remember, too, that Lefebvre-Desnouettes was one of the founding members of the Vine and Olive Colony in Alabama with Lallemand.

- The doctor who signed Ney's death certificate was completely fictitious.[6] There was no doctor in the area by that name.

- Ney's wife apparently never grieved and suddenly became very wealthy after his passing.[7] Also, none of his family members attended his funeral the day after his execution.[8]

- Both Marshal Ney and Peter Stuart Ney had physical characteristics in common, along with many other similarities. Both had flaming red hair. Both shared very distinctive scars on their faces and bodies that were clearly from combat. Both were master fencers. Floyd also points out that both men spoke Hebrew, Latin, Greek, French, and English.[9]

- In the mid-1830s, several men attempted to convince the Chamber of Peers in France to reverse Ney's death sentence[10]—more than ten years after he supposedly died. This would have been completely unnecessary for a man who was actually dead but would have been incredibly useful for a man who was still alive and hoping to one day return to his homeland.

- The birthdate for Marshal Michel Ney was January 10, 1769, the same birthdate listed on Peter Stuart Ney's tombstone.

French documents also tell us that many other Napoleonic followers were forced to flee under similar circumstances to save their lives, as they were all marked men facing death if they remained in France. In *History of the Third Creek Presbyterian Church*, Fleming writes that, "[a]t the time of Ney's alleged execution, many of Napoleon's followers who were condemned to execution by the Bourbon Courts did escape, and their escape has been acknowledged in history, especially in the case of Marshal LeFebre Desnouettes,"[11] Ney's reported shipmate during his escape. And there was an additional very powerful force at work here that cannot be glossed over: the Freemasons.

In F. F. Rowe's article "Was Marshal Ney in America?" published by the Davidson College Historical Association in 1898, Rowe recounts the testimony of Basil Jones of South Carolina, a contemporary of Ney who claims Ney told him how he escaped. Jones said, "He fell by preconcerted arrangement as if he were dead, was taken up, disguised, and finally escaped to the United States, the Ancient Fraternity aiding in his escape from the first."[12] This reference to the "Ancient Fraternity" is critical, as Marshal Ney and the high-ranking French officials who could have helped stage the mock execution were all known Freemasons. Rowe also references an 1891 article that tells the story of a man named George Melody going to Paris and meeting with King Louis Philippe. When Melody asked the king if Ney was actually shot, the king retorted,

> Mr. Melody, I know the fact that you are one of the highest Masons in America. I am known as one of the most exalted Masons in Europe. Marshal Ney held a position among Masons equal to either of us. The prisons were full of men condemned to be shot. These men were daily being marched out to meet their fate. Some other man may have filled the grave intended for Marshal Ney.[13]

Murat cites a Boston magazine article from 1920 that proclaims, "Freemasons know about Ney's escape, especially those of the Grand Orient Lodge of France."[14] Studying the fraternity alongside several longtime Freemasons as we have for the past two years, it is very easy for us to imagine a situation in which the Brotherhood could arrange Ney's rescue so adeptly, especially considering his position of importance to the French people. Next to some of the other operations the Freemasons are known to have successfully maneuvered, Ney's rescue and relocation would have been child's play. We believe he may have been brought into port in Charleston and given orders to lead a quiet life and wait—mainly because so many French exiles had relocated to the United States by that point, and he needed a low profile in case any of them were enemies with designs to do him harm. Charleston at the time was a Freemason stronghold, a place where many powerful people could keep him safe. What Ney was waiting for is perhaps the most intriguing thread of his story.

It is a known fact that Luciani and Lefebvre-Desnouettes, who came over on the rescue ship with Ney, had a hand in forming a French colony of exiles at Demopolis, Alabama.[15] This colony was just like Champ d'Asile—the French Bonapartist colony Jean Laffite supported. Remember these colonies were established with the hope of creating spaces where French exiles could find refuge to wait—either for Napoleon to ascend the throne in France again or to set up a new French kingdom in North America with his followers.

After a dreadful military defeat in 1813, Napoleon was forced to sign an abdication agreement and live on the island of Elba. With Napoleon out of the picture, Ney fell under the command of the Bourbon King Louis XVIII. Once Napoleon left Elba, he put together another army and tried to come back on the scene and reclaim his position. Robert Williams writes, "Ney was ordered by King Louis to take his own troops and march to meet Napoleon, conquer him, and bring him to Paris in an iron cage, like some savage animal."[16] When Ney and Napoleon met on the battlefield, Ney refused his orders and instead, "he knelt before Napoleon, offered him his sword and services, and the two old soldiers were reunited once more. And again, Europe trembled as both Ney and Napoleon marched toward Paris."[17] Of course, Waterloo followed along with Napoleon's penultimate loss of power. But Marshal Ney was true to the end and risked his own life for his friend.

The reader should not be surprised to learn that the people who knew Peter Stuart Ney in the United States commented on his passionate love for Napoleon and his distress upon learning that the emperor had died. According to multiple reports, Ney got word of Napoleon's death while he was teaching a class. West writes, "[W]hen news arrived that Napoleon had died, he fainted dead away in his classroom, dismissed the classes when he was revived, and that night attempted suicide."[18] In *Marshal Ney, A Dual Life*, Legette Blythe describes the classroom scene in more vivid detail: "The scholars see their master's face go pale, see it drained of colour even in the thinning hair above his high forehead. They see him reach for the table to steady himself, miss it, and crumple to the floor."[19] Rowe reports the suicide attempt was accompanied by Ney uttering the phrase "Oh colonel, colonel, with the death of Napoleon my last hope is gone!"[20] Some sources say the suicide attempt involved slitting the throat. Any soldier who had served in the French Revolution would have been grieved by the emperor's demise, but it is clear that Ney's dramatic response and subsequent suicide attempt went much further than the devotion an ordinary soldier would have felt.

As Ney continued to follow the political happenings in France, those around him claimed that he had similar reactions to other news:

> In 1830, on learning that Louis Philippe, Duke of Orleans, had ascended to the throne of France and that the Bourbon line was therefore well entrenched, he flew into a rage and could not be consoled for days thereafter. When news arrived that Napoleon's son, L'Aiglon, had died in Vienna, Ney went into a deep depression which took months to dispel, months during which his friends feared he would try to kill himself, for he declared that he had nothing to live for anymore.[21]

Interestingly, the Rowe article claims that after Napoleon's death, when it was clear that the vision of the French exiles in the United States would never be seen to fruition, Peter Stuart Ney "burned a large quantity of his papers—perhaps everything that he thought might lead to his identity. Among other things burned was a very exact likeness of the Emperor Napoleon."[22]

No Cover in the United States

Numerous accounts indicate Peter Stuart Ney was *repeatedly* recognized by former French soldiers while on American soil. He was apparently noticed in Charleston as soon as he got off the boat, which likely prompted his move to a smaller town in South Carolina. Whenever French exiles who served under him during the French Revolution saw him and spoke to him openly in public places, witnesses reported Ney usually sought to cut the encounter short and disappear into the crowd. He was said to have avoided "prominent Napoleonic exiles in the United States" anytime they were around him.[23] His repeated moves from small town to small town would certainly indicate a person who wanted to be as inconspicuous as possible.

Most significantly for our story, Ney was recognized on the streets of Lincolnton in a now famous encounter with one Lorenzo Ferrer. Ferrer was in Lincolnton by 1839, and Ney died in 1846, so the two overlapped in the area by roughly seven years. Like so much of the Lorenzo Ferrer lore in the area, the stories that have been handed down by the locals are oddly parallel. The story goes that Ferrer and Ney met on the Court Square in Lincolnton—either by chance or on purpose, brought together by friends who thought they should meet. The narratives below illustrate what is said to have happened.

From Robert L. Williams's
People Worth Meeting and Stories Worth Repeating

"On one occasion Ferrer had a visitor named Peter [Stuart] Ney. Yes, this was the same man described in an earlier part of this book, a man who was undoubtedly Marshal Michel Ney, commander of the troops of Napoleon Bonaparte. When Ney met the peaceful pirate, the tempers of both men flared almost instantly. One report stated that the two men were on the brink of a sword fight."[24]

From Gaither Schrum, quoted in Jim Mathews's "Was Resident a Legendary Pirate?"

"Peter Stuart Ney, who was one of Napoleon's exiled marshals, came to Lincolnton and was taken to see Ferrer. When the two Frenchmen met, they squared off, stared at each other, drew back in clenched fists and began yelling at each other in French. A man in the crowd, realizing that something was wrong, grabbed Ney and led him away. Ney told his companion that Ferrer was a 'damned renegade and a traitor and should be hung.' Ferrer never commented on the incident."[25]

From David C. Heavner's "The Story of Wallace Reinhardt"

"During his lifetime, Wallace Reinhart befriended two rather mysterious, well-educated Frenchmen. The first was Peter Stuart Ney. Legend has it that he, in reality, was Marshal Ney, a marshal of Napoleon's army. . . . Here is where the life of Wallace Reinhardt was touched by this man. As a young man, Reinhardt was sent to study under Ney in Iredell County. This was probably the one-room brick school—still standing—at Third Creek Presbyterian Church. [This is also Ney's burial site.] Reinhardt stated that he studied under this man in 1836 and was highly impressed by him. . . . In the mid-1800s, Reinhardt's life was touched by another Frenchman, Lorenzo Ferrier. Ferrier came to Lincolnton and showed the prospect of having great wealth. This caused a great deal of speculation about his origins, as he was not gainfully employed in the many years he lived in Lincolnton. There were many who believed he was, in fact, Jean Lafitte—the pirate. This feeling grew after he and Ney met on the street in Lincolnton and engaged in a vehement argument—in French!"[26]

From Victor Fair's *The Hills of Home*

"On one occasion Peter Stuart Ney, the mysterious old school teacher who was believed to be Napoleon's great Marshal Ney, visited Lincolnton and was taken to see Ferrer. When these two Frenchmen met they squared away, glared at each other, drew back with clenched fists and began to jabber angrily and excitedly in French. The Lincolntonian who had arranged this interview saw at a glance that something was wrong between them, so he grabbed Ney by the arm and hastily led him away. Ney told this citizen that Ferrer was a 'damned renegade and a traitor and should be hung.' It was quite evident that these two Frenchmen had known each other under some unhappy circumstances, no doubt in another part of the world. Ferrer could not be induced to comment on the man who was supposed to be Marshal Ney."[27]

From Gladys Childs's "Lincolnton's Pirate"

"On one occasion, as told by Wallace Reinhardt to his grandson Victor N. Fair, Peter Stuart Ney, believed to be Napoleon's exiled marshal, while visiting Lincolnton, was taken to meet Lorendzo Ferrer. When the two met, antagonism flared between them, and both Frenchmen began an angry confrontation in French. A man standing by grabbed Ney and led him away. Ney said Ferrer was a renegade and a traitor and should be hanged. Ferrer could not be induced to comment on the happening."[28]

While these accounts may appear to create more questions and offer few answers, we believe, based on all that we know of both Ney and Laffite/Ferrer, that the story makes perfect sense, providing clues via the behavior of both men.

First, to Ney. By the time this incident occurred, there were ample other accounts of Ney's short-tempered confrontations with those who appeared, in his estimation, to have been disloyal to France. His fierce dedication to the cause made it impossible for him to remain silent. Therefore, the fact that Ney quickly became so enraged at Ferrer after a brief and heated conversation in French—and also after apparently recognizing Ferrer—is no surprise and appears to have been completely in character for Ney. He was reacting to someone who, in his own words, was *a traitor and a renegade who should be hanged.* There is no record of Ney having reacted so strongly toward anyone who he thought was a traitor *to the United States*, therefore we must assume that he considered Ferrer a traitor *to France*. The use of the word "renegade" is also interesting, given that the term was commonly used to describe pirates like Jean Laffite in those days.

Second, to Ferrer. According to the story, Ferrer was no less enraged than Ney during the confrontation. The heated words, spoken in French, were mutually fired off by both men. And yet, once the two were separated by bystanders, Ney was the one determined to have been ready to strike blows while Ferrer appeared to be interested in nothing more than putting the incident to bed with no further discussion—this in spite of the fact that he was being pointedly questioned by friends who witnessed the quarrel. Indeed, Ferrer refused any further comment on the matter and never spoke of it again. This is completely in his character, when you take into consideration Ferrer's efforts at discretion about his past. These were traits consistent with Ferrer from the day he arrived in Lincolnton until the day he died.

When the account of Ferrer and Ney was first read, we had not yet benefitted from information that we later discovered concerning the actions of Jean Laffite as they related to the French exiles and their efforts to regain a firm footing here in the United States. If you believe the claim that Laffite may have made a rescue attempt that failed to bring Napoleon to the United States alive, this could have added an additional reason for Ney to harbor anger toward Laffite. This last story, if true, would have been more than enough to provoke an encounter such as the one that occurred, but even if the failed Champs D'Asile colony was the source of Ney's anger, the blow-up could have been triggered when Ferrer, perhaps foolishly, introduced himself to Ney, in French, as Laffite. It would also have probably occurred to both men that blowing either of the other's cover would only result in retaliation in like kind—and what would have been the point?

Therefore, we would reasonably be left with a tale of an encounter between two Frenchmen who supposedly had never met, followed by a heated conversation in French that quickly escalated into a near altercation, followed by an intervention and a few words of heated innuendo, resulting in nothing beyond that. And, indeed, that is exactly what happened.

NEY'S DEATH

The final chapter in Peter Stuart Ney's life closed in Cleveland, North Carolina, a tiny community in Rowan County. In the year 1846, stricken with pneumonia, he lay dying at the home of Osborne Foard, where he lived. Blythe recounts the scene in the book *Marshal Ney: A Dual Life*. One of those in attendance was Ney's friend, a physician named Matthew Locke. Locke spoke to Ney: "Mr. Ney, there is something that has been puzzling us for years. And now we want to have the truth from your lips. We want to know who you are." Blythe writes the old man's eyes lit up, he raised himself upon his pillow and looked Locke squarely in the face, saying "I will not die with a lie on my lips. I am Marshal Ney of France."[29] Ney was interred at the Third Creek Presbyterian Church Cemetery.

Physical evidence and eyewitness recognition aside, the words and actions of Ney during his time in the Carolinas pointed to a man who never lost hope of returning home to France once the danger of imprisonment and death had passed. Many of those hopes hinged on Ney's belief that Napoleon, his old commander, would soon be returned to power. For instance, while living with the family of Colonel Benjamin Rogers in Florence, South Carolina, as a teacher to the Rogers children, Ney spoke at length of these hopes. Blythe writes, "Peter Ney talks hour after hour on long winter nights before the Rogers fire. In spite of his caution it is not difficult to see

Ney Grave Marker at Third Creek Presbyterian Church

that all his hopes are centered on the Emperor's return. Guardedly, but in detail, he talks of his past life; of battles he has fought, of friends he has known, the Emperor, Josephine, the great men and women of France. Always the talk reverts to the Emperor."[30]

Ney was given to great volumes of correspondence during those days, often staying up very late in order to write letters which were sent off in sealed envelopes the next day, most often to Philadelphia. Concurrently, letters, and sometimes more than one per day, arrived from Philadelphia addressed to Ney.[31] It is not unreasonable to suppose that he was corresponding with other French exiles in an effort to remain abreast of the latest developments in their ongoing hope of establishing either a return to power in France or a new base of power somewhere in the United States. Residents of Cleveland also noted Ney had frequent visitors, most of them coming at night and leaving before sunrise.[32]

Perhaps not coincidentally, these years of feverish correspondence by Ney (somewhere around 1819) directly correlate with Jean Laffite's involvement in the Texas settlement of French exiles at Champs D'Asile, an involvement that did not end well for the French refugees, who ultimately returned to New Orleans and other locations, their numbers having been greatly reduced by sickness and death during the effort.

It also appears that Ney spent his later years working on a memoir. Friends asserted that he had a "propensity for writing to late hours at night in some secret journal."[33] He supposedly reported to Foard that he had written a manuscript that he wanted him to retrieve and translate after Ney's passing. According to Ney, it would contain a story that would "astonish the world."[34] Then on the night of Ney's death, a trunk that he had kept with him for many years vanished from the Foard home. According to several sources, the chest was eventually tracked down in New York City and shipped back to Cleveland to be opened. On the first night that it was back, the Foard cottage was destroyed by a fire. Davidson College, where Ney taught for a time, actually owns one of Ney's trunks, along with several books about French history and Napoleon that contain his original comments and drawings. Ney also has a fascinating connection to the Davidson College seal.

The local story goes that the school put out a public call seeking designs for a new logo. A local man offered a submission that was accepted and used as the college's new seal. Robert Williams writes that many years later, "a goldsmith in France . . . saw the [Davidson] letterhead and demanded to know how the college obtained the design which was, he insisted, an original rendering that he had done at the request of Napoleon Bonaparte. The design was used on a special medal to be awarded to Marshal Michel Ney, the Bravest of the Brave."[35]

Just as Lorenzo Ferrer's sudden and mysterious appearance in North Carolina has always been a matter of conflicting expert opinion, the same holds even more true for Ney. Polarizing opinions are held by scholars on both sides of the Ney question—even to the point that his body was exhumed twice in an effort to gain further clarity about his true identity. Both exhumations were accomplished long before modern DNA and other technological advances, and both attempts proved inconclusive. Given all that we have read about Ney, especially in light of our parallel research into Lorenzo Ferrer, we stand with those who assert that Peter Stuart Ney was

This bust stands in the Davidson College history room at the E.H. Little Library. Interestingly, the statue is identified as "Marshal Ney 'Designer of the College Seal' Horace Marvin Hicks, sculptor Presented to Davidson College Charles W. Allison, Class of 1904." He taught at Davidson under the name Peter Stuart Ney.

Marshal Ney and that the Freemasons were the major facilitators of his rescue, his escape from France, and his successful relocation in the United States. They had that power at their disposal. Furthermore, taken in concert with the story of Laffite/Ferrer, the notion that Ney was Marshal Ney gains even more credence. The chances of two enigmatic Frenchmen landing in tiny Lincolnton truly defies the odds—until you consider the two records side by side. At that point, the improbable begins to look more like truth than fiction.

CHAPTER SIXTEEN

FROM THE DESK OF JEAN LAFFITE

It is a truth universally acknowledged that critics will never agree about Jean Laffite's handwriting. If you find a handwriting expert who says a sample of the buccaneer's writing is authentic, you will likely find two who disagree. Much speculation has centered on the question of Laffite's command of the written word across the various languages he knew, his proficiency likely varying from tongue to tongue. Everywhere he went, he was identified by his accent as a Frenchman, so we agree with the scholars who suggest he was more comfortable writing in the French language, which we suspect was probably his mother tongue.

The writing samples that are available in archival libraries across the country are difficult to verify because many have suggested Pierre Laffite or a secretary penned the majority or even all of Jean Laffite's writing for him. If true, that would mean that only the *signatures* on official documents bearing his name are actual samples of his writing. We have seen many of these documents in person in Texas and Louisiana and can attest to the fact that when you compare them side by side, it is clear that multiple writers were probably involved.

Handwriting analysis—even under perfect conditions and using the latest methods—is also still an inexact science. A person's handwriting also changes significantly over time. The handwriting of a young man will look very different from that same man in his older age. These are just some of the reasons that make us very hesitant to venture too deeply into this territory.

Consequently, this chapter will not draw any conclusions or make any assertions about what is authentic, though we feel an extended study of all the known documents by a team of handwriting specialists is warranted. What we do want to emphasize in this short chapter, though, are some circumstantial facts that will crystalize a few things in our concluding chapter. As well, we will offer several textual samples that grabbed our attention as we were comparing the handwriting of Jean Laffite and Lorenzo Ferrer. We will simply present the pictorial comparisons with minimal commentary so the readers may draw their own conclusions.

NEW ORLEANS NOTARIAL ARCHIVES

Laffite scholars have a bona fide gold mine of information about the brothers during their Barataria days in the New Orleans Notarial Archives Research Center, including seventy detailed notarial acts which are explored in the article "Cruising Contractual Waters: Searching for Laffite in the Records of the New Orleans Notarial Archives," composed by the now-retired director of the archives, Sally Reeves. This collection is extraordinary and exists today only due to the historically stringent requirements of Louisiana notaries to keep records of every transaction in a ledger and then pass along those records to another notary upon their retirement. The result is a building on Poydras Street in New Orleans filled with every notarial transaction in New Orleans from 1735 to 1970.

While we disagree with Reeves's basic premise—that the information housed in the archives supports the notion that the Jean Laffite "journal" is authentic—her piece does shed very interesting light on the history of his signatures. Reeves highlights several contradictions in stories that the Laffites gave notaries about their origins and their age, inconsistencies which make it impossible for scholars to place much credibility in anything they said. Reeves also notes that both of them signed their name spelled "Laffite," though that was not the conventional spelling of the name at the time.[1] In summarizing the signatures, Reeves also points out how this spelling contradicts the spelling the notary sometimes used, a discrepancy that should have been noticed by a notary.[2]

All of the archives are organized into the ledger books of the individual notaries. For the general researcher, there is unfortunately no index to the collection. However, the Laffite researcher upon request will be given a handy chart that lists all of the known notarial agreements involving the Laffites. On the following page is a signature that appears on one of the notarial documents in French that Jean Laffite signed. It is dated February 5, 1813, from the ledger of Narcisse Broutin.[3]

Laffite's signature was known to evolve over time, with examples ranging from relatively plain to quite stylized. Note the signature from October 20, 1805, (shown on pp. 194–99) written at Grand Terre. Titled "Jean Laffite's instructions to Henri [Saybatier]" in the Historic New Orleans Collection

Signature from the Ledger of Narcisse Broutin, 1813

catalog, this document offers a detailed listing in French of orders for the ship *Pomona* and how it is to work with the *Monoterix* and the *Saturnia*—all in the Laffite fleet.[4] It is signed "Jn Laffite," and to our untrained eyes, it appears that the whole document and the signature were written by the same person, though we do not claim to know whether that was actually Jean Laffite or not.

Laffite to Madison 1815

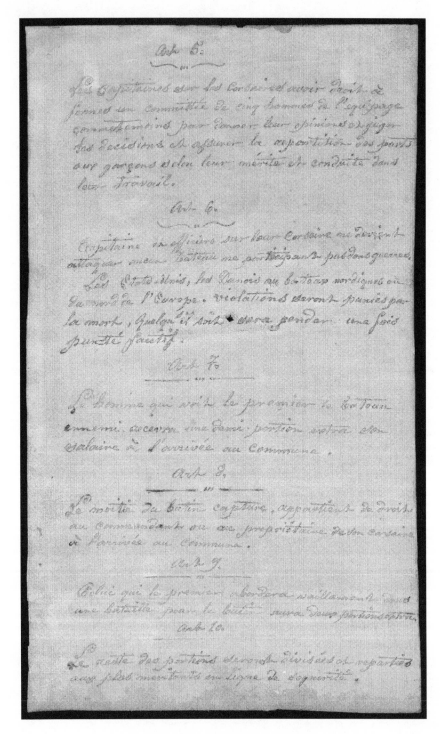

Jean Laffite's Instructions to Henri [Saybatier]
Courtesy of the Historic New Orleans Collection

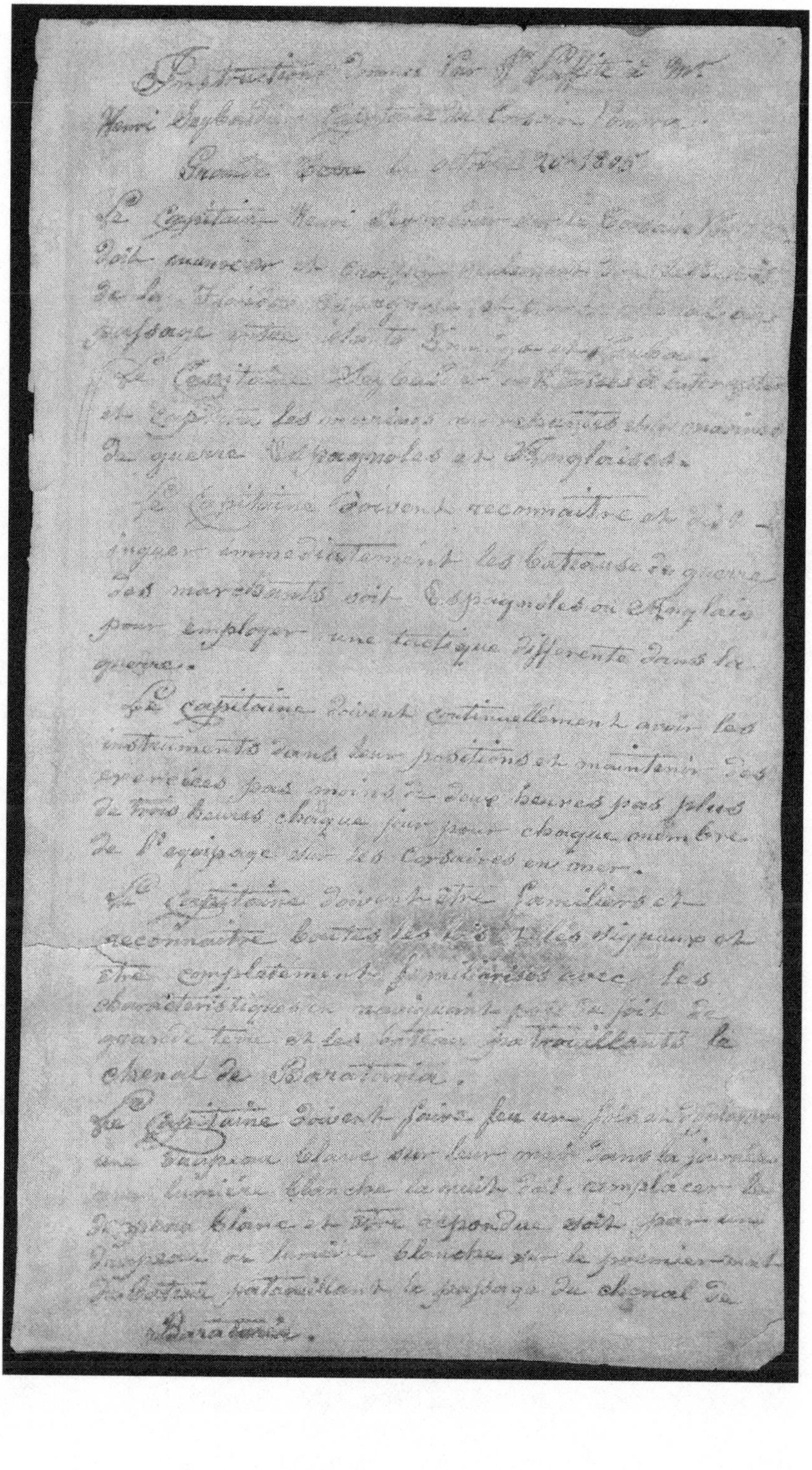

Art 1ᵉʳ.

Les Capitaines Jⁿ Barbie Warvien et Alcade Gervien
Gonebal sur le Corsaire Saturnia et Corsaire Monterria
Fait manœuvrer et croiser seulement du nord ouest
du chenal de Yucatan jusqu'au rio Grande.
Le Capitaine Warvien fait manœuvrer entre la Jamaique
et Cartagène en Colombie.

Art 2ᵉ.

Les Corsaires "Pomora", "Monteria", "Saturnia", partirent
le 23ᵉ Octobre 1805 pour voyés avec toutes les
necessitées, provisions et etc... pour naviguer et
croiser respectivement pour leur assignation
dans les endroits dans les différentes instructions
au frais du Commandant.

Les Capitaines pourvoyeront les coffres de médicines,
un docteur sur chaque Corsaire avec les
instruments chirurgiens les quels seront au frais
du Commandant.

Art 3ᵉ.

Chaque Capitaines de Corsaire et son équipage
seront complètement equippés et fournis
avec Cannons, trembleus, ammunitions et
nourriture pour une période de 80 jours poiles-
suivants, chevres, batails, maïs, farine de
blé, molasse, noir, fruitières, vin, et lignes de
pêche.

Art 4ᵉ.

Chaque capitaines de equipage auront deux
cuisiniers et assistants dans leur galeres et les
quartiers du manger, des garçons 12 et 16
ans accompagnés par leur père dans
l'équipage pour faire les tits, nettoyages etc...

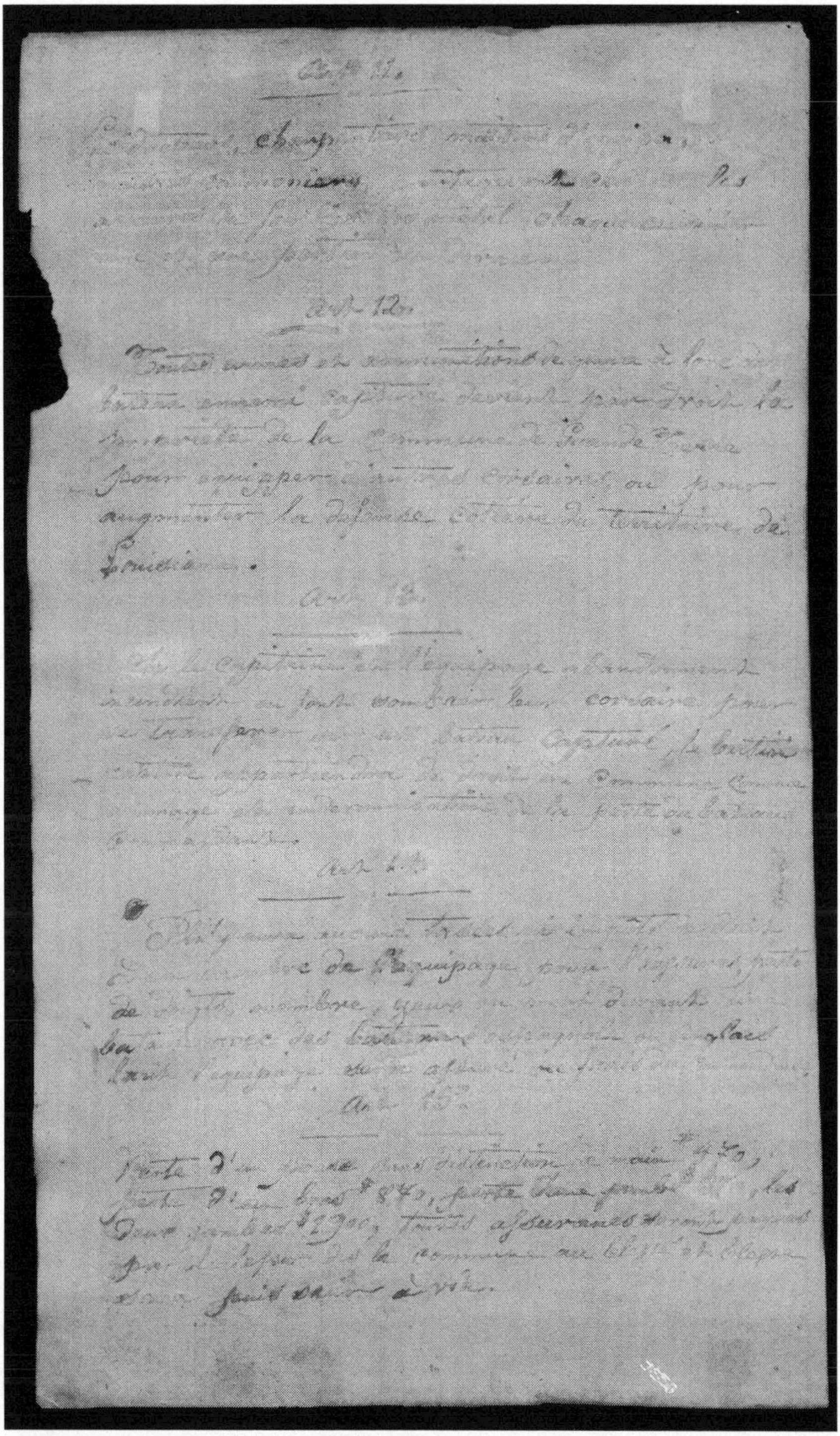

Art. 26.

Celui qui mourra de cause naturelle sous l'acte de Dieu pendant la croisière, sa femme et ses héritiers, ses exécuteurs ou s'il n'y a pas d'— Dartification, et administrateurs seront nommés pour localiser des proches parents, qui recevront alors $1500.

Art. 27.

Les femmes d'officiers ou, de membre de l'équipage privées pour cause de mort en action de leur soutien, recevront $1900, et une annuité de $100 par mois pour toute une autre année.

Art. 28.

Au bord des corsaires, par l'usage fréquent de boisson intoxiquante sera interdit ainsi que durant le temps au port aux membres de l'équipage de garde.

Art. 19.

Patroner ou fraterniser avec des maisons de mauvaises réputations ou de prostituées, ou avec les occupants de dit endroit sera interdit au membres de l'équipage

Art. 20.

Les violations des articles 18 et 9 respectivement démena pour une période de 6 mois le membre de l'équipage de ses droits et il sera suspendu de la Commune de Grande Terre.

Art. 21.

Quiconque instigant mutinité troublée, mauvaise conduite, petit larcin, vol pendant la croisière sera jugé et confiné à une cellule des corsaires et perdra ses droits, il sera déporté ou expulsé à son retour, de la Commune de Grande Terre.

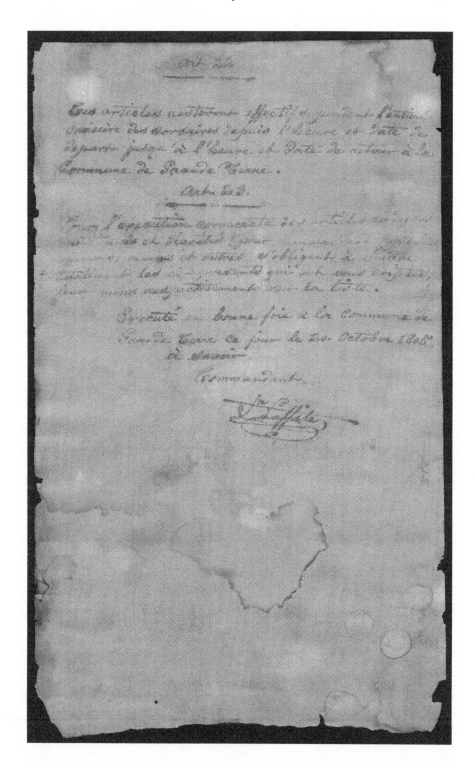

Compare the signature on the December 27, 1815, letter from Jean Laffite to President James Madison housed in the Library of Congress.[5] As with all Jean Laffite signatures, he never signed his name "Jean"—always "Jn."

The capital "L" in this signature (minus the large circular flourish at the top) caught our eye. Compare it to the composite signatures from Lorenzo Ferrer in the figure below. The first example is from an 1844 North Carolina General Assembly petition that Ferrer signed along with most of the other influential men of Lincolnton during that time.[6] The petition advocated against the formation of neighboring Catawba County to the north of Lincoln County. The second example comes from Ferrer's original Lincoln Lodge 137 petition in 1852.[7] The final example was taken from a January 26, 1859, receipt from the lodge records.

Focusing on the capital "L," you will notice that Ferrer signed it a bit differently each time, except for the v-shaped dip in the lower part of the "L," which also appears in Laffite's capital "L." While Ferrer is older with each successive signature in the chart, one thing that does remain consistent is his distinctive lower-case "r's." These "r's" can be compared to the text of Laffite's instructions to Henri Saybatier introduced earlier. Note the "r" in

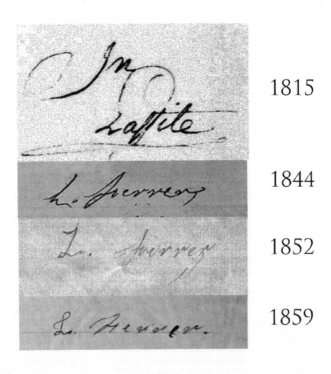

1815

1844

1852

1859

words like "extra" from page two and "membre" from page 4. Also, in all three Ferrer signatures, he attempted to make a flourish at the end every time. In 1842 it appears as a comma, in 1852 it is an actual flourish, and in 1859 it looks like a period—but some sort of emphasis is attempted each time, even when he is an old man.

Like Jean Laffite, Lorenzo Ferrer never signed his full first name. He always abbreviated "Lorenzo" with an "L"—with one important exception.

The original copy of Lorenzo Ferrer's will, housed in the North Carolina Archives in Raleigh, is transcribed in its entirety in Chapter Seventeen. After examining the pages in August 2019, we have reason to believe that Lorenzo Ferrer, in seriously declining health in 1873 two years before his death, composed the document himself.

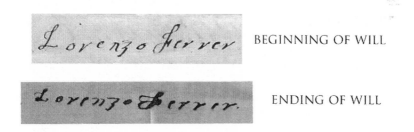

BEGINNING OF WILL

ENDING OF WILL

We were actually thrilled to find as many textual samples written in Ferrer's hand as we did. But as you will see in Chapter Nineteen, the old Frenchman had one more ace up his sleeve for us.

CHAPTER SEVENTEEN

THE LAST WILL AND TESTAMENT OF LORENZO FERRER

W e chose to begin this book by taking you to the end of the story, and for good reason. That is where we began our search. Within just a few days of the beginning of our project, we were given a copy of Lorenzo Ferrer's last will and testament written in his hand.[1] Reading it then was like looking at a pile of jigsaw puzzle pieces and having no picture on the box to follow. The most important components of it were impossible to see without the full context of all the players. Reviewing the same text after conducting a full investigation was quite another story altogether.

The will was written in the presence of two witnesses in 1873—two years before Ferrer died. We do not know whether the two men who signed as witnesses watched the writing of the will or merely observed the signing of the document. One of the witnesses, Robert Sowers, was the son-in-law of Charles C. Henderson. Henderson himself had passed away in 1869, but the family connection to Ferrer remained. Henderson's children, presumably including Sowers's wife (Theodora Henderson Sowers), inherited vast tracts of land in his will. For that fact alone, Sowers's witnessing of Ferrer's will should be viewed by the reader with more than a passing interest. In fact, we will not be surprised if we learn during future research that the thread connecting Ferrer to the Hendersons not only carried right up to his death but continued well beyond that, even though we do note that none of the Hendersons were named as beneficiaries in the document. Perhaps that is because there was no need. The Hendersons were wealthy enough in their own right. Any inheritance from Ferrer would most likely have only been a token of esteem. On the other hand, given the history laid out in this book, we have asked ourselves if there was more to the story. For every connection that we were able to establish, how many more were hidden? Not all deals were recorded for posterity in legal documents. In fact, many deals

I Lorenzo Ferrer here write my last will
and testament whilst I am in possession of my
faculties. As I have shortly to appear, at the
Tribunal of St. Peter, at the gate of Eternity, where St. Peter is to pronounce according to my mer-
its or demerits. For our Lord Jesus Christ, intrusted the Key of Heaven to St. Peter and enjoined
him to admit the deserving to enter into Heaven
and enjoy an eternal happiness, but to condemn the
undeserving depraoudes, to the everlasting sulphyrous
ous flames, in the devil's abode.
Therefore, I am endeavouring, to comport
myself in such a manner, in order to merit
an eternal happiness, in the presence of God and
his Angels, and in company with St. peter,
St. Paul, St. Titus and the other Saints. For I
am anxious to converse with these happy
martyred Saints, and rejoice with them, at
the firmness patience, and willingness, they
endured at their martyrdom, for the sake
of our Lord Jesus Christ. And I am
also in hope to see and embrace, my kind
friend Michael Hoke, William Lander,
and others good and honest friends,
with whom I hope to enjoy an eternal felicity.
I here charge the two joint executors,
the first thing they do to pay my debts,
should there be any. I said should there
be any, because, at present I am not indebted of a single dollar.
I here will and bestow to Mistress
John Maclean, Major Augustus Maclean
I daughter Mary, five hundred dollars; for
I am highly indebted to her, for her kind
ness.
I will and bestow to the deceased William Lander I daughter, Miss Ella and Miss
Clara, one hundred dollars to each one.

Lorenzo Ferrer Original Will

I will and bestow one hundred dollars to
Miss Nancy Swanze Charly Swanze's
daughter in Cattawba County.
I will and bestow to Catharine Sullivan
in this County, to her and to her only, my
house and lot, Number 25th in the South
West Square in this place, together with
my lot Number 43 in the North west
of this place, and also one hundred dollars.
I will and bestow to Mistress Solomon
Futherow, one hundred dollars.
I will and bestow to James H. White
of Long Creek about Gaston County three
hundred dollars
I will and bestow to honest George Kaon
one hundred dollars.
I will and bestow to the good Pastor Samuel
Lander one hundred dollars
I will and bestow to Wallace Reinhardt
in this place, my tract of land, in the
vicinity of the farmer poor house in
this County; and a note on Ellam Cald
well, in this place, Callop Mutz security
for the sum of two hundred and thirty three
dollars, and 53 cents. due on the first day
of March 1867. together with my house and
lot, in the South west square in this place, Number 28th and all the articles found therein, either
in the house, or on the lot and also one
hundred each, to two of his daughters, one
is named Annie Lee, the other is named
Pinkie. I will and bestow to James
Wilkie, and Thomas Wilkie, one
hundred dollars, to each one- in this pl.
I will and bestow to John Anthony
in this place, one hundred dollars.
I will and bestow, to a colored woman
named Fanny M. Bee, Peter M. Bee's
wife. at present, at Mr. Leard re.
M. Bee's fish pond, one hundred dollars.

I will and beston to my former slave Noticus Sextius, to him and to him only one hundred Dollars.

I will a sufficient sum, for a durrable marble tomb stone and six marble pillars to support the tomb stone, erected over my grave, and also, for the expense of engraving.

I here name James, Willhie, and Wall are Reinhedt in this place, to be joint executors, to this my last will and testement. After having executed my will and testament, as herein prescribed. Then, the surplus of money remaining in their hands, I will it and beston it to be divided between the two executers above named.

Perhaps it is not improper in me here to mention, in case of some mistake in taking one person for another on account of the same name. That is I had a cousin of the same name, age, and profession of mitself. He resided at the south and south west. He contracted the consumtion, and he returned to France, and he died. This the first day of May, Anno Domini 1873.

I here affix my name and seal.

Lorenzo Berrer. (seal)

Robt. Lawrie
Thomas Mills

involving land, and sadly, the brokering of enslaved people, were accomplished in secret. It is therefore not unreasonable to ask if the Henderson/Ferrer connection was entirely friendly, especially in light of the 1859 North Carolina Supreme Court ruling which pitted this family against Ferrer in a very high-profile dispute. There is the possibility that the stronger ties may have consisted of secrets that both sides had a vested interested in keeping hidden. The Hendersons unquestionably had a lot to lose should word get out that their expansive wealth had come because they had been in bed with a pirate for decades.

Ferrer's will named a pair of co-executors, Wallace Reinhardt and James Wilkie. In *The Hills of Home*, Fair (a grandson of Reinhardt) noted that, to his knowledge, Ferrer had not left a will, this after he presumably searched county court records for such a document. A copy of the will was later discovered in the archives of neighboring Gaston County, having been probated there because Reinhardt had served as Lincoln County's Clerk of Superior Court since 1874. As an executor and beneficiary of the will, he was not allowed to handle probate. Fair likely did not realize this, which might explain why he never thought to search probate records in any neighboring counties for this document.

In Chapter Twelve we quoted the assertion in Fair's book that a letter Ferrer wrote just before his death says, "the negro hussy that stays with me is stealing all my money."[2] In the same book, Fair reported, "In his late years [Ferrer] was bedridden, and was waited on by his negro woman."[3] We know from Census data that this was Eliza. While there is no record of what specifically ailed Ferrer, the simple fact of old age would seem to point to any number of plausible reasons. Ferrer lived to the age of ninety-six and wrote this will at age ninety-three or ninety-four.

Fair's account of the letter is similar to information we received from multiple local sources during the research of this book concerning a handwritten letter on old paper composed by Ferrer that had long been housed in the archives of St. Luke's Episcopal Church in Lincolnton, where Ferrer is buried. According to these sources, the letter resided for many years in a yellow file folder clearly marked "Jean Lafitte" in a locked filing cabinet that required a key to access. Longtime church staff members—more than one of them—remember the letter well because they used to take it out of its envelope on occasion and read it, simply because it was old and interesting. These same sources confirm that it was a letter and not a will and that it laid out some past life history and offered details about Ferrer's burial wishes. Sometime around 2010 or 2011, the letter went missing. (It is important to note the letter went missing <u>after</u> a water problem under the rectory caused flooding and some items were lost.) Staff members one day found the empty "Jean Lafitte" folder on top of the filing cabinet. Someone had apparently taken it out of the archives before we had a chance to see it. Having spoken with one staff member who had described the letter and also its folder in detail, we decided to go to St. Luke's and search through every piece of paper in the files, knowing exactly what to look for and hoping that the letter had simply been misfiled. In spite of a complete search of the archives that even extended to the church attic, and with the full cooperation of and kind assistance from the staff at St. Luke's, we found nothing but the empty "Jean Lafitte" folder, just as it had been described to us. In short, the letter appears to have disappeared.

It is impossible to know if the St. Luke's letter and the letter cited by Fair are the same. It is conceivable there were two separate letters, maybe even more than two. However, we felt so strongly that this letter held valuable information about Ferrer (and possibly his past life, even including references to a past identity) that we asked everyone in town who had ever had any connection to historical records—not only at St. Luke's but also within the Lincoln County Historical Association and the Lincoln County history room at the local library—if they had seen any such letters. Aside from our sources (who preferred not to be named), nobody had knowledge of where the letter might be.

You will forgive us as researchers and authors if we give fair warning here that should this letter miraculously appear after the release of this book, it will be clear indication of willful intent to withhold information from other researchers, if not implied evidence of theft, should the holder not be able to prove that he or she came by the letter via honest means.

What we do have in our possession, of course, is a copy of the actual will, a document that is not without its own wealth of clues. One of those clues may well turn out to have been a misstep by Ferrer or possibly those advising him—a careless and overcompensating attempt to direct eyes away from a fact that no one had even noticed. Before we get there, however, we should look at the will.

We quote the document here in its entirety. The words of the will are in smaller size type, while our commentary appears in regular text.

> I, Lorenzo Ferrer here write my last will and testament whilst I am in possession of my faculties. As I have shortly to appear at the Tribunal of St. Peter at the gate of Eternity where St. Peter is to pronounce according to my merits or demerits. For our Lord Jesus Christ intrusted [*sic*] the Key of Heaven to St. Peter and enjoined him to admit the deserving to enter into

Heaven and enjoy an eternal happiness, but to condemn the undeserving defrauders to the everlasting sulphureous [*sic*] flames in the Devil's abode. Therefore I am endeavouring to comport myself in such a manner, in order to merit an eternal happiness, in the presence of God and his Angels, and in company with St. Peter, St. Paul, St. Titus and the other saints. For I am anxious to converse with those happy martyred Saints, and rejoice with them at the firmness, patience, and willingness they endured at their martyrdom; for the sake of our Lord Jesus Christ. And I am also in hope to see and embrace my kind friend Michael Hoke, William Lander and other good and honest friends with whom I hope to enjoy an eternal felicity.

Note in this passage that the will uses the British spelling of "endeavouring" instead of the American spelling of "endeavoring."

I here charge the two joint executors, the first thing they do to pay my debts should there be any. I said should there be any, because at present, I am not indebted of a single dollar.

I here will and bestow to Mistress John Mclean, Major Augustus Mclean's daughter Mary five hundred dollars; for I am highly indebted to her for her kindness.

We are unsure about the significance of Ferrer's friendship with Mary McLean. Five hundred dollars was a large sum of money to be left to someone simply because of her "kindness." Mary appeared to be an upstanding citizen of Lincolnton and was only thirty-one years old at the writing of Ferrer's will. We know that she and her husband lived only about a block away from Ferrer on the corner of West Main and South Government Streets, so it is possible that she was a good neighbor who went above and beyond to make sure that the elderly Ferrer was properly looked after. Having said that, Mary had only married her husband in 1865, so her tenure as a good neighbor could not have been long-standing. Sadly, Mary died the year after this will was written—and Ferrer actually outlived her by another year. Mary's sister, Violet J. Hoke, did receive $40 from the will.

I will and bestow to the deceased William Lander's daughters, Miss Ella and Miss Clara, one hundred dollars to each one.

Ferrer held William Lander in high regard—so much so that he is mentioned in the opening paragraphs of this will as one of those men who Ferrer looked forward to reuniting with in Heaven. Lander was a fellow Mason with Ferrer, though Ferrer had exited the lodge in 1857. Lander passed away in 1868, and his wife had died five years prior to that, so Ferrer likely gave each daughter this gift as a token of his friendship with their father.

> I will and bestow one hundred dollars to Miss Nancy Swanze, Charly Swanze's daughter in Catawba County.

Nancy, a young woman of twenty-three, was living with her father, Charlie, aged seventy-two. We are unclear why Ferrer left any money to Nancy, and of course, he does not bother to explain. The surname *Swanze* was actually a mistake. The correct spelling of the name is *Scronce*—and when the will was probated, *Scronce* was the spelling that was shown. Ferrer spelled the name phonetically (as it sounded). This is further evidence that solidifies our belief that Ferrer wrote the will himself.

> I will and bestow to Catherine Sullivan in this County, to her and to her only, my house and lot, Number 25 in the Southwest Square in this place, together with my lot Number 43 in the Northwest of this place, and also one hundred dollars.

Ferrer owned two houses in the same city block in Lincolnton. His primary residence was located on lot eighteen of that block. Based on other property records for Lincoln County during this time, we believe that Catherine Sullivan was possibly Catherine Mauney Sullivan, also known as Katy Sullivan, who was living elsewhere in Lincoln County with her husband, Jerry, when Ferrer penned his will. Ferrer offers no explanation for the gift, and our research turned up no Ferrer relationship with her or any member of her family. If this Catherine Sullivan is indeed the woman who received the house, we do wonder why it was left "to her and to her only" and not to her husband as well. Our research did find that Katy Sullivan was notoriously contentious and was involved in numerous lawsuits in Lincoln County during the last quarter of the nineteenth century, often representing herself in court. With that in mind, it is not unreasonable to speculate that perhaps Mr. Sullivan was quite happy to send her to a new home on lot twenty-five in Lincolnton, all by herself. Indeed, perhaps Lorenzo Ferrer was bestowing the greater gift to him.

> I will and bestow to Mistress Solomon Tutherow one hundred dollars.

We have no record of any relationship that Ferrer had with Sarah Hauss Tutherow, who was fifty-eight years old at the time the will was written.

Like some of the other women mentioned in his will, it is possible that he transacted local business with her. Many Lincolnton residents relied upon local farmers (and their wives) for such things as fresh meat, fresh produce, milk, butter, and eggs. Additionally, Ferrer, as a single man (who may or may not have had a permanent, live-in housekeeper after Louisa passed away in 1858) would have also needed services such as laundry, tailoring, and house cleaning.

> I will and bestow to James H. White of Long Creek Shoal Gaston County three hundred dollars.

Mr. White was a farmer from neighboring Gaston County whose farm was located near the town of Dallas. We do not have a record of any business dealings between Ferrer and White, and we cannot say for sure why he left this gift, other than as a token of friendship or perhaps, as mentioned previously, as thanks for services rendered.

> I will and bestow to honest George Koon one hundred dollars.

George Koon, who was himself up in years at the writing of this will, was also a local farmer, living in the Howard's Creek section of Lincoln County. In *The North Carolina Booklet: Great Events in North Carolina History*, Martha Helen Haywood et al. write, "An old Frenchman in Lincolnton, Lorenzo Ferrer, often bought farm products from Mr. Coon, and so admired his perfect integrity, and 'full measure of potatoes,' that one of his bequests was: 'I will and bestow to honest George Koon one hundred dollars.'"[4]

> I will and bestow to the good pastor Samuel Lander one hundred dollars.

Reverend Lander was a Methodist minister, just as his father before him had been. He was also a noted educator, associated with Davenport College in Lenoir, North Carolina, as well as several colleges in South Carolina. Both father and son are mentioned in local newspaper accounts of the day as being active in the community. We searched the Samuel Lander ledgers (spanning the years 1838–1865) in the UNC Chapel Hill library and found no references that connected Lander and Ferrer.

> I will and bestow to Wallace Reinhardt in this place my tract of land in the vicinity of the former poorhouse in this County; and a note on Ellam Caldwell in this place, Callap Mutz security, for the sum of two hundred

and thirty three dollars and 53 cents due on the first day of March 1867, together with my house and lot in the Southwest Square in this place Number 18th and all the articles found therein, either in the house or on the lot and also one hundred each to two of his daughters, one is named Annie Lee, the other is named Pinkie.

We have established Jean Laffite was not 100 percent comfortable writing in English, and indeed Ferrer's will, while making great use of some eloquent language, also displays an abundance of misspelled words, like that of his friend Caleb Motz's here, which is spelled phonetically. Perhaps Ferrer in later life was no different than Laffite—reluctant to write and thus unaccustomed to spelling the names of his friends. This could also explain the complete lack of correspondence associated with him. Despite the spelling errors, Ferrer's use of classical language—antiquated even in 1873—is striking. Fair noted it as distinctive in his book as well.[5] It is also worth pointing out that Caleb Motz was a brother of both George W. Motz (who went belly-up financially in Mississippi while working with Lawson F. Henderson) and Andrew Motz (whose suspicious death many people believe was a murder that was precipitated by a business conflict with William Slade, who was part of the Slade-Henderson slave-trading company, and/or some sort of conflict with Motz's own business partner, Elisha Barrett). Both Caleb Motz and Elam Caldwell were also involved in Mississippi business transactions with the Hendersons.

> I will and bestow to James Wilkie and Thomas Wilkie one hundred dollars
> to each one in this place.

The Wilkie brothers were carriage makers and local blacksmiths. They came to Lincoln County from Rutherford County. Their business was located on West Main Street just a couple of blocks away from Ferrer's house. James Wilkie was named as one of Ferrer's co-executors. In the years following Ferrer's death, James Wilkie also served as Lincoln County Treasurer.

> I will and bestow to John Anthony in this place one hundred dollars.

John Anthony was a Lincolnton furniture maker who also made coffins.

> I will and bestow to a colored woman named Fanny McBee, Peter McBee's
> wife, at present at Mr. Veardre McBee's fish pond, one hundred dollars.

Fanny McBee is listed on the estate distribution as Fanny Middleton, and her husband, Peter, as Peter Middleton. *Mr. Veardree McBee's fish pond* actually refers to a prominent and well-known Lincolnton citizen named Vardry McBee who lived on East Main Street one block east of the Court Square. The exact location of Vardry McBee's fishpond is apparently lost to time, as no local historians we consulted had any idea of its whereabouts. We do know from local newspaper accounts of the day that McBee's pond was a favorite local hang-out. An April 26, 1889, *Lincoln Courier* article reported, "Colonel McBee's fishpond seems to be a favorite resort, and feeding the fish, a pleasant pastime on Sundays. There are some large carp in the pond. Col. McBee caught one last week that weighed nine pounds."[6] The *Courier* also offered this story on January 13, 1893:

> The extreme cold weather has brought into use the skates that have been allowed to rust for the want of ice during the past several years. Mr. Motz's pond and Mr. McBee's fish pond are loaded with skaters. By the way, we are told that Mr. S.G. Finley fell out with the ice the other day on Mr. McBee's pond and set in to beating it, whereupon the ice dodged from under his feet, letting him gently down into the water up to his shoulders. The ice kept cool all the while and Mr. Finley became so immediately. Since the foregoing was put in type we learn that Mr. Finley denies the allegation, except as to one foot.[7]

As for Fanny McBee (Middleton), we have no understanding of how she connected to Ferrer, other than our previous mention of many local residents providing services such as fresh produce and dairy products, housekeeping, laundry, etc.

> I will and bestow to my former slave Vatinius Sextius, to him and to him only one hundred dollars.

We already outlined Vatinius's story and would only add here that the mention of his full name in this will is the only time it occurred in any document we located. It is very likely that Vatinius no longer lived in the area when Ferrer's will was written. If he was the son of Louisa and Ferrer, and if his age in 1860 (two years after her death) was indeed sixteen, he would have been thirty-five years old when Ferrer died. Many local anecdotal accounts claim that Vatinius was gone from the area after Ferrer's passing, possibly returning briefly in the very late 1800s—but there is no concrete evidence that this actually happened. For what it is worth, this "former slave" was the only person of that designation to receive anything at all from Ferrer, even though he owned many enslaved people during his lifetime. If Vatinius was Ferrer's son, $100 was a paltry inheritance.

> I will a sufficient sum for a durable marble tombstone and six marble pillars to support the tombstone erected over my grave, and also for the expense of engraving.

The famous tombstone, described here by Ferrer and for which provision was made in his will, still remains today on his grave and will be discussed in a moment.

> I here name James Wilkie and Wallace Reinhardt in this place to be joint executors to this my last will and testament. After having executed my will and testament as herein prescribed, then the surplus I will and bestow it to be divided between the two executors above named.

As cut-and-dried as this provision of Ferrer's will may seem, the very facts outlined in our book would dictate all manner of questions surrounding the matter of "the surplus" that was left over after all disbursements had been accomplished, the most notable one being the local legend about the chests of gold and jewels Ferrer apparently brought with him to Lincolnton, which will be discussed in full detail in Chapter Eighteen. Consider, too, that it appears Ferrer at the very end of his life died with around $4,000 cash in hand. That was a lot of money in 1875. We also came upon several references to Ferrer giving away large sums of money to friends before his death—transactions that were not recorded in an official capacity.

And then there is this.

For whatever reason, at the end of a very fluent and articulate statement of his last wishes, Ferrer chose to include a startling final thought that would come to puzzle and confound every researcher whose future path it would cross. It reads as follows:

> Perhaps it is not improper in me here to mention in case of some mistake in taking one person for another on account of the same name, that is, I had a cousin of the same name, age, and profession of myself [*sic*]. He resided at the South and Southwest. He contracted the consumption [*sic*] and he returned to France and he died. This the first day of May, Anno Domini 1873. I here affix my name and seal. Lorenzo Ferrer (seal).

As mentioned in the opening pages of this chapter, this passage proved curious at first reading and even more intriguing as our research progressed.

It ended up serving as a catalyst for more questions—questions which ultimately led us to Mississippi and the revelations of Ferrer's dealings there, his mysterious marriage, and his connections to the Hendersons. How ironic that Ferrer's attempt—an overcompensation at best and a very revealing mistake at worst—would end up being the undoing of a very carefully kept secret identity that had endured for nearly fifty years. Not only do we believe it was a foolish mistake (either by Ferrer or someone advising him), but it happened at the end of Ferrer's life—almost at the eleventh hour and fifty-ninth minute.

For starters, our approach to Ferrer's story began from an entirely different angle than that of previous approaches—all of which were based only on local research. Very few local historians had a deep knowledge of the life of Jean Laffite *before* approaching the record on Ferrer. At best, one or two of them sought information on Laffite after the fact, and then only in an effort to verify his death in order to discount what was being said of Ferrer in Lincolnton. By contrast, our first reading of the passage came after extensive study of Laffite and his established record of aliases throughout his time as a privateer in the Gulf. Laffite was a man who devoted considerable energy to the pursuit of "mistaken identity," viewing the use of different names as an asset and employing them often. Parsons even classifies Laffite as a man of "various alter egos."[8] Therefore, while most local historians looked at Ferrer's final passage and scratched their heads, we read it and immediately saw an attempt to distract and distort. The behavior did not seem to us to be inconsistent at all with what we knew of Jean Laffite.

While we had not yet run across the critically important revelation of Lorenzo Ferrer's early years in Mississippi, the passage already made sense to us in the larger context of Jean Laffite's known habit of posing as someone other than who he actually was.

The obvious next clue came in the relation of this passage to the rest of the will. What bearing did these words have on any of Ferrer's final wishes? None that we could discern. Did this paragraph bear any connection to Ferrer's money or any of his properties? No, it did not. Did it mention any living relatives? No, none were mentioned. In fact, the larger "why" had to do with the cousin himself. If the man was in fact dead, as Ferrer reported, then why bring it up at all? Furthermore, why the vague reference to "the South and Southwest"? South and Southwest of *where*, pray tell—Lincoln County—or North Carolina—or the United States? It stood out to us that Ferrer, who had just gone to great lengths to provide details about leaving Wallace Reinhardt not only a house and land but also everything in that house or on the land, was *deliberately* giving vague details about this long lost cousin who shared his age, his name, and even his "profession"—which, by the way, was what—rich old Frenchman? By all accounts, Ferrer had not worked a single day during the thirty-three years he had lived in Lincolnton. As well, there was only one Lorenzo Ferrer in the United States who was anywhere close in age to him. We found him. And he had Louisa with him.

For all these reasons, we knew immediately that the last passage held significance and secrets yet to be unlocked. It would be another two months before we uncovered Ferrer's Mississippi past and his deep connections with the Henderson family—a past that placed him within five years or so of Jean Laffite's last reported death, and even more importantly, in extremely close proximity to the Mississippi River—a body of water Laffite knew like the back of his hand and could navigate in his sleep. Not only that, but Ferrer in Mississippi behaved exactly as we would have expected an aliased Jean Laffite to behave—keeping a low profile, maintaining himself as a moving target yet engaging in the same business pursuit that had made him infamously wealthy in the first place—slave trading. This was the only thing Laffite knew—profiteering—by whatever means necessary and available at the time. When we did discover the truth, this final passage became even more clear. At the end of his life, Lorenzo Ferrer was trying to sever any cord of recognition between his later life in Lincolnton, North Carolina, and whatever had happened during these years in Mississippi. We still are not thoroughly convinced of the reason for his desperation to cut this tie, though we have a theory that we will discuss. At the very least, it seemed to us that this was a completely unnecessary attempt to turn attention away from something that no one was watching to begin with. In fact, Ferrer says this in his own words: "Perhaps it is not improper in me here to mention in case of some mistake in taking one person for another on account of the same name." In our minds, this raised a rhetorical question for Ferrer and also to ourselves as researchers. Why do you care if someone mistakes you for a cousin of the same name who no longer lives where you are pointing, and in fact, no longer lives, period? According to you, he died. So, why?

Toward the end of our research, we believe the collected weight of the facts may be pointing us to that answer. There is the possibility this passage was not even Ferrer's idea, but was forced into the will by a third party.

A strong indication of this theory is demonstrated in the voice of the passage itself. The cadence of the text—the disjointed use of prose, awkward sentence formation, and abrupt statements seemingly thrust into the passage in a clumsy attempt to get all the facts in—points to authorship by someone different from Ferrer, whose smooth and flowing prose is unquestionably present in the preceding words of the document.

As we have demonstrated, and as the record underscores, the Henderson family was a common thread in Ferrer's life for a span of more than fifty years. Given all that we now know and have outlined in this book about the financial dealings across the South during the nineteenth century, and given the fact that so much money and so many deals were never even documented beyond a hidden handshake and money that passed under the table, it is not unreasonable to suppose that there were remaining loose ends in Mississippi and the surrounding area that, had they somehow been unearthed or connected to Ferrer, would have caused either financial loss or even some sort of legal jeopardy or exposure for those whose interests in these loose ends was still very much alive. Our belief in this theory grows stronger as our research into this incredible story continues.

For now, we will simply point to the two men who witnessed Ferrer's will—two men who were present in the room. One of them, Thomas Wells, was a local carpenter. The other, a man named Robert Sowers, had recently taken a bride. Her name was Theodora Henderson. Her father, recently deceased, was Charles Cotesworth Henderson.

FERRER'S TOMBSTONE

As enigmatic as Lorenzo Ferrer was in life, it is only fitting that his grave marker should be a story in and of itself. We know from his will that Ferrer designed his own tombstone. His seal on the will indicates his name is "Lorenzo Ferrer." Yet, the inscription on his tombstone reads, "*Lorendzo Ferrier, born in the city of Lyons died on the 16th of April, 1875, aged 96 years.*" Perhaps the engraver simply made a mistake after Ferrer's death, but it is bizarre that both his first and last names would be spelled differently than they were on his will. In fact, throughout his time in Mississippi and Lincolnton—even as he was approaching the turn of the twentieth century, when the time of spelling fluctuation ceased—the spelling of his first and last name just never seemed to regulate.

For more than one hundred years, Ferrer's remains have rested in St. Luke's cemetery, his elaborate tabletop monument regularly drawing interested history buffs who want to see the grave of the mysterious old Frenchman. Several generations of children who grew up in Lincolnton—including these two writers—have memories of their parents bringing them

St. Luke's Façade. Courtesy of Mary Whisonant

to St. Luke's to view "the pirate's grave." Indeed, there are many other notable people buried there, including Confederate Major General Stephen Dodson Ramseur and a whole host of individuals from the most prominent families in Lincolnton beginning in the 1840s. The St. Luke's property is picturesque beyond words, and the mystique of Ferrer's burial there adds to the wonder experienced by visitors to the grounds.

In January 2019, we spoke with Dr. Michael Trinkley of the Chicora Foundation of Columbia, South Carolina, the company hired by St. Luke's to restore Ferrer's tombstone in 2007. According to the fabulous Mary Whisonant, a historic photographer and a longtime preservationist at St. Luke's whose deep love for the church's rich history is evident in everything she does there, Chicora was hired because there was "a dangerous crack on the [Ferrer] stone."[9] The church's Preservation Committee was determined to do everything within its power—including fundraising—to enlist the services of professional preservationists. Chicora's final report, which we have read, says the original tomb marker was a "marble ledger set on six tapered marble legs with 5x5 top caps."[10] The report noted that the "ledger rocks slightly and is unstable."[11] Over the years, dim-witted vandals have unfortunately struck the historic St. Luke's property, and Ferrer's tombstone became a target for folks who insist on sitting and even standing on top of the

Ferrer Grave Before (above) and After (below) Restoration

monument. Chicora had been called in to both clean the monument and stabilize it. The report indicates that as they began to dismantle the tombstone, it was discovered that the marble legs had been resting on a block that had shifted, revealing the reason for the ledger's instability.

Unfortunately, as the company was swinging the tabletop back into place after it was cleaned using an antimicrobial solution, the report says, "a crack/break developed almost centered in the ledger."[12] The stone slab broke into two pieces. Chicora then had to make two repairs that permanently altered the tombstone but stabilized it enough to save it. First, they had to use a marble repair mortar to bond the two broken slabs of the ledger and prevent further damage. Secondly, an epoxy was used to affix the repaired slab to a new marble ledger underneath it for support.

It is regrettable that our team was unable to view the underside of the tabletop ledger to search for any secret markings before the original slab was glued to the new supporting marble slab. We asked several members of the team who helped with the restoration if anyone looked at or took photographs of the underside of the marker, as we were interested in seeing if Ferrer possibly included markings there, which Freemasons of his time were sometimes known to do. Unfortunately, nobody on Dr. Trinkley's team had any reason to look under the stone, and other project volunteers we spoke with said they did not examine the opposite side of the ledger either. Trinkley advises that if such an examination was attempted, it would require using acetone between the two slabs in order to loosen the epoxy, but he does not advise that action for the sake of the preservation of the stone. As much as it pains us, the reality is that what is on the underside of the monument will forever remain unknown.

The history of Louisa's tombstone is also worth recounting here. Whisonant explains that sometime in the 1950s, Louisa's monument was moved by vestry request to the very back wall of the graveyard, where historically the black congregants were buried. Remember she died first in 1858 and was buried in the plot right beside where Ferrer would be buried seventeen years later. Louisa's stone was moved by Ray Hoffman, the man who built the brick wall around the cemetery. The original request to move the stone was due to the difficulty of mowing the grass between Ferrer's monument and Louisa's gravestone. Many people erroneously report that Louisa's grave was *originally* in the lower part of the cemetery, the area known as the "colored" graveyard, because custom would not allow her to be buried next to a white man. The vestry records, however, contradict this narrative. Until ground-penetrating radar (GPR) was used to map the cemetery, even the folks at St. Luke's thought Louisa was buried in the lower graveyard. However, Ferrer and Louisa have been side by side in death since his passing in 1875. While the decision to move her stone in the 1950s may have been influenced by the belief that a mistress should not be buried next to her lover, it appears that the reason for the stone's relocation was a practical one related to groundskeeping.

In January 2016, the St. Luke's Preservation Committee (with Whisonant acting as chair) decided to right the wrong related to the removal of Louisa's stone. After soliciting private donations, the vestry approved the plan to hire Jason Harpe of Harpe Consulting to move Louisa's monument from the lower part of the graveyard to its original location beside Ferrer's. At the time, Harpe was the Lincoln County Historical Association director. He also volunteered his time in the 2007 Chicora restoration project for Ferrer's tomb. The work on Louisa's grave marker commenced in early February 2016. The restoration effort included the use of GPR to determine where Louisa's body was actually located in relation to Ferrer's. The team made the decision to adjust the stone slightly from its original 1858 location to allow enough space between the monuments for mowing. Present-day visitors to the graveyard will now see the tombstones of Ferrer and Louisa side by side.

We are aware that the revelations revealed in this book are going to inspire new interest in Ferrer's story, and historic sites in Lincolnton with a connection to his life like St. Luke's will ultimately receive many new visitors, some of whom will be out-of-towners and may not have the respect for Lincolnton's heritage that residents do. Before publication of this book, we gave the St. Luke's vestry an opportunity to review our findings and work to make a plan for handling the possible influx of curious graveyard pedestrians while still protecting the property. We wanted to ensure that our book did not create problems for the St. Luke's congregation or cause harm to the graveyard.

First, let it be known that it is the firm belief of all involved with this project that there is *no treasure buried in or near Lorenzo Ferrer's gravesite.* St. Luke's has used sophisticated GPR a number of times to identify the precise locations of the remains of those buried in the cemetery. Those results revealed *nothing other than human remains.* Any kind of treasure would have been revealed on the scans. Anyone caught desecrating the graves at St. Luke's by digging will be arrested and prosecuted, a risk that is certainly not worth taking, considering the fact that we know for sure there is no treasure buried there.

If you are inspired to visit the St. Luke's graveyard, please be respectful of not only Ferrer and Louisa's final resting places but of all the departed souls who are buried there. Do not for any reason sit on, climb on, or touch the monuments, as many of them are already in poor condition. The Preservation Committee is working diligently to care for the monuments, and any interference from visitors will make their job even more difficult.

Finally, St. Luke's is a small congregation with an expansive property on the National Register of Historic Places. Maintaining the church and the graveyard using best practices in historic preservation and artifact care is enormously expensive. When damage is done to the property, the church must come up with the money to repair it. If you are able, please consider donating to the church, and mail it to St. Luke's Episcopal Church, 315 N. Cedar Street, Lincolnton, NC, 28092. Please add a note that says the donation is for the preservation of the grounds. The St. Luke's property is one of Lincoln County's finest, and it needs to stay that way for generations to come.

CHAPTER EIGHTEEN

LAFFITE'S TREASURE

In a classic word association game, the majority of participants who hear the word *pirate* are going to answer with the word *treasure*. The two ideas will always be synonymous. We recognize the connections made in this volume between Laffite and Ferrer will in all likelihood inspire treasure hunters to consider Lincoln County a new potential hunting zone, so it is important to address here why it would be wise for them to expend their energies elsewhere, if for no other reason than the fact that the mother-daughter duo who penned this book would be all about digging up some pirate gold if it existed. Yet, after researching this mystery exhaustively for almost two years, believe us when we say that if we thought there was any treasure to be had in the area, we would have gone out under cover of night with our husbands' shovels and scooped it up long before this book was published.

Applying some commonsense logic to the question of pirate treasure reveals why burying it and leaving it unattended was simply not prudent and probably was not common practice. First, remember pirates risked their lives to obtain their ill-gotten gains. It would not make much sense for them to face the prospect of hanging for their crimes only to then leave their treasures behind without stationed guards. It is important to point out as well that pirates during the Golden Age of Piracy and afterward tended to frequent the same hot spots—islands close to shipping lanes and havens with lax governments where they could set up base camps, like the Bahamas and Jamaica, at least until officials got their act together and pushed the scallywags out. Pirates would have to go way off the beaten path to find a place that no other band of pirates might visit and discover their X marking the spot. The literature offers very few accounts of pirates actually burying their treasure, and the credibility of most accounts of buried treasure in existence can be questioned and ultimately unraveled. After all, if there were witnesses to treasure being buried, they would recover it instead of reporting the location to others.

Consider, too, the logistics of burying treasure. One man cannot unload a chest full of treasure from a ship, lug it to another location, and then lower it into a deep hole all by himself. This project would require several men, which creates a situation in which more than one person knows where the fortune is buried. The chances of at least one of the men going back in secret to try to retrieve the chest are extraordinarily high. And honestly, what pirate would bury treasure and then not go back to get it or tell someone else to get it? The history of the documented recoveries of pirate treasure proves our point: there is no history. The researcher will be hard pressed to find a story about pirate booty found buried on land in the United States or the Caribbean islands. One does not have to look far for stories about the retrieval of sunken treasures that went down *accidentally* on doomed ships. Despite hundreds of years of looking, ordinary people have not made such discoveries on land.

The Booty

If you believe Lorenzo Ferrer was Jean Laffite, the question of what Laffite's treasure was like and where it could have ended up would naturally be foremost in your mind. There is no doubt that the Laffite brothers in their heyday—most prominently in Barataria but to an extent again in Galveston—were *incredibly wealthy*. Their operations, carried out at sea by pirates operating basically as contractors, had fairly low overhead, so profits were tremendous. However, in both Barataria and Galveston, the Laffites were estimated by many to employ a thousand men or more. Even with vast profits, that is a big payroll to maintain, and it was reported that one of the reasons Laffite kept his men in line so well was because he paid them handily, far decreasing the possibility of mutiny. Spreading the wealth in this way meant that the scale of Laffite's personal fortune was probably much smaller than the treasure-hunting lore speculates.

We know that fortune, whatever the size, was decimated in 1814 when Louisiana officials raided Barataria, and the brothers and their lawyer tried unsuccessfully for years to convince someone in authority in Washington to get their confiscated goods back after their valiant service in the Battle of New Orleans. It was clear in the historical moment after the war that it would never be possible for Laffite to set up operations in Barataria again, so we put the probability of him leaving any treasure in that area at next to nothing. Saxon, Dreyer, and Tallant in *Gumbo Ya Ya: Louisiana Folktales* concur with our theory about Laffite's diminished riches after Barataria: "Tales of hidden Lafitte treasure increase from year to year, yet, on the other hand, authorities agree that Lafitte was without funds when he departed the Louisiana scene, and that it is decidedly unlikely that he would have left such immense wealth behind."[1] Knowing the backwaters and bayous as he did, Laffite could have returned in the years following his exit in order to recover items he might have buried.

Similarly, as the Galveston chapter closed in 1820 and Jean Laffite sailed away from the island for the last time having lost another hideout, he likely took everything he had with him. We have no doubt that it was a fortune of enough value for him to live comfortably (if not extravagantly) for the rest of his life, but beyond that we feel his net worth was suffering, and he knew that pirating was changing, likely never to be what it was ever again. Because of this, the prospect of him having massive wealth seems far-fetched. He knew without question at that point that he would never return to Galveston. The United States government would see to that. When he sailed that day with his skeleton crew, he left no treasure behind. Even so, Yoakum writes that after Laffite's exit, "Galveston was again desolate. The town of Campeachy was laid waste, and the island only visited by occasional hunters for Lafitte's buried treasure."[2] Perhaps these hunters were spurred on by accounts such as those of J. O. Dyer from the Galveston *Daily News* in 1920. With conditions in Galveston deteriorating due to a number of factors, Dyer writes:

> In 1820, mutiny was rife, and the men, of whom but 400 remained, not only grumbled, but clamored for permission to become pirates. It was then that Laffite again showed his masterful way of handling rough men. There were still about forty men who could be trusted, and these secretly buried the private treasures of Laffite and his partner—shipowners as well as those of some of the officials. Three places were selected on the island and one on the mainland, and the chief articles of value, plate, jewels and bullion, were duly buried.[3]

By the time he would have permanently vacated the island a year later, though, any treasure that may have been buried was certainly dug up by one of these forty men.

As much as our book has talked about the intricate web of Freemasonry in the 1800s, we should also point out the possibility that the pyramid of the Laffite operation was never really fully controlled by the Laffites themselves; they may have just been the face of a larger Freemason effort involving command of the Gulf. Many of their men, including Dominque You, were known Freemasons, as were all the high-level figures who they associated with: Jackson, Livingston, and Latour. You even has a Freemason lodge named after him: Dominique You Lodge 468 in Arabi, Louisiana. It could be that any existing treasure was never really the property of the Laffites but that they were the men in charge of collecting it, protecting it, and then moving it, likely up the muddy Mississippi and its tributaries that they knew better than anyone. Freemasonry sprang from the Knights Templar, and people are obviously still looking for that treasure, which, if it was kept intact, would have been absolutely massive. The Freemasons were—up until the October 13, 1307, betrayal by the French government and the Catholic Church—the richest and most powerful entity on Earth, so it is not outside the realm of possibility that the Brotherhood could have been calling the shots among the band of pirates.

It is also possible considering what we know from the correspondence of Edward Livingston and Arsène Latour that the majority of the Laffite fortune may have been spirited away to safety in another country like France. Remember we found evidence in the Princeton University Library that as late as 1834 Laffite was trying (with the help of his longtime lawyer) to recover assets from France.

Another twist in the folklore posits that Laffite may have been in the possession of a huge fortune not of his own making, but one he rescued and then hid for a friend: Napoleon Bonaparte. In "The Legacy of Jean Lafitte in Southwest Louisiana," W. T. Block relays a legend passed down by the Louisiana family of a man named Charles Sallier:

> According to Sallier, a French agent contracted with Lafitte, following the Battle of New Orleans, to hurry to Bordeaux, France, on a top secret mission. During June, 1815, at the end of the famed 'One Hundred Days,' Lafitte one night loaded aboard a score of sea chests which contained the Emperor Napoleon's personal fortune. In the aftermath of the Battle of Waterloo, the emperor had hoped to avoid retribution by escaping to Louisiana, but when he failed to arrive at an appointed hour, Lafitte sailed away from Bordeaux without him.[4]

The story goes that Laffite and his men then brought the treasure back to Louisiana and buried it in the marshes of Barataria, though no narrative resolution is offered to account for what happened to the treasure after that. Such a claim is something to think about in light of the story of Peter Stuart Ney screaming that Lorenzo Ferrer was a "traitor" on the streets of Lincolnton. Maybe he was a traitor who did not try hard enough to rescue the emperor but managed to rescue the emperor's money without a problem. This legend, if true, could be another possible source of the Ney/Ferrer squabble.

Still, the facts and suppositions outlined above have not dissuaded treasure hunters or dampened the vivid folklore that has sprung up around the Laffite legend. Anyone who encountered a famous figure like Jean Laffite would naturally spend the rest of his or her days telling stories—likely numerous versions of those stories—to any and all willing to listen. And for the record, we are not opposed to the folklore because our investigation has revealed that folklore is often based upon a kernel of truth that simply needs further study or clarification. In *Florida Pirates: From the Southern Gulf Coast to the Keys and Beyond,* James and Sarah Kaserman write that Laffite "once stated that, along the coast of the Gulf of Mexico, he had buried enough gold to build a solid-gold bridge across the Mississippi River."[5] They report the unsubstantiated Laffite boast that he had buried treasure "in every inlet and on every island along the entire coast of the Gulf of Mexico," along with the Galveston legend that Laffite sold his soul to the devil in exchange for his grand Red House there.[6] Such stories have value in that they have captured the imaginations of generations of readers who keep the legend alive and continually renew interest in the history of the locations where the tales are centered.

Block's article outlines the story of a formerly enslaved man named Wash who claims to have seen Laffite and his men in the act of burying treasure. Block says Wash died at age 104 in the year 1880 and that he had been born in Africa but sold by Laffite when he was young. Wash apparently saw Laffite and his men coming in and out of the swamp, and he says he witnessed a murder. Three men were coming to retrieve what he thought was treasure, and only two came out of the woods. A body was later found. Wash concluded, "And that's why there ain't no more known about that big pirate than there is. People were afraid to open their mouths those days unless it was to eat. There's that old Catalon that died here about four years ago. Why, that poor old darky was scared to death of his life most of the time, because everybody knew that he was one of Laffite's cooks and knew more than anybody else alive about where the money was buried."[7]

At this point, the fiction of Laffite's treasure is nearly impossible to separate from any fact that may exist, and if he indeed did have enough gold to build a bridge across the Mississippi and he buried it in Louisiana, Texas, or somewhere in the Caribbean as the legends say, nothing has yet been found. Maybe he never buried it and instead kept at least a portion of it in his possession. That possibility has become part of the rich folklore surrounding Lorenzo Ferrer in Lincolnton and his elusive treasure chests.

FERRER'S CHESTS OF GOLD

It has already been established that Ferrer came to Lincolnton without a profession and never worked. Gladys Childs's article "Lincolnton's Pirate" asserts that "Lorendzo Ferrer, believed to be Jean Lafitte, bought property in Lincolnton; lived well, but in seclusion, in a two story house back of the century old Lincoln County jail."[8] Nobody could explain how he had the means to own two houses and numerous properties and live so well, which caused suspicion among the townspeople of his day, many of whom offered accounts after he died. One story, though, is of particular importance here. In it, Ferrer enlisted the help of a friend to help transport and then hide several mysterious chests in the vault of the old courthouse when the Yankees were expected to invade Lincolnton during the Civil War.

Truly, every written local account of Ferrer's life in Lincolnton tells some version of the story, but we were able to track down the genesis of the tale: George Kizer. According to a Kizer relative, Carole Hoffman Howell, her Uncle Fred's father George Kizer was a groundskeeper at St. Luke's.[9] George was born in 1859 and died in 1940. Kizer is the one who passed down the story of the chests of gold. He was a contemporary in Lincolnton with Ferrer for sixteen years before Ferrer's death, and he remembered talking to Ferrer as a young boy. Childs writes in her article "Lincolnton's Pirate" that Kizer "was up in years" when she arrived in Lincolnton. Childs says Kizer told

Old Lincolnton Courthouse

her that "in his boyhood, he and his buddies would gather around Ferrer on the Court House Square and listen to the fascinating tales he told them of piracy. The boys called him 'The Pirate.' He let them see and handle the coins and jewels in his treasure chests."[10] A claim in Robert Williams's *People Worth Meeting and Stories Worth Repeating* supports Kizer's assertion that Ferrer was not shy about showing off his treasure. Williams explains, "At his home Ferrer kept several chests filled with gold and other valuables. He did not mind showing these trinkets to his friends."[11] Anyone who had the chance to see such a sight in Lincolnton in those days would have certainly remembered it, so it makes sense that the stories about Ferrer's maneuver to protect his assets would be passed down through the generations.

In 1865—the end of the Civil War—reports indicated that the Yankees could invade at any time. According to the story, Ferrer asked his good friend Wallace Reinhardt for help moving iron treasure chests to the vault of the courthouse, as there was no way for him to protect his valuables at home. All the local accounts are strikingly similar. It was not lost on us how unified in the details they were. The case can be made that various authors have simply taken the facts from what they have read and reported them that way, but our experience tells us that usually when folks retell a story, new embellishments are added.

Below is a selection of what is said in printed publications about the treasure chest stories.

From Scotti Cohn's
It Happened in North Carolina: Remarkable Events

Not long after Wallace Reinhardt . . . got word of the possible [Yankee] assault, he received an urgent message from his friend and fellow resident, a Frenchman named Lorendzo Ferrier. Ferrier wanted to move his valuables into the Lincoln County Courthouse vault for safekeeping. As Reinhardt helped his friend load his three iron chests onto a wagon, he thought about the theory he had begun to form about Ferrier's true identity. The tall, dark-haired, handsome Ferrier had arrived in town about twenty years earlier under a cloud of mystery, accompanied by a strikingly attractive young woman of African descent. As the couple rode down the street in their fine carriage, the people of Lincolnton stood in doorways and on corners, watching and wondering. Even more intriguing to them than the dashing man and his lady were the three huge iron chests stacked on the back of the buggy. The man introduced himself as Lorendzo Ferrier from New Orleans.[12]

From David C. Heavner's "The Story of Wallace Reinhardt"

[Speculation] was also fueled when word got out that [Ferrer] and Reinhardt carried chests of gold to the basement of the courthouse as they feared the approach of Yankee troops during the Civil War.[13]

From Therne Dellinger's "Ferrer or Lafitte?"

An interesting tale is that when the Yankees were coming, Ferrer, with the aid of Wallace Reinhardt, hid some large heavy chests in the basement of the courthouse. This is supposed to have contained jewelry and gold.[14]

From Victor Fair's *The Hills of Home*

When it was reported that the Yankees were about to invade Lincolnton in the closing days of the Civil War, Ferrier sent for his closest friend, Wallace Reinhardt, and requested him to help move his treasure to the Court House for safe keeping. This was done, by use of a wagon team, and when the several large and heavy iron chests were placed in the vault of the Court House, Ferrier opened one of these chests, scooped up a double handful of gold money and presented it to his friend for his services. He also gave this citizen a very handsome and massive gold watch to which was attached a heavy gold chain which evidently was intended to be worn around the neck. This chest contained much gold coin, many articles of rich jewelry, including diamonds, rings, brooches, etc. Ferrier never made any explanation to how or why he was in possession of all this wealth.[15]

From *Lincoln County Heritage, 1997*

Ferrer lived to the ripe old age of 96. No one ever saw him work a day in his life. He loved to sit on the courthouse steps and tell the old men and boys of his pirating days. His wealth was apparently in the three large chests he brought with him, which [were] stored in the courthouse. The Huss house on the west court square is located on lot #18 where he lived.[16]

From Ralph Farmer's "Lorendzo Ferrer & Jean Lafitte . . . One in the Same?"

During the closing days of the Civil War word came through Lincolnton that the Yankees were about to invade. According to Wallace Reinhardt, Ferrer sent for him and requested his help in moving his 'treasure' to the Lincoln County courthouse for safe-keeping. A wagon team was used to accomplish the task and once the heavy iron chests were placed in the vault Reinhardt was rewarded. Ferrer opened one of the chests, scooped up a double handful of gold coins along with a gold watch and chain and gave them to Reinhardt. According to Reinhardt Ferrer never offered an explanation as to where the gold, coins or jewelry which filled the chests came from. To Reinhardt this was proof that Ferrer and Lafitte were one in the same.[17]

You can see from six different accounts of the same event that none of the storytellers put extra jam on the bread. They are very similar in content and basically tell the same story. The reader can thus draw his or her own conclusion about whether these stories ring true.

Lest we forget, Reinhardt—not coincidentally—was one of the executors of Ferrer's will, yet these supposed chests of gold were never mentioned in that document. Was the report of this event true, or was Reinhardt simply indulging in a bit of exuberant storytelling in the wake of Ferrer's death? On the other hand, if true, then what happened to those chests and their contents? In late nineteenth-century Lincolnton, they would likely not have blended in. For instance, how does one put such "treasure" to practical use? If a run to the local hardware store was in order, did Ferrer plunk down a diamond brooch on the counter as payment for a few pounds of ten-penny nails, asking for his change in small bills? Even more so, if someone made periodic deposits into a local bank for the purposes of converting gold to currency, word would have leaked out. And yet none of this shows up on any record of the day that we have found, the only remotely plausible exception being the stand-alone and unsubstantiated legend coming from Milton that Ferrer deposited a large sum of money in the local bank. These clues, or lack thereof, lead us to believe that Ferrer's chests of treasure were either greatly exaggerated, spirited away from Lincolnton and placed in safe-keeping somewhere else, stolen, or never existed to begin with. The only other option would have been that Ferrer and Wallace Reinhardt (who already knew about the chests and had been taken into Ferrer's confidence, if you choose to believe his story) had prearranged for Reinhardt to retrieve whatever remained from its hidden location on the property that was left to him in Ferrer's will. A bit of credibility does attach itself to this last option as evidenced in the will itself. In his remarks about the house and land that he leaves to Catherine Sullivan, Ferrer's language is straightforward. In similar remarks regarding his gift to Reinhardt, however, Ferrer goes to extra descriptive trouble—denoting not only the house and land, but also "all the articles found therein, either in the house or on the lot."[18] Legally, that would certainly cover chests of gold and jewels, though the fog of history has obscured the truth to the point of oblivion. And we are not 100 percent certain the will was not written in some sort of code that Reinhardt would have understood.

While we may never know the truth, the stories in Lincolnton about the treasure chests have never settled down, and locals continue to speculate about what could have happened to them. One of our sources claims that in 1989 when Hurricane Hugo came inland and did severe damage in the Piedmont of North Carolina, including Lincolnton, a tree fell on North Aspen Street near Lincolnton High School and hit a house. On the porch of the house was a big trunk described as having "heavy iron handles and a camel top." Our friend stopped and asked if it could possibly be one of Laffite's three chests, but she was not given a straight answer. When she returned a few days later to inquire again, it was gone, and nobody could provide information about where it went.

If the chests did exist, and we think there is a decent chance they did, Wallace Reinhardt was probably directed to their location around the time of Ferrer's death. When he passed, Ferrer had no living family that we know of, so everything he owned likely passed into the possession of close friends, and local history tells us he had no closer friend than Reinhardt.

So where does this leave those adventurers who will forever be on the hunt for Laffite's fortune? The answer is probably not Lincolnton.

CHAPTER NINETEEN
THE SEARCH FOR ARTIFACTS

As our many months of research concluded, we had sufficient evidence in hand to make the case that Lorenzo Ferrer was Jean Laffite. However, two pivotal late discoveries that occurred while we were polishing the final manuscript moved us from an incredible case backed by a mountain of documents into the realm of an incredible case backed by *physical artifacts* as well.

When we first began our quest to uncover every shred of available evidence about Ferrer in Lincolnton, we heard mention of a poem that was supposedly found at the old man's house after he passed. It was not until November 2018 just before Thanksgiving that we finally tracked down Lincoln County historian Ralph Farmer's obscure article "Lorendzo Ferrer & Jean Lafitte . . . One in the Same?" published in *Footprints in Time*, a newsletter of local lore. At the end of his article, which recounts many of the stories that have become part of the Jean Laffite oeuvre in Lincoln County, Farmer includes the typed words of a poem "by an unknown author found in Lorendzo Ferrer's house, lot #18 Southwest Square, Lincolnton."[1]

Though we pride ourselves on being professional researchers and generally very composed women, we will admit to throwing a little hootenanny right there in the North Carolina Room at the main branch of the Gaston County Public Library when we flipped to the page containing the long-sought verses. The content of this poem—and the fact that it was found in Lorenzo Ferrer's house—made the perfect connection for our hypothesis.

Below are all nine stanzas of the untitled poem transcribed in full.

> Come all you good people and hear me relate
> Concerning Great Britain and her dismal state
> The British and Savage they make a great show
> But brave General Jackson has laid many low

It has been but lately as I have heard tell
A number of British in action have fell
It was General Jackson on liberty side
Killed eleven hundred and then was not tired

It was near Pensacola this battle was fought
The British began it but little they got
The British commanders say what do they mean
Such others as Jackson I never yet seen

For his metal from cannons like thunder doth fly
Which caused the hosts of Great Britain to die
And the British general was first for to yield
He says he will fight him no more in the field

For he looks like a man that was raised in the dirt
Though he'll whip the British in his hunting shirt
Although that their coats they were bordered with gold
He'll drive them before him he won't be controlled

His arms are extended he works them by slight
Slips into their camps and sells eggs in the night
His hat it was ragged his coat it was thin
The British and Savage did let him in

He ranged through their camps as I have been told
Until all his poultry by art he had sold
His army lay muted until he was done
Then took Pensacola without firing a gun

Come all you that got wives and sweethearts at home
Remember the hour when you will return
And if your companions you never more shall see
You rest in the arms of sweet liberty

Farewell to all cowards I bid you a dieu [*sic*]
The days of pleasure you will not pursue
The war is not ended its only begun
God spare General Jackson until it is done.

To begin, nine stanzas is a fairly lengthy poem, especially considering that each stanza contains two sets of rhyming couplets. The creation of rhyming verse is obviously much more complicated than blank (un-rhyming) verse, so the writer invested time in the composition of the poem. Additionally, it can be concluded with confidence that the writer of the poem was well-read, as the verse is constructed in iambic tetrameter (four feet/iambs [unstressed/stressed syllables] per line). Iambic tetrameter is not nearly as common a poetic structure as iambic pentameter (five feet per line). Anyone who has ever taken a literature course has studied Shakespeare, who was famous for using iambic pentameter in his plays and sonnets. Any novice poet could get by writing in iambic pentameter, but it would require a more sophisticated thinker to even know that iambic tetrameter was a thing—much less to have the confidence to attempt to use it to compose verse. Further supporting the assertion that the writer was well-educated is the way in which the verses rhyme—usually in unforced pairings that work with the content of the lines. In other words, most of the rhyming words feel natural in this poem, whereas when very inexperienced writers attempt to rhyme, their pairings often feel forced, as they rhyme for the sake of rhyming because they believe that is what poets do. Furthermore, this writer demonstrates an understanding of inexact rhyme, which is a more refined rhetorical strategy. This can be seen with the rhyming of *side* and *tired* in the second stanza and *fought* and *got* in the third stanza. The writer of this text even goes so far as to break the rhyme scheme in stanza eight with *home* and *return* ending the first and second lines. An immature poet would not have known that it was okay to break the rhyming scheme to call attention to the content of a specific passage. This writer had read enough great poetry to be familiar with the strategy of breaking the rhyme scheme.

In stanza one, the writer opens with a call for the readers to gather around to hear the story about the haughty English, who he compares to savages. For several centuries, this introductory call to attention was a method used by the great poets, a history this writer has clearly studied. The reader is informed of the prowess of General Andrew Jackson, who has "laid many low" on the battlefield. The writer makes clear in the first four lines that the purpose of the piece is to criticize the British and exalt Jackson. In this way, it is a rhetorically tight composition, as it tells the reader exactly what the poem will be about in the exposition.

The second stanza boasts of the forces under Jackson's command killing 1,100 British soldiers and yet still not being tired. The tense of this stanza is also noteworthy: "It has been but lately as I have heard tell / A number of

British in action have fell." This text was either written around the time the 1,100 British soldiers were killed in combat, or it was intentionally written to evoke that moment in time and take the reader there—to the actions of Jackson in the *present* rather than the *past*. The tense puts the reader in the scene to witness Jackson's glory, which implies that the writer was there to experience it.

In stanza three, the location of the action is revealed: Pensacola, or more specifically, the Battle of Pensacola. The conflict, which took place in November 1814, was part of the War of 1812 and led up to the final British/American skirmish at the Battle of New Orleans in 1815. The writer describes the British as the ones who "began it," but "little they got" for their efforts. The British had never seen a leader of Jackson's caliber, the writer suggests, which leads to the surrender of the British in the fourth stanza.

The best descriptive details of the poem come in stanza five, where the writer explains Jackson "look[ed] like a man that was raised in the dirt." Even so, he was able to "whip the British in his hunting shirt." The writer then mocks the fancy British uniforms "bordered with gold," implying that fine clothes cannot bring victory to an inferior force, while ragged clothes do not matter when the force is led by a capable commander. The next stanza further describes Jackson's appearance: "His hat it was ragged his coat it was thin." Again, these are the kinds of descriptions that sound like a man who had seen Jackson on a battlefield. For this writer, the details are personal and intimate.

The final two stanzas speak directly to fellow soldiers in the Battle of Pensacola, which is something that only a fellow soldier would feel comfortable doing. Again, the tense chosen implies that the poem was written contemporaneously with the battle. The writer says, "Come all you that got wives and sweethearts at home / Remember the hour when you will return." The writer did not phrase this to say *when you did return* but *when you will return* in the future. The final stanza rebukes any cowards who are unwilling to finish the war with the English, as "The war it is not ended its only begun." At the time of the events in the poem, several more years of conflict were ahead before the Battle of New Orleans ended the war. The writer closes with a prayer for Jackson, who is idolized throughout the text: "God spare General Jackson until it is done."

We made two important decisions once the text of this astonishing poem was discovered. First, we contacted a colleague with connections to a listserv of nineteenth-century American literature scholars, and she posted the poem for identification and debate. We learned that the poem was a ballad, a genre of writing that was very popular in the 1800s, especially among men who had been to war. These ballads were usually set to music and sung around campfires. We also learned that ballads like these were written to commemorate great bravery, particularly that of valiant commanders and other leaders. Of all the specialists who responded to the query, none of them recognized this particular text, even though it is about a very specific historical event, suggesting that the poem was written by someone who never published the work. This was a homegrown ballad—one composed by someone who absolutely adored Andrew Jackson. Judging by the level of sophistication the work reveals, it is clear that the writer was not Joe Blow from the militia, called up from his rural farm to serve in the conflict. Furthermore, the kind of adoration of Jackson demonstrated in the poem seems unlikely in a foot soldier who probably never had the chance to interact with Jackson or even see him.

The next good decision we made after discovering Farmer's article was to continue to pursue *the original copy* of the poem. While finally having a transcribed copy of the text in hand was a delight, we wanted to see the original to examine the handwriting. Luckily, it did not take long for our wish to come true. It was tucked away in a folder in the Lincoln County Historical Association's archives on the third floor of the Cultural Center on Main Street in Lincolnton. This part of the collection was donated by Bette Morris of Lincolnton, whose husband was also a local Freemason. It is unclear how she came into possession of the document.

We spent considerable time viewing the original because Farmer's transcription had corrected inconsistencies and spelling errors for the sake of publication. The original is a fascinating artifact for a number of reasons, including the fact that the reader can also see several edits the writer made during the composition process. What drew our immediate and prolonged attention, though, were the misspellings and errors made by the writer, the same kinds of errors made in the Ferrer will. Notice the use of "the" instead of "they" in line three ("The Brittish and Savage the make a great show"). Also noteworthy is the inconsistent spelling of "British" throughout the poem.

For several weeks we were perplexed by the writer's use of "Jeneral" in reference to Andrew Jackson (lines four, seven, and thirty-nine). However, it eventually occurred to us that the letter "J" in this instance is entirely consistent with a person whose native language is not English.

This poem paints for the reader a picture of a writer who understood a complex poetic tradition enough to mimic its form in a number of ways, who clearly had a wartime experience with Andrew Jackson that inspired tremendous adoration, but who demonstrated a slight deficiency in his mastery of written English. We conclude, therefore, that Jean Laffite was the author

Original Poem Possibly Written by Ferrer

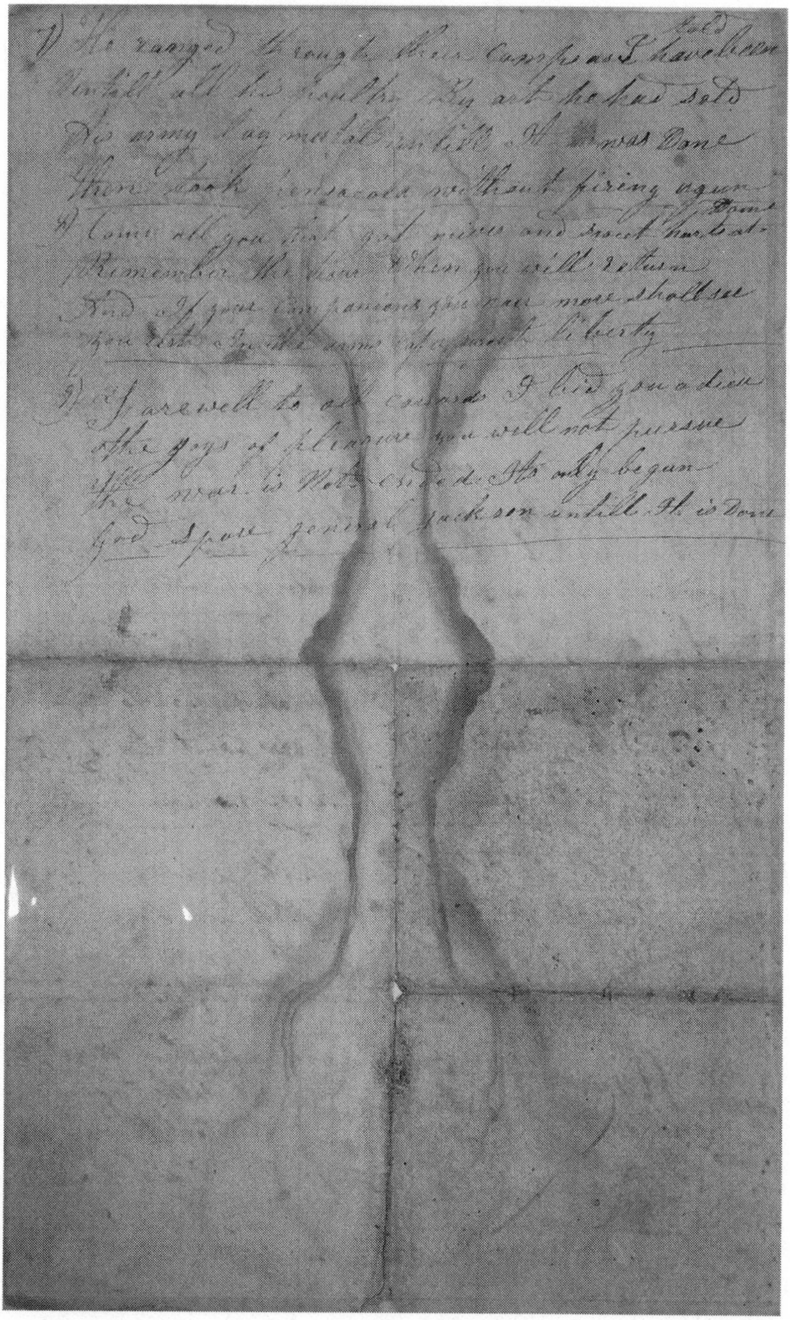

of the poem, though we cannot say whether he wrote the text whilst living under that identity or as his alter ego Lorenzo Ferrer. We are also confident that this document was written in his handwriting, just like the will.

THE PIÈCE DE RÉSISTANCE

In June 2018, we received a text message from our favorite Freemason, Brent Turner, telling us that we needed to get up to the lodge as soon as possible. All of our research trips to Lincoln Lodge 137 had stirred interest about the captivating story of Brother Ferrer. One of the younger Brothers, Lynden Berry, who had already been working with us to glean everything we could about Ferrer from the lodge's historical documents, had just made a discovery. While they already knew their third-floor meeting chamber was filled with marvelous history and all kinds of interesting artifacts, Berry had for the first time noticed an old sword in an iron scabbard that hangs on the wall above where the Tyler guards the door during ceremonies. A sixty-year Freemason in the Lincoln Lodge confirmed that the sword has always been there, and nobody to his knowledge has ever taken it down for examination—until Brother Berry decided to do so that night following their regular meeting.

"Looking at it, I figured it must be old," Berry explained, "so I became interested in finding out just how old. I began looking into it by the letters on the sabre, and the research I found indicated the sword was made between 1812–1813, specifically for the War of 1812."[2] The maker's mark on the blade of the sabre reads "HHP" in capital letters above the designer, "N. STARR," for Nathan Starr, the top American sword maker in the early 1800s. The model is known as the Nathan Starr Model 1812 Contract Cavalry Sabre. The "P" that appears above the "HHP" mark indicates it was "proved" by military inspector HHP, Henry H. Perkin, who worked with the Nathan Starr factory. Starr signed a contract with the US government to create five thousand of these "horseman's swords," but after one thousand were manufactured around November 1812, a design change was implemented for the remainder of the run. One of the changes was the scabbard material being changed from leather to iron. The sword in Lincoln Lodge 137 is part of the second run produced sometime after November 1812 but before 1813 came to a close, meaning it could have been part of the Battle of New Orleans in 1815. Groom makes the point that the Battle of New Orleans was largely fought with rifles, muskets, and cannons.[3] This opens up the possibility that Laffite may have been awarded a sword like this as an honorary weapon. Knowing too that he was possibly away from the front

Laffite Sword. Courtesy of Lynden Berry

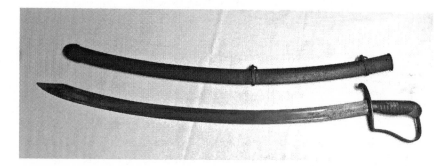

lines while the actual battle was going on, it would stand to reason that a sword like this (if it was in his possession) could have escaped the war in such good condition save for some leather loss on the handle and a few stains on the blade. A more down-to-earth and likely explanation is the notion that Laffite came into possession of this sword by virtue of the large cache of smuggled and stolen weapons in his warehouse in Barataria. He could simply have appropriated this sword for his own use long before the Battle of New Orleans. Given that there is no documentation that his role in that conflict included any hand-to-hand combat, it is possible this sword never factored into that battle at all.

The discovery of a War of 1812 sword was exhilarating, and it immediately set our wheels spinning about whether Lorenzo Ferrer was the one who donated it to the lodge. We also considered Lieutenant Colonel James Henderson, who was killed in 1814 just before the Battle of New Orleans. However, since he died in the conflict, we quickly concluded that the sword (if it was his) would have become a treasured family heirloom, and the Henderson clan definitely had enough fine houses among them to display such a symbol of a soldier's courage. Also important was the fact that Henderson lived in Tennessee. Only his nephews were members of the Lincolnton Lodge, so displaying the sword of someone who was never a member would be very strange. We then thought about the fact that there were Lincolnton troops sent to fight in the War of 1812. Turner explained to us that the first Lincolnton Lodge was opened in 1803, but it lost its charter right after the War of 1812 and closed in 1816.[4] Internal lodge documents indicate that the war directly impacted the financial problems that plagued that first lodge. It closed and was reopened in 1851. Even though it was a long shot that maybe someone involved in the War of 1812 came back home and donated the sword, which was kept until the lodge reopened thirty-nine years later, we still wanted to investigate names to see if any soldier may have had connections to Lodge 137. Before we could begin that research, however, we were informed of our approval to come to the lodge to view the sword in person.

Our husbands, now thoroughly bewildered by our antics with this project, were not surprised when we began digging through their toolboxes looking for a blacklight. While they knew deep down we were not capable of murder and thus should not need a blacklight to detect and conceal blood splatter, their curiosity was definitely piqued. The afternoon of June 16, 2019, when we turned out the overhead lights and used the blacklight to thoroughly examine the sword and scabbard carries with it perhaps our most vivid memory of our research adventure. As we moved on to the scabbard, which Berry and others had understandably not thought to examine closely, our eyes all landed on the same spot—the spot where an inscription not fully visible to the naked eye had clearly been etched by hand into the iron.

With the lights turned out and a flashlight in hand, Berry, who leaned in to get the first close look with a magnifying glass, remarked that it looked to him like someone had etched the letters "capital J and then a small n. After that it looks like a space and a capital L."

Having no knowledge of how Jean Laffite commonly signed his name, Berry could not understand our sudden keen interest, but we recognized

Laffite Sword Inscription

the significance immediately. We knew Laffite always signed his name *Jn. Laffite*. Our research never uncovered a single example of his signature with the name "Jean" fully spelled out. Not only that, but a further examination indicated that the surname had been spelled *Laffite* with two "f's" and one "t." The clear implication was that Laffite himself was the likely source of the inscription. And it had been hiding in plain sight for two hundred years in Lincolnton Lodge 137.

Since the discovery of the sword, we have contacted numerous experts to learn more about it. We have confirmed with antique arms experts that we are correct in our dating of the piece. It is what is known as an M-1812 contract cavalry sabre. To gain further insight, in January 2020, we took the sword to the North Carolina Museum of Art and met with Noelle Ocon, the senior conservator of paintings. Ocon was kind enough to x-ray the sword and scabbard for us to determine if that technology might reveal a better view of the inscription. When we realized the scan was not picking up details on the surface, we scheduled a consultation with metals expert Mark Erdmann, the owner of Erdmann Art Conservation. Using a microscope, Erdmann was able to draw the following conclusions:

- Though faintly visible to the naked eye, the letter markings that we saw are indeed an inscription.

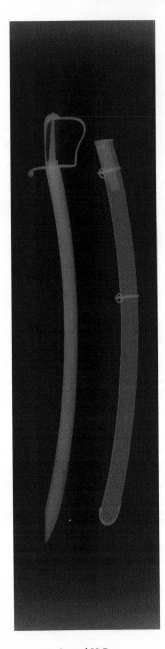

- Erdmann was able to identify the nature of the inscribed marks as separate and distinctly different from the accidental marks, dents, and scratches made by random use and wear, noting that the differences between the two were clearly visible under magnification. While the accidental scratches were shallow, the inscription was quite deep.

- The residue of some sort of aged coating appears on the surface of the scabbard, possibly either a varnish or oil which was applied *after the inscription*. Both the inscription and the coating are very old in Erdmann's opinion, but the inscription definitely came before the coating.

- The coating partly obscures the inscription in some spots.

- The inscription was scratched by hand by an individual using some sort of sharp metal tool. It was not made by a professional engraver with specialized equipment.

- Erdmann was able to confirm the same letters we detected under blacklight. He said the "Jn" was clearly visible at the beginning. Following that is a space. The next letter appeared to him to be a capital "L," though part of it was not legible due to age. Several of the following letters were obscured by the varnish, but he confirmed either two "f's" or two "t's" followed by a very clear and legible lower-case "e." Erdmann said the "e" was definitely the last letter of the inscription. (We note here that in most of Laffite's known signatures, he used a long swipe across the "t" in his last name that extended backwards over the tops of the preceding "f's." Unless further enhancement proves definitively one way or the other, it is reasonable that this inscription shows two "f's" with a swipe across their top, which would be consistent with Laffite's signatures.)

- The ending conclusion from the consultation was that the inscription reads "*Jn L . . .tte.*"

Sword X-Ray

Additionally, via correspondence about this sword with various museums, including Colonial Williamsburg, the Metropolitan Museum of Art, the Smithsonian, and others, we have determined that a process called Reflectance Transformation Imaging (RTI) may provide further enhancement of the inscription. However, that technology is somewhat inaccessible to the general public, and as yet we have been unable to gain access to it.

The sum total of the information gathered about this sword, beginning with its accidental discovery all the way through to the expert verification, leaves us with extremely high confidence that it was the personal property of Jean Laffite and that it stayed with him until he donated it to the Freemasons late in his life. The traditional use of a Tyler's sword in Masonic meetings is long-standing, so it is reasonable that one would have been needed in this newly formed lodge in Lincolnton. Ferrer, as a founding member, may have been happy and even more honored to donate this sword for that purpose. For those who may still be in doubt about Lorenzo Ferrer's identity, we ask how it is possible to explain that a sword with Laffite's virtually invisible inscription made it into a Freemason lodge in a tiny little town in North Carolina.

THE LOST INKWELL

The final Ferrer artifact that we are still on the hunt for is his famed inkwell, which we have read about in numerous Lincoln County sources. Fair explained, "The fact that Lorenzo Ferrer was a seafaring man is without doubt. The writer has in his possession Ferrer's old inkwell, given by the mysterious Frenchman to Wallace Reinhardt. This inkwell is made of solid lead and weighs four and one quarter pounds. It has only a small recess for holding ink not much larger than a thimble. It is of the common type used by ship captains in the old days, so constructed of lead with a wide bottom in order to prevent it from easily overturning or being rocked from the table by the motion of the ship. It is now being used as a doorstop."[5] Remember Fair was Wallace Reinhardt's grandson, and the inkwell clearly had been handed down to him. Cohn says of the elusive inkwell, "More than a hundred years later, Reinhardt's descendants proudly display Ferrier's old inkwell made of solid lead—2 inches wide at the base, weighing 4 pounds—the type of inkwell used by ship captains in days gone by."[6] Lincolnton historian Therne Dellinger refers to "things now in the Victor Fair . . . family that lead to the fact he was a seafaring man. For instance, a 4-pound . . . inkwell, flat bottomed so as not to tip at sea."[7] Other sources give more details about the inkwell. We have read that it was two and three-quarter inches wide with a top that was one and three-quarter inches square with a precise weight of four and a quarter pounds. Some have suggested it looks more like a candleholder than an inkwell. After reading another local source that claimed it was once in the possession of Victor Fair's wife, we made every effort to find ancestors who could help us track the inkwell's location. We spoke with Fair Whitley, Victor Fair's granddaughter, and she did not have any information regarding its whereabouts.[8] And so, the search continues.

CHAPTER TWENTY

CLEAR VIEW IN THE REARVIEW

Ascertaining the absolute truth of a mystery that had its origins nearly 240 years ago somewhere between Europe and the Caribbean, spanning the next century before finally coming to rest in a North Carolina town, is preposterous on its face, especially when taking into account the various twists, turns, and opportunities for misinformation that marked its progress. Having said that, we will offer a word here in the spirit of Katherine Hepburn as she portrayed the iconic Rose Thayer in the movie *The African Queen.* When incredulous German military officials tried to argue the probability of Rose and her partner, Charlie Allnut, succeeding in navigating the impossible journey down the Ulanga River, past too many obstacles to count, citing all the ways in which it could not have happened, Rose simply lifted her chin and said to the assembled group, "Nevertheless."[1]

Here is the summary of what we believe to be the truth, based on everything that we have discovered and recounted for you in this book. Sometime around the year 1780, the man who lived his life using many names, two of which were Jean Laffite and Lorenzo Ferrer, was born. In the absence of birth records, that birth could have happened in France, Spain, or possibly on the present-day island of Haiti. Sometime shortly after the turn of the nineteenth century, that man, now using the name Jean Laffite, made his way to New Orleans and began doing business as a privateer. His partner, a man named Pierre Laffite, was most likely his brother. Along with a third trusted friend and possible brother, a man calling himself Dominique You, the three made a significant impact on the history of the Gulf region of the United States in the years leading up to the War of 1812, amassing a great fortune by trading in smuggled goods and enslaved people, neither of which placed them in high regard in the eyes of American officials.

Even so, immediately preceding the definitive Battle of New Orleans, the assistance that they lent to an extremely vulnerable American army likely turned the tide of that battle. Had they not supplied General Andrew Jackson and his troops with expertise, extra manpower, and more critically, with desperately needed flints, the battle could have gone the other way, and the British would have taken control of the mouth of the Mississippi River, not to mention the western boundary of the United States, subsequently bringing a young nation to its knees for good. In exchange for their help, the men were granted high praise and full pardons for past deeds, but little else after that. Their fortunes seized and disbursed, they were left with no choice but to begin again. They did so by offering their services as double agents, both as spies for Spain and also as partners with a group of highly placed and powerful New Orleans investors intent on seizing control of the remaining portions of the Gulf Coast that were still up for grabs—the same areas that were also the desire of Spain. The Laffites were on the payroll of both. Part of that process also provided the Laffites with the opportunity to reestablish their privateering empire on the island of Galveston, Texas, where Jean Laffite became the leader of the settlement, living prominently in a large house known as Maison Rouge because of the bright red color he chose to paint it. However, the Laffites' dreams of renewed glory and the resurrection of their privateering empire came up against an increasingly effective United States government, which succeeded in forcing them to abandon Galveston in 1820 with greatly decimated resources and no immediate Plan B. Consequently, they wandered. Pierre Laffite died of yellow fever and was buried on Isla Mujeres in the year 1821, following which Jean ended up in Cuba under the sheltering wing of his old and powerfully connected friend, Arsène Latour. After twice getting himself captured and thrown into jail and twice escaping, it became apparent to Laffite that there would forever be a price on his head and that his days of operating as a privateer were never going to return. His options had narrowed considerably.

With Pierre dead and his surrounding posse of loyal underlings and politically powerful wingmen shrinking down to only one or two, Laffite faked his death at sea, went underground in Cuba, and disappeared, almost surely with the help of Latour—a man whose reputation was still intact and whose connections with Laffite's former attorney, Edward Livingston, were still very strong. Livingston had parlayed a good relationship with Andrew Jackson into a rising career that moved him out of Louisiana permanently, landing him in various roles in Washington, DC—first as US congressman from Louisiana, then US senator, then as secretary of state under now-President Andrew Jackson, and finally as ambassador to France. During all of this, while Laffite stayed underground, Livingston and Latour stayed in touch. Finally, in the year 1830, a new opportunity presented itself in the form of the burgeoning cotton trade in Mississippi—an area well-known to both Laffite and Latour as a result of their exploration of the area in 1815. While no planter, Laffite would have immediately seen the potential for profit in Mississippi. Cotton would be impossible to grow without slave labor, and slave labor was something that Jean Laffite knew how to market. He also understood how much money could be made under the table in such an environment—one that was not yet benefitting from government regulation in any meaningful sense. Having now been out of sight for at least six years, Laffite (no doubt in concert and in consultation with Latour) decided that the time was right to reenter the United States. For Latour's part, he reached out to Livingston in Washington, speaking of Laffite in code as *Maison Rouge* (a clear indication that Livingston must have also been aware all along that Laffite had not died at sea), asking for Livingston's help in recovering some of the former pirate's assets that were currently being held in France. With the hope of that help, Laffite reentered the United States via the back door, probably putting Bayou Lafourche to good use as his port of entry. The bayou was an old favorite of the Laffites because it was too shallow to permit large boats, yet extremely navigable for small ones, and a foolproof way up the Mississippi River without having to touch New Orleans.

Once inside the United States, Laffite simply came ashore somewhere between Baton Rouge and Natchez and began again, this time using the name Lorenzo Ferrer. He quickly set up shop in the area between Natchez and present-day Jackson—right in the heart of the Mississippi cotton boom and right in the lap of the slave trade. From 1830 until possibly 1837, he bounced around several counties in Mississippi—Copiah, Hinds, and Madison—buying and selling land and enslaved people. At one of the many slave markets along the established route between Virginia and Mississippi, he purchased an octoroon woman, a "fancy girl" named Louisa, so called because of her mixed race and exceptional beauty. Louisa was a teenager at the time, and her status as a fancy girl made her a lucrative asset. On at least one occasion and possibly two, Ferrer likely rented her to other owners for the horrific purpose of birthing more enslaved people. Also, in a matter still under scrutiny, Ferrer took a wife. Now aged fifty-four, he married a young seventeen-year-old girl named Nancy Alford, who was the daughter of a man Ferrer likely had done business with, either as a slave broker or as a land speculator or possibly both. The marriage did not last, and yet there is no record of divorce or annulment. Less than two years later, Nancy Alford Ferrer married a man named John Mounger and ended up living happily ever after in Mississippi, bearing eleven children along the way. While there are two or three good explanations for why the marriage with Ferrer failed, we lean toward the theory that because of their age difference, it seemed more an opportunistic arrangement for some purpose other than love. We also believe Nancy made one of two discoveries—or maybe both—but either of them could have ended the marriage. It is probable that she learned some time after the wedding that she was married to Jean Laffite. It is also probable that by this time, Ferrer and Louisa were romantically involved—either with Louisa's consent or without. In any event, these discoveries could have precipitated some sort of a threat from Nancy—or even from her well-connected father—to leave or else face exposure. The discovery, even without a threat, could have aroused enough fear for Ferrer that he simply picked up Louisa and abruptly left, abandoning Nancy in the process. Whatever the case, Ferrer left Mississippi with Louisa by his side and never returned. And, as luck would have it, he left Mississippi having regained his financial footing—not coincidentally right ahead of the collapse of the cotton boom—with a new fortune intact. While it does not appear to rival the size of his former fortune, it could easily have been substantial. A tremendous amount of money was made in Mississippi in the years between 1830 and 1837, and a good deal of that money was made illegally and in private. Add to this the possibility that Livingston had indeed been able to recover Laffite's assets from France in whatever amount, and it is easy to see how Lorenzo Ferrer arrived in Lincolnton, North Carolina, with Louisa and a small fortune to his name.

And neither was Lincolnton a coincidence. Having met and likely done business with the various Henderson men who had made their way to the exact same area of Mississippi at the exact time when Ferrer was there doing business, we believe that he not only arrived in North Carolina with a beautiful woman and a fortune, he came with a new set of well-placed friends at his disposal, friends who very possibly knew his real identity and understood and appreciated his talented connections to the slave trade and his familiarity with how to make money in the shadows. In whatever form the friendship took, we believe the Hendersons paved the way for Ferrer to relocate to Lincolnton and made sure to keep his secret for the rest of his days. During the next thirty-six years, Ferrer appears to have found the safe harbor that always eluded him in his younger years as Jean Laffite. He was finally able to relax and live as an accepted member of society within the high circles that had always attracted him. Those years were not without a few alarming hiccups, however. Within the first five years of his arrival, he was unexpectedly confronted by Marshal Michel Ney in an incident that quickly turned volatile and could have actually exposed his secret—had Ney not possessed his own reasons for wanting to maintain a secret identity. Also during these years, it appears that his appetite for operating just outside the bounds of propriety—especially where finances were concerned—was a continuing hallmark of his personality. We do not discount the possibility that he continued his activities as a slave trader, though none of that was ever made public. Lincolnton resident William Slade was a known broker. The likelihood of an old slave trader such as Laffite/Ferrer not knowing of this and taking advantage of the various opportunities presented by Slade and others is slim to none. All of this sheds light on how the "mysterious Frenchman" managed to arrive in town with money and never work a day for the rest of his life.

A final bit of Jean Laffite's past may have reached out to him in the matter of the 1859 murder at Woodside. We are fifty/fifty on whether or not the entirety of that tale is true—but if true, we believe the attacker could have been William Mitchell, the brutal sociopathic murderer and former pirate whose death was never recorded and who maybe held a festering grudge against Laffite from his days of running contraband in the Gulf for the Laffite operation. Along the way, of course, the Freemasons were ever-present. From the earliest days in New Orleans until just a few years before his death, Laffite/Ferrer benefitted from and interacted with that organization in ways that are still revealing themselves. His love for the Masons was most apparent in the gift of his sword to the lodge. Because it bore the inscription of his former name, *Jn Laffite*, it would not have been an item that Ferrer could have safely displayed in public at his own home. But within the confidential confines of the lodge (whose Brothers may have known his true identity), the weapon would have been safely displayed, according an honor to Ferrer that he perhaps felt he never received after the Battle of New Orleans.

After Louisa's untimely death in 1858, it appears to us that Ferrer finally lost heart and began his slow decline. He left the Masons, never to return, and his health apparently began to fail. At the end of his life, he was bed-ridden and being cared for by his servant, Eliza, a woman that he clearly did not trust. Perhaps for that reason alone, Ferrer took pen in hand and composed his own last will and testament, two years before his actual death. We are not sure if the final paragraph in the will was his idea or was perhaps the idea of one of the Henderson heirs, Robert Sowers, who witnessed the signing of the document. Looking at the original, the last paragraph appears to be written with a different quill, because the ink is heavier. This may or may not have a bearing on anything at all—but no matter whose idea, the final paragraph was obviously meant to erase any link to the story that you have just read.

The similarities between Lorenzo Ferrer and Jean Laffite were ample. Based on documented evidence of their actions, professions, personalities, and physical descriptions, below is a list of those commonalities.

- Born between 1778–1782

- Native tongue—French

- Member of Freemasons

- Tall, well-dressed, dark complexion, and handsome

- Outstanding conversationalist

- Commanding personality

- Fondness for mixed-race women

- Slave trader

- Land buyer

- Socially astute

- Surrounded himself with powerful, well-connected, wealthy friends

- Ferocious and stubborn when it came to his money

- Loved an audience

- Always had money

- Idolized Andrew Jackson

- Clever and secretive

- Pushed claims to higher courts or authorities when he did not agree with outcomes

- Similar handwriting

- Deficient in English spelling

- Penchant for beaver-skin/otter-skin caps

We have no idea why the task of discovering this story fell to us, but we do know that we are grateful to have been given the opportunity to tell it. Life is much stranger than fiction, and we do not discount the notion that the man known as Jean Laffite and Lorenzo Ferrer somehow decided from beyond the grave that it was time for the truth to come out. If that is the case, then we hope that we have told it well.

The late Gaither E. Schrum, who was on the Lorenzo Ferrer case long before we were, was a beacon for us on this journey, as his work kept falling into our laps at very important junctures. His granddaughter, Mecca Whitesides Simmons, shared with us that he always told his children and grandchildren, "History only lives on if we continue teaching it."[2] We would add to that, saying history only lives on if we continue to inspire the curiosity necessary to keep others engaged with it—and we truly hope that our manuscript inspires other Laffite and Ferrer researchers to add on to the work represented here. We are still amazed at how many people in Lincoln County do not want to talk about Lorenzo Ferrer. We encountered more than we can count on one hand who provided information but did not feel comfortable being named in the book. It is our sincere hope that this text will loosen the logjam that has existed for almost 150 years since Ferrer's death. True historians want to collaborate with others to find out more. In that way, books are never really finished. The project does not end here—it is actually just beginning.

AFTERWORD

Crafting the final few sentences of such a gratifying research project gives us ample reason to be thankful for the ride. We ran full throttle for two years and went to great expense to travel all over the country in search of Jean Laffite. We bought dozens of books (some quite rare) and consulted hundreds of others, not to mention the tub full of articles we amassed. We requested close to one hundred interlibrary loans. We consulted with historians, archivists, museum curators, librarians, and experts all over the world. We read literally thousands of primary documents that turned out to have no information for the sake of finding the few buried nuggets that we needed. We traveled the backroads of the United States to access the rural libraries and courthouses without digitized files.

While the publication of this book will be recognized as a bombshell by many Laffite scholars and local historians alike, we readily admit that what we have composed here is just a start. Our book will likely reignite interest in what can be found about Lorenzo Ferrer not just in North Carolina or Mississippi but elsewhere. Therefore, we anticipate in the coming months and years that more documents will be uncovered, especially in private or forgotten collections that were not available to us. Such discoveries will thrill us, and we look forward to seeing how our research may make it possible for unknown documents to be brought to light. We ask any reader who has knowledge of any document that may add to the Lorenzo Ferrer literature to please contact us. We believe Ferrer's inkwell still exists, and we have strong suspicions that it is in private hands possibly in Lincoln County. We know there was an original handwritten Ferrer letter in the archives of St. Luke's Episcopal Church in Lincolnton that was removed, and we very much want to see it. Likewise, if that letter was different from the one Victor Fair referenced in *The Hills of Home*, we want to see that letter, too. We need the help of Mississippi historians who may be able to shed more light on Ferrer's business there. We welcome the assistance of any Mississippi or Louisiana Freemasons with access to private files that may inform our continuing research. The Henderson boys did not leave behind very many letters that made their way into archival repositories, so we would be delighted to hear from anyone who has any such correspondence in a private collection. And if anyone knows where Vardry McBee's fishpond is, for heaven's sake, please get in touch with us. We have done all we know to do in order to find it. You may reach us at jeanlaffiterevealed@gmail.com.

APPENDICES

CHAPTER TEN: NEW BEARINGS

Learning a bit about the Mounger family helped us to determine how the rest of Nancy Ferrer Mounger's life unfolded. She did not leave Mississippi with Ferrer, and we do not believe she even went up to Madison County with him. John Mounger (1786–1847) married Tabitha Brewer (1780–1855) in 1807, and they had Sampson, Martha, George, John Brewer, Susan, Henry, and James Mounger. Like most surnames in early American history, the Mounger name has various spellings, including *Monger* and *Munger*. It appears as though after John Brewer Mounger married Nancy Ferrer, they settled in the Big Creek area, near Calhoun, Mississippi, where he was born and raised. John B. Mounger lived from 1810–1860, and he and Nancy had many children together beginning in 1837 (*immediately* after they wed): John Adams H. (born 1837), Tabitha (born 1838), Caroline (born 1840), James Henry [Jim] (born 1842), Jesse (born 1842), Greenberry B. (born 1845), George William (born 1847), Sampson Anthony (born 1848), Bethania Ann (born 1857), Walter (born 1860), and Martha Susan (date unknown). Considering this number of children, we can conclude either that Lorenzo and Nancy Ferrer did not keep a common marriage bed or he was infertile. The Moungers appear in the 1850 Yalobusha County Census, with John's occupation listed as "planter," and they are in the 1860 Census in Calhoun County, Mississippi, listed as farmers. John Mounger died in 1860, so he is not in the 1870 Calhoun County Census. The head of household is Benjamin Mounger, who must be a relative but not John's brother. Nancy, who was born in 1818, died in 1870 at the age of fifty-two.

CHAPTER ELEVEN: KEEPING UP WITH THE HENDERSONS

The thirteen Henderson children, all born at Woodside, included ten boys and three girls. Two of the girls died in infancy, and one of the boys only lived to the age of ten. The Henderson children are as follows, with those whose names emerged in our Ferrer research being designated with an asterisk. This brief summary is an amalgamation of numerous online genealogy sources related to the Henderson family, handwritten notes graciously offered by Lincoln County historian Ann Dellinger, several other print sources, and a document found in an 1878 deposition given by Ann E. Henderson (Lawson Henderson's granddaughter) in the Tennessee court case *W. C. & J. W. Vaulx et al vs. Mary C. Burtwell.*

1. *Wallace Alexander Henderson*, 1799–1823, studied medicine as a young man and even went north for medical training. After an educational trip to New York in the winter of 1822, he caught pulmonary consumption and subsequently traveled to Havana, Cuba, in an effort to recuperate. He never returned home, dying at the house of Dr. L. Les Dalley in Havana on April 24, 1823.[1]

2. **John Carruth Henderson**, 1801–1833, married Nancy Riley Gaffney in 1828 but died five years later.

3. *Charles Cotesworth Henderson*, 1803–1869, was as successful in his own right as his father Lawson had been before him. C. C. Henderson was a very prominent local merchant whose reputation and wealth extended into large portions of western North Carolina and beyond. He is one of the Henderson brothers who chose to stay in Lincoln County. Among other things, he owned a local tannery that produced shoes and harnesses, was a major investor in the developing railroad industry across the Carolinas, and made very astute investments in large tracts of land. Although he lived his entire life in Lincolnton, Henderson's business interests took him as far away as New Orleans. Sherrill references an interview with Henderson family friend George M. Lore in which he remembers C. C. Henderson in 1856 or 1857 saying that he had recently been conducting business in the Crescent City.[2] C. C. Henderson was a student at the Pleasant Retreat Academy in Lincolnton along with many of the sons of the town's finest families. The 1822 roster alone included the names George W. Henderson, John L. Ramseur, Hugh L. Henderson, John Motz, George W. Motz, James P. Henderson, Charles C. Henderson, Michael Hoke, Jacob Ramseur, George Hoke, and John Hoke.

4. *Lawson Franklin Henderson*, 1806–1858, outlined in detail in Chapter Eleven.

5. ***James Pinckney Henderson,*** 1808–1858, outlined in detail in Chapter Eleven.

6. **Jared Irwin Henderson**, 1810–1821, died at the age of ten.

7. ***Hugh Lawson Henderson***, 1812–1837, never married and had no children. He is said to have died on the *Brig Orson* as it traveled from St. Croix to Savannah. We found evidence of him in Canton in the 1830s when his brother Lawson was in business there.

8. ***George William Henderson,*** outlined in detail in Chapter Eleven.

9. **Mary Graham Henderson Herndon,** 1816–1877, married Thomas N. Herndon, a Lincolnton attorney, in 1835, following which they moved to New Orleans, where Thomas practiced law. Mary died in New Orleans in 1877.[3]

10. **Logan Barry Henderson,** 1818–1844, was embroiled in scandal after being accused of murdering a young man named Marcus Hoke in Lincolnton. Daniel W. Patterson's *A Tree Accurst: Bobby McMillon and Stories of Frankie Silver* provides an account of what happened:

> A fiery nineteen-year-old named Logan Henderson returned to Lincolnton in 1837 after serving in the Texas Rangers. He learned that one Marcus Hoke had called Henderson's father a "damned liar," a "damned old scoundrel," and a "damned old grayheaded rascal." Henderson could perhaps have borne a thousand injuries, but when Hoke ventured upon insult to his family, he vowed revenge. He sought out Hoke and beat him with a cane that shattered, revealing that it sheathed a sword blade. Hoke drew a pistol and Henderson his Bowie knife, the two grappled, and as they tussled, Henderson stabbed the other man. Hoke died from the wound nine hours later. A court found Henderson guilty of manslaughter and sentenced him to six months in jail and to be "burned on the hand" [or branded].[4]

The Lincoln County Historical Association archives also contain a compelling letter from Lawson Henderson (Logan's father) to Beverly Daniel, marshal of the District of North Carolina in Raleigh, on December 8, 1837. In it, Henderson explains what actually precipitated the fight:

At the time I was sick at Raleigh I had went there to attend to a suit in Equity which I brought in that court against Col. John Hoke which was decided at the summer term of 1835, the report of which case no doubt you have seen among the reports of the cases tried at that term in which the conduct of said Hoke is so glaringly exposed by the court that it hath brought down the displeasure of him and family against me and which last August led to an affray between my son Logan B. Henderson and Marcus L. Hoke dec'd, the son of said John Hoke. I having met the dec'd in the street on the morning of the 19th of that month, upon my inquiry at him why he was taking liberties of abusing me in my absence, he gave me much insulting and abusive language, and before my return home information of the abuse was communicated to my son Logan B. Henderson by two gentlemen who heard it.[5]

The senior Henderson then goes on to explain the details of the altercation in vivid detail and then asks Daniel to use his position to try to persuade the governor to act on Logan's behalf.

Logan Henderson died in Texas in 1844 (apparently of natural causes though at a young age), during the time of his brother James's rise to prominence. He never married. Marcus Hoke's grave is in the Old White Cemetery in Lincolnton (just off the Court Square). Note the style of his tabletop grave marker with his death date of 1837. Ferrer's tabletop grave marker erected thirty-eight years later is almost identical in design—the only two markers of their kind in the area.

1. *Walter Carruth Henderson, 1820–1850, also died in Canton, Mississippi, having never married. He was thirty.

2. Margritt Sarah Henderson, 1822–1823, died in infancy. She is buried in the Old White Church Cemetery in Lincolnton.

3. Jane Eliza Henderson, 1824–1825, died shortly after her first birthday.

4. *Wallace Alexander Irwin Henderson, 1827–1851, died at the age of twenty-four in Canton, Mississippi, as a bachelor. He is the brother who is shown living with George in Canton tax records, both listed as merchants/clerks. In his will he left a share of a Rutherford County, North Carolina, gold mine, a house in Lincolnton, and a

big tract of Louisiana land to his inheritors. He never married. The Sherrill book cites an advertisement from 1830 that announces, "a large vein of gold has been discovered in the Henderson and Wilson mine in Lincoln County near Kings Mountain and the ore is worth $3.20 per bushel."[6] Further investigation is needed to determine if the Hendersons were invested in other mines.

Two more Henderson family members are integral to Ferrer's story as it unfolded after his arrival in Lincolnton in 1839.

1. **Lawson Pinckney Henderson,** son of Charles Cotesworth Henderson and Barbara Glen Bryden, was born in 1829. He was in the 1850 Lincoln County Census as living with his parents. He was an influential member of Lincolnton Masonic Lodge 137 from its founding in 1852. He married William Cornelia ("Willie C.") Caldwell, daughter of John Caldwell and his wife Hannah P. Robinson of Burke County. He was on the 1880 Burke County Census living with his wife and their nine children. He died in 1887 and is buried in Cherry Fields Farm Cemetery in Burke County.

2. **Robert Sowers,** son-in-law of Charles Cotesworth Henderson, was a Lincolnton attorney. He married Theodora Henderson, daughter of C. C. and Barbara Henderson, in 1871. He witnessed the writing of Lorenzo Ferrer's last will and testament along with Thomas Wells. The executors were James L. Wilkie and Wallace M. Reinhardt.

The Hendersons in Madison County

While the Henderson children all originated in Lincolnton, several of them moved to Mississippi—to the same area where Lorenzo Ferrer was living. And it just so happens that they were doing the same kind of work as Ferrer. All deed books referenced in the charts below are from the Madison County Chancery Clerk's Office in Canton. The Chancery Clerk's website (https://www.madison-co.com/elected-offices/chancery-clerk) contains links to all the old deed books in digitized form. With our notations for book and page number, you can quickly access these original deeds by using the "Search Historical Records" tab. This timetable, which only offers a selection of the deals we found involving the Hendersons, makes it clear just how prolific they were in their business transactions in Madison County. As well, we have included all of our discovered references to Lorenzo Ferrer's activities in Madison County at the same time the Hendersons were living there and doing business. The reader will again note how varied the spellings of Ferrer's name are during this time frame. We argue he needed to change up his name to make a clean break from the unresolved marriage (and Lord only knows what else) he left behind in Hinds and Copiah counties.

1832:
May 27, 1832: William Walker enters into an agreement with L. F. Henderson. The document says Walker was indebted to Henderson in the amount of $6,957.13 (Book M, p. 214).

1833:
Lorenzo D. Farrar stands as bondsman in September 1833 in Madison County for Zadock Parish to marry Elizabeth Hurst. The marriage takes place in the same year when we found a land deal for Ferrer in Copiah County.

The first deeds involving the Motz Henderson Company, which was formed by Lincolnton friends George W. Motz, Hugh Henderson, and George W. Henderson, show up in 1833. Motz Henderson actually sold the land that was used to lay out the town of Canton.

1834:
This is the year *Lorenzo Ferror* marries Nancy Alford in Copiah County and is simultaneously in the 1834 tax rolls for Hinds County (as *Lorenzo Ferrow*) and Madison County (as *Lorenzo D. Farrow*).

June 6, 1834: *L. D. Farrar and wife Mary* deed to William Walker and William Anthony land in Town No. 11 Range No. 3E near Love's Creek for $2,000 (Book B, p. 400–401). See the full discussion of this issue in Chapter Ten.

November 1, 1834: Joseph Carson and his wife Elizabeth deed to *Lorenzo D. Farrar* ten acres for $800 (Book B, p. 392–393).

1835:
L. D. Farror is in the 1835 Madison County tax rolls. There are no headings, so the document is difficult to read. It appears he paid one white poll tax and 38 cents in other taxes.

June 5, 1835: William H. Bole and his wife complete several land transactions with Lawson F. Henderson for the sum of $600. (Book C, p. 159).

September 30, 1835: *Lorenzo D. Farrow* buys thirty-nine acres in the Mt. Salus land office.

November 25, 1835: Lawson F. Henderson and James P. Henderson make a land deal with F. W. Davie and William F. Jones of South Carolina for $16,800 (Book C, p. 566). Notably, this is the only land deal for James Pinckney Henderson in Canton. After this, he moves on to Texas. Lawson F. Henderson stayed in Canton and continued to buy and sell land, with his company ending in controversy with the insolvency of his partner.

1836:
L. D. Farror is on the 1836 tax roll in Madison County. He pays one white poll tax. This is the last Mississippi hit we have for him. March 3, 1836: Lawson F. Henderson and Samuel F. Feamister record a land transaction for $1,000 (Book C, p. 552–533).

1837:
Lawson F. Henderson is on the 1837 Madison County tax roll with 160 acres.

January 22, 1837: Lawson F. Henderson enters into a deed in trust with Jefferson Law, William Keeney, and A. F. Hill (Book L, p.632–633).

October 20, 1837: Lawson F. Henderson and George W. Henderson agree to a land transaction for $500 (Book E, p. 170).

1838:
Lawson Franklin Henderson is on the Madison County tax roll for 1838 with 160 acres.

January 1, 1838: John Briscoe and Lawson F. Henderson sign a deal for $1,500 (Book I, p. 106–107).

March 8, 1838: S. M. Flounery and wife and Lawson F. Henderson enter into a land deal for $2,000 (Book E, p. 405–406).

November 27, 1838: Albert G. Forney of Burke County, North Carolina and Motz Henderson ink a land deal for $2,000 (Book F, p. 131).

1840:
Lawson F. Henderson is in the 1840 Madison County tax roll with 480 acres.

January 9, 1840: Henry Heamblin and Lorenzo Latham (administrators of the Andrew E. Beattie estate) execute an agreement with Motz Henderson (Book G, p. 605–606).

April 2, 1840: Motz Henderson enters into an agreement with Thomas Mullin and his wife Elizabeth (Book G, 609–610).

May 2, 1840: Samuel D. Livingston and his wife Phebe Ann sign a deal with George Henderson, George W. Motz, and Jesse Heard that includes a promissory note to the Branch of the Commercial Bank of Natchez for $7,561.65. It involves 160 acres (Book G, p. 696–698).

May 4, 1840: John Munn enters into an agreement with George W. Henderson. Henderson became the security of Munn in several promissory notes payable to the Branch of the Commercial Bank in Natchez (Book H, p. 141–142).

December 10, 1840: Lawson F. Henderson gets a land grant in the Mt. Salus office for thirty-nine acres. This parcel was likely purchased earlier and just approved in 1840.

1841:
Lawson F. Henderson has 400 acres in the Madison County tax roll. George Henderson is also listed.

1842:
Both George Henderson and Lawson F. Henderson are in the Madison County tax roll for 1842.

July 12, 1842. G. W. Motz, George W. Henderson, Jesse Heard, and Jacob L. Mitchell are involved in a mortgage with the Commercial

Bank of Natchez (Book I, p. 478). This deal relates to a deed of mortgage conveyed from Samuel D. Livingston and his wife Phebe Ann bearing the date May 2, 1840 (Book G, p. 696).

September 9, 1842: George W. Henderson, Lawson F. Henderson, and Ann Henderson are involved with a mortgage to the Community Bank of Natchez (Book I, p. 328).

1843:

Both George Henderson and Lawson F. Henderson are in the Madison County tax roll for 1843.

1844:

Lawson F. Henderson is in the Madison County tax roll for 1844.

1846:

April 8, 1846: John H. Rollins and his wife enact a deed to L. F. Henderson for $3,300 (Book K, p. 154–155). This transaction relates to a deed recorded in April 1839 in Book F, p. 311–312.

April 8, 1846: William Bailey and George W. Henderson enter into a deal related to assets held by Robert Lassiter but belonging to the heirs of James A. Blanton (Book K, p. 805–806).

1847:

This is the year that Motz Henderson Company begins to unravel. March 6, 1847: A document filed on this date lists all of George W. Motz's debts, including to members of his own family in North Carolina. He is listed as living in the Parish of Livingston in Louisiana. He may have been financially ruined and needing a place to live outside of Canton (Book K, p. 437).

1848:

Many documents outlining the demise of Motz Henderson Company are filed in this year.

Lawson F. Henderson is in the 1848 Madison County tax roll.
February 21, 1848: Andrew Motz, John Motz, and Elam Caldwell of Lincoln County and Asa Fleachman and his wife (formerly

Caroline R. Motz of New Orleans) deed to George W. Henderson lands that were involved in an 1847 deed with George W. Motz (Book K, p. 759–760). This appears to be a liquidation or repayment of some kind from the failing business. (Elam Caldwell's name emerges again in Ferrer's will.)

June 12, 1848: Lawson Franklin Henderson inks a deal with L. W. Petrie for twenty-four acres in Canton. There was a condition involving a note in favor of Henderson in the amount of $9,339.59 with the Bank of the Metropolis at Washington, DC (Book K, p. 862–863).

March 16, 1849: The dissolution of Motz Henderson Company continues in this deed of trust between George W. Motz and G. W. Henderson. The original deal was made in 1848 between Motz and his wife Mary Angeline of the state of Louisiana and George W. Henderson. It revolved around several tracts of land in or near Canton. On April 14, 1848, Motz and Henderson executed several promissory notes payable to Charles H. Fisher at the Bank of Louisiana New Orleans. Lawson F. Henderson had served as securities. Motz also owed many debts, including a large one to the Bank of Natchez (Book L, p. 112–113).

1849:
February 27, 1849: George W. Henderson and wife Amanda execute a deed of trust to Henry R. Coulter. This was part of the Motz Henderson liquidation (Book L, p. 118–119).

May 20, 1849: Keightly Sanders agrees to a mortgage with a group trading under the name Motz Henderson Merchants and George Calhoon. The deal includes 400 acres (Book L, p. 234–235).

August 18, 1849: Lawson F. Henderson serves as the security on a note involving John Stone and his wife Eliza, David Dean, Perry Cohen, and Henry Coulter (Book L, p. 309–310).

1850:
This is the year George W. Henderson dies. He is in the 1850 Madison County tax roll aged 35.

April 28, 1850: Lawson F. Henderson writes the security for a deal involving George Calhoon and Albert Hill. Calhoon was indebted to S. D. Livingston as president of the Board of Trustees for a school in the sum of $1,500 (Book L, p. 509–510).

1851:
March 10, 1851: Lawson F. Henderson is the security on a deal between George Calhoun and Cameron Coulter (Book L, 691).

1855:
Lawson Franklin Henderson is in the 1855 Madison County tax roll.

1865:
December 1865: H. L. F. Henderson and C. C. P. Henderson along with his wife Fannie B. Henderson come before the Madison County justice of the peace in December 1865 to file a financial agreement (Book Q, p. 211).

1866:
February 20, 1866: H. L. F. Henderson and C. C. P. Henderson and his wife Fannie enact a deed to David Bell involving several large sums of money. $6,885, $4,285, and $2,600 is secured by note payable on the first day of January 1867 with interest (Book Q, p. 209–210).

1874:
April 14, 1874: William R. Parker and his wife Laura sign a deed of trust to C. C. P. Henderson trustee to secure Hugh L. F. Henderson in a promissory note (Book BB, p. 590).

To sum up, it appears that Motz Henderson Company ran from about 1833 (when Canton formed) to 1847. Lorenzo Ferrer—with the many variations of his name—was in the area and documented in the 1830 Copiah Census, the 1831 Copiah tax roll, the 1831 Louisa document, the 1832 Copiah tax roll, the 1833 Copiah land deals, the 1834 marriage to Nancy Alford, and various land deals in Copiah. He was simultaneously on the 1834 tax rolls in Hinds and Madison and then only Madison for 1835 and 1836. Then he is gone right before the Panic of 1837 hit. While we did not find any business deals that connected Lorenzo Ferrer directly with the Hendersons in Mississippi, he was buying land in the same land office with them, and they were conducting business with the same local men.

Though the deals outlined in the chart above appear to be mostly related to land speculation and promissory-note underwriting, we had a strong suspicion that the Hendersons were also slave traders like Ferrer. Our suspicions were confirmed in the summer of 2018 when then Lincoln County Historical Director Jason Harpe forwarded the newspaper clipping below from the December 1, 1854, edition of the *Western Democrat*. It certainly appears that Slade, Henderson and Company in Lincolnton were in the business of trafficking human beings.

CHAPTER TWELVE: A PIRATE COMES TO LINCOLNTON

Listed below are more detailed annotations grouped by decade for many of the source references to Lorenzo Ferrer in Lincolnton from Chapter Twelve. All deed books referenced in the charts below are from the Lincoln County Register of Deeds website (http://www.co.lincoln.nc.us/index.aspx-?NID=214). Upon entering the inquiry system portal, use the "Old Index Books" tab to search for the documents related to Ferrer's lifespan.

1840s:
- *Lorenzo Ferrer* was listed in the 1840 Census alone—with no other people reported as living in the household. This data could support the assertion from the *Lincoln County Heritage, 1997* volume that he first came to Lincolnton alone.

- Our first indication that Ferrer became involved in business pursuits in Lincolnton came with two hits in the Lincoln County Register of Deeds office. On February 25, 1843, *Lorenzo Ferrier* entered into an indenture between Dr. Samuel P. Simpson, H. W. Guion (Simpson's lawyer), Lawson Henderson, and others (Deed Book 38, p. 664). The agreement involved 110 acres and several smaller tracts, enslaved people, twenty-five vehicles/carriages, livestock and other items. *Lorenzo Farrier* is included as being owed $829.09 from what appears to be a promissory note on March 31, 1842.

- On November 17, 1843, Guion, the trustee for Simpson and his creditors, sold lot twenty-two in the southwest square of Lincolnton to *Lorenzo Ferrier* for $150 (Deed Book 40, p. 495).

- *Lorenzo Farrier* appeared in the 1844 Lincoln County tax roll having paid poll tax for two enslaved people and possessing one lot worth $150.

- In November of 1844, *L. Ferrer* signed a petition that was submitted to the General Assembly of North Carolina in protest of neighboring Catawba County being formed out of lands taken from Lincoln County.

- On May 22, 1847, *Lorenzo Ferrer* sold Jacob A. Ramseur lot twenty-five for $350 (Deed Book 41, p. 154). Five days later, on May 27, 1847, *Lorenzo Ferrer* sold Ramseur lot twenty-two for $150 (Deed Book 41, p. 152). This was the same price Ferrer bought it for in 1843.

- *The Lincoln Courier* on July 7, 1847, covered the Lincolnton Independence Day celebration. Townspeople gathered for a speech from Thomas Slade on the courthouse lawn before moving to Johnson's hotel for a dinner filled with toasts by men such as Major W. J. Hoke, L. P. Henderson, William Lander, and Ferrer.

- On October 16, 1847, *L. Ferrer* bought lot eighteen from Allen Alexander for $600 (Deed Book 41, p. 214).

- *L. Farrar* appeared on the Eckles Company 1848 tax roll in Lincoln County. Both lots eighteen and twenty-five are mentioned as valued at $375 and $250, respectively.

- *L. Ferrer* participated in Lincoln County's Fourth of July celebration in 1848. According to the July 7 *Lincoln Courier*, the event included another large gathering on the courthouse lawn, and the rhetoric focused on the "war with Mexico" and welcoming home the "Lincoln boys." A motion was made to assemble a committee that would be tasked with "designating the manner in which the Regulars and Volunteers of this and the surrounding counties shall be received."[7] "L. Ferrer, Esq." was listed as a member of the committee.

1850s:

- *Lorenza Ferrer* appeared on the 1850 Lincoln County tax roll owning both lots.

- *Lorenzo Ferrer* was included in the 1850 Census for Lincoln County. Just like the previous Census records in Mississippi, no occupation was listed. His place of birth was marked as France. His age was fifty-seven, though this was clearly incorrect. He would have been around seventy. His real estate was valued at $800.

- *Lorenzo Ferrer* petitioned to join Lincoln Lodge 137 A. F. & A. M. on February 6, 1852. The Lincoln County Historical Association has a copy of the original petition.

- On April 26, 1852, Jacob A. Ramseur co-signed for A. J. Hobbs to borrow $100 from *L. Farrier* (Deed Book 43, p. 213).

- On May 30, 1853, C. C. Henderson paid *L. Farrier* $1,000 dollars for a twenty-five-year-old enslaved male named Ephraim (Deed Book 42, p. 415). There is no other reference to Ferrer owning Ephraim unless he is one of the unnamed enslaved people listed in the Census.

- In 1854, Ferrer was part of the Freemason proceedings to expel H. W. Hudson from the lodge for "unmasonic conduct."

- *L. Ferrer* was in the 1856 tax roll in Lincoln County. He was listed as owning lot eighteen (valued at $400) and lot twenty-five (valued at $400). He paid three slave polls.

- *Lorensoe Farrer* was in the 1857 tax roll in Lincoln County. His real estate was listed as lot eighteen ($400) and lot twenty-five ($400). In a duplicate tax roll for 1857, he was listed as *L. Ferrer*. He paid three slave polls.

- Ferrer quit Lincoln Lodge 137 on January 11, 1858.

- On April 23, 1858, *L. Ferrier* was listed in a deal with A. L. Hobbs and J. C. Jenkins. It involved $100 and a tract of land adjoining the Poor House (Deed Book 43, p. 348). The document also mentioned a deed on June 12, 1856.

- Ferrer's black mistress Louisa died November 29, 1858. She was buried in the St. Luke's Episcopal Church graveyard the next day.

- *Lorenzo Ferrer* was in the 1859 tax list in Lincoln County owning lots eighteen and twenty-five and the lot where the Poor House sits.

1860s:

- *L. Ferrier* was in the 1860 Census in Lincoln County. He listed one enslaved female aged thirty-five and one enslaved male aged sixteen. These could be Eliza, the woman who remained as his servant until his death in 1875, and Vatinius, who some suggest was his son with Louisa.

- *L. Ferrier* was included as a slave holder in the 1860 Lincoln Slave Schedule. He documented one twenty-five-year-old enslaved female (which may be Eliza, but she is listed as forty-six years old in the next Census) and one sixteen-year-old enslaved male (possibly Vatinius).

- Numerous stories indicate Ferrer hid treasure in the vault of the courthouse in April 1865.

- *Lorenzo Ferrer* was listed in the 1868 tax list in Lincoln County. The notation says he owned fifty-eight acres, with land worth $100. He was listed as owning town lots eighteen and twenty-five worth $500. The location of the land was noted as "Near Poor House."

- On October 10, 1868, B. S. Johnson and his wife Barbara sold *L. Ferrer* parts of lots eight, twenty-one, twenty-two, and forty-three for $1,600 (Deed Book 45, p. 271).

1870s:

- *Lorenzo Ferrier* (aged eighty-seven) was in the 1870 Census in Lincoln County. For the first time, Eliza was named with him aged forty-six. She was listed as a black female whose occupation was "Domestic Servant." Her birthdate was about 1824 in North Carolina. As usual, no occupation was listed for Ferrer. Both of them were documented as "cannot read and cannot write," though this may have been a mistaken assumption by the census taker. Ferrer was listed as having a mother and father of foreign birth. He cited Leon, France, as place of birth. The value of his real estate was $400, and the value of his personal estate was $3,000. Eliza became part of Ferrer's life not very many years before his death. If Ferrer was bedridden, he needed constant help. Even less is known about Eliza than is established about Louisa. By the time Eliza began helping Ferrer, he was way too old to be involved in a physical relationship. The first solid hit for her does not come until 1870. She also appears as Eliza Ferrier on the list of "coloured" parishioners in the St. Luke's records in 1871 and 1874. These records were not gathered every year. We know that Ferrer did not leave Eliza anything in the will, which leads us to believe another interesting notation in Fair's book. He writes, "there is a letter in existence which Ferrer wrote just before his death in which he states that 'the negro hussy that stays with me is stealing al my money'" (160).

- On August 26, 1870, *Lorenzo Ferrier* sold (but basically donated) two acres (the old Poor House tract) for $1 to the trustees of the Episcopal Diocese of North Carolina (Deed Book 46, p. 400). This land, about three miles out of town, was used to build St. Paul's Church.

- On May 1, 1873, Lorenzo Ferrer handwrote his will. His instruction included specific directions about his tombstone. Witnesses were Robert Sowers and Thomas Wells.

- Lorenzo Ferrer died on April 16, 1875, at the age of ninety-six. No details about his death are available. He is buried at St. Luke's Cemetery under a tombstone with the name *Lorendzo Ferrer*.

- Approximately a year after Ferrer's death, on June 14, 1876, Eliza entered into a deal with S. P. Sherrill and his wife, Barbara. For $30 they bought half an acre of land in the southwest square of Lincolnton (Deed Book 49, p. 538). It is unclear how Eliza came to be in possession of any land. (Interestingly, Barbara Henderson Sherrill was Charles Cotesworth Henderson's daughter. Her sister, Theodora, is the woman who married Robert Sowers, witness to Ferrer's will.)

During these Lincolnton years, Ferrer's name is represented eleven different ways: *Lorenzo Ferrer, Loranzo Ferrer, Lorenzo Ferrier, Lorenzo Farrier, L. Ferrer, L. Farrar, Lorenza Ferrer, L. Farrier, Lorensoe Farrer, L. Ferrier,* and *Lorendzo Ferrer.*

ACKNOWLEDGMENTS

The pursuit for the information contained in this book took us to archival repositories, local libraries, churches, graveyards, museums, historical societies, and Freemason lodges in seven states and put us in contact with scholars all over the globe. We owe a deep debt of gratitude to the countless individuals who offered assistance along the way, some in their capacities as county and state employees and others who joined in our adventure simply because they shared our passion and curiosity.

To **Brent Turner** and the **Freemason Brothers of Lincoln Lodge 137 A.F. & A.M.** You had absolutely no reason to let two wild women on a historical mission into your archives, but we sure are glad you did. Brent's efforts were especially helpful because his research unlocked a number of mysteries about life in early Lincolnton and about Lorenzo Ferrer's business there. Brent, we consider you to be an honorary member of our research team now. We also appreciate the efforts of **Joey Mathis**, who sat side by side with us and dug through all of those records. And to **Lynden Berry**, our official Jean Laffite Sword Whisperer. Your research on the sabre and your willingness to share it is so appreciated. It was and is an incredible discovery.

To **Jason Harpe, executive director of the Lincoln County Historical Association** for more than twenty years. Your guidance and knowledge of Lincoln County in the 1800s was indispensable to our project, and your early and ongoing encouragement as we began and continued this journey made all the difference. You were there from the beginning and truly helped chart our course. Considering how many times we blew up your telephone with text questions, we should have probably paid your bill for the entirety of 2018 and part of 2019.

To **Bill Beam and Tina Guffey at the Lincoln County Historical Association**, for assistance in studying the archives available in your collection.

To **Heather Szafran and Robert Ticknor at the Historic New Orleans Collection**. You never lost patience with us when we repeatedly forgot how to use the microfilm machine, and you pulled so many resources for us. Special thanks for granting permission to view several original documents for the purposes of handwriting analysis.

To **Darlene Mott at the Sam Houston Regional Library and Research Center** in Liberty, Texas. When we dropped in on you, we were in an incredible rush to get to Austin. You showed us exactly what we needed to see in the library and gave us the best possible directions to circumvent Houston traffic to boot.

To **the staff of the Notarial Archives Research Center in New Orleans**, especially our new friend **Siva Blake**. Your collection has to be one of the most amazing notarial archive repositories in the United States, and we feel lucky to have seen it.

To **the staff of the Dolph Briscoe Center for American History at the University of Texas at Austin**. Seeing the Bibliotheca Parsonia collection in person was truly marvelous.

To **Joy Pitts** and **Tina Oswald at the East Texas Research Center at Stephen F. Austin State University** in Nacogdoches. Due to time constraints on our trip, we were unable to make it to your library, and you were gracious enough to scan and email several items that were crucial to our research, including the document that connected Louisa to Lorenzo Ferrer in Mississippi and North Carolina.

To **the staff of the University of North Carolina at Chapel Hill Louis Round Wilson Library Special Collections Department** for their help in August 2018 with the McBee family papers and the Samuel Lander ledgers.

To **the staff of the Gustavus Adolphus Pfeiffer Library at Pfeiffer University**, especially the fabulous **Lara Little**. There has to be a special place for you in a librarian's hall of fame somewhere.

To **Mark Erdmann** of Erdmann Art Conservation, for your assistance in authenticating the inscription on the sword found in Freemason Lodge 137 in Lincolnton. We knew what we saw, but it sure was nice to have an expert agree.

To attorney **Alton Reeder**, who decoded a complicated legal decision so that our two non-legal minds would be able to understand what the courts had decreed. Your gift of time and expertise will forever be appreciated.

To **Bronson Pinchot**, actor, dear friend, and expert wingman, for your starring role in the promotional video for this book which still has us in stitches. We know you are in total disbelief with us that Jean Laffite lied.

To **Ann Dellinger**, who we have officially crowned the queen of Lincoln County history. Your research methods are among the best, and we are incredibly grateful that you were willing to share your expertise with us—along with decades of your own research. You told us on the day we first met that in order for stories to become history, they needed to be supported by documents and facts. We hope the case we presented in this volume makes you proud.

To **Sherry Zhang, Jena Mayer, and Brianna Cregle at the Rare Books and Special Collections department of the Princeton University Library**. We appreciate your help in finding the "Maison Rouge" letter we had so hoped was in your collection.

To **the staff of the EH Little Library at Davidson College** for access to materials related to Peter Stuart Ney.

To **Eleanor Barton**, the curator of the Rosenberg Library in Galveston, Texas, for your assistance with the Lafitte oil paintings in the collection.

To **the staff of the Charles R. Jonas Library** in Lincolnton. We spent a great deal of time in the North Carolina Research Room, and everyone there was always so helpful.

To **Thomas Cumberland in the Office of the Grand Lodge of Mississippi**. We called you—a lot—and peppered you with questions each time. Thank you for humoring us and always returning phone calls.

To **Rose Diamond** of Pittsboro, Mississippi, and **George M. Mounger**, of Calhoun City, Mississippi, for help with Mounger family genealogy, and especially to George for loaning us his comprehensive Mounger family history book.

To **Allison Dillard**, a reference and cataloging librarian at the **Georgia Historical Society** in Savannah, for consulting with us on several ship log questions early in our research process.

To **Father Steve Hines and the office staff at St. Luke's Episcopal Church** in Lincolnton. You had every reason to be suspicious of two blonde women wandering through your lovely graveyard at all hours, but you took us in anyway and allowed us free access to your archives. Thank you for being such good stewards of Lincoln County history and for caring for the St. Luke's facility with the honor it deserves.

To **Alex Bravo**, Spanish instructor at Pfeiffer University, for your translation of several Colombian documents related to Laffite.

To **Dr. William Felsher**, for your assistance with the translation of numerous original documents written in French.

To **Dr. Karen Leathem, historian at the Louisiana State Museum**, for your assistance with several Cabildo photographs and corresponding historical details. **Kira Kikla** and **Tom Strider** were also a great help.

To **Tricia Nelson with the Copiah County Mississippi Historical & Genealogical Society** for offering contact information for local historians and providing land deed details. And many thanks to **Paul Cartwright** for offering information about Thompson's Store.

To **the staff of the Lincoln County Register of Deeds** office for helping us navigate through the information in all of those big beautiful books.

To **the staff at the State Archives of North Carolina in Raleigh** for their consistent help on many research days.

To **the staff at the Mississippi Department of Archives and History** in Jackson for retrieving numerous boxes of materials, including several rare and fragile documents that required special permission.

To **Elsie Keever**, whose interview early in our research process led us in a number of worthwhile directions. You are a hoot and a half.

To our distant cousin **Rick Ramseur**, for allowing us free access to your family home, Woodside, for pictures, and for sharing a number of leads that helped us along the way.

To **Oscar Foster**, the secretary of **Freemason Lodge 25 in Hazlehurst, Mississippi**. We really enjoyed hearing about the history of your town, and you were so gracious to search the lodge records for us.

To **the staff in multiple departments at the Raymond, Mississippi, courthouse complex**, especially **Chris**, who went down to that creepy basement with us to dig through dozens of dusty volumes.

To **Noelle Ocon**, the senior conservator of paintings at the North Carolina Museum of Art. Your willingness to x-ray our sword was very generous. Getting to see an Auguste Rodin sculpture up close in your amazing conservation lab was a bonus we never expected.

To **Isabelle Bouillet**, citizen of Saint-Marc-le-Blanc, France, who answered our emergency call for help more than once and whose middle-of-the-night translation of a 200-year-old letter handwritten in Old French was nothing short of heroic. Merci beaucoup, Isabelle.

To **the staff at the Madison County Public Library** in Canton, Mississippi. Thank you for allowing us to rummage through your filing cabinets.

To **Katrina Kalda at the Université de Tours** in Tours, France, for connecting us to local Freemason lodges in the area.

To **photographer and St. Luke's Episcopal Church historian Mary Whisonant**. Your love for St. Luke's is unparalleled, and we greatly appreciate your willingness to help us, even through your doubts about the impact our project might have on the church grounds. We hope the outcome of our findings will spur new sources of funding for the historic preservation of your lovely church.

To **Oliver Pinchot, Director of Auctions Imperial**, for your assistance in authenticating Jean Laffite's sabre.

To **Lonnie**, the angel who came to our rescue by the side of Highway 18 just below Raymond, Mississippi on the 95-degree day when our tire blew out. You poured sweat as you changed our tire—just because you are a kind soul. We will never forget you.

To **Michael Trinkley**, the **Director of the Chicora Foundation**, the group that conserved Lorenzo Ferrer's tombstone in the St. Luke's Cemetery, for information about the project.

To **the staff at the Gaston County Library** in the North Carolina Collection Room for assistance with several articles and books.

To **Steve Amos, Kim Hemphill, and the staff at the Copiah County, Mississippi, Chancery Clerk's office** for assistance with many old deeds and patents.

To **Reverend Scott Oxford**, the volunteer archivist for the **Episcopal Church Western North Carolina Diocese**, for his assistance with several questions about the records at St. Luke's.

To **Lincolnton Freemason Tommy Smith** for arranging access to the United Daughters of the Confederacy building, which used to be the meeting location for local Masons.

To **the staff of the Copiah-Jefferson Regional Library** in Hazlehurst, Mississippi, for assistance over the phone and in person.

To **the staff at the Madison County, Mississippi, Chancery Clerk's office** in Canton, for pointing us in the direction of numerous documents we needed.

To **Darin Panel** at **Freemason Lodge #28 in Canton, Mississippi**, for searching your records for both Lorenzo Ferrer and the Henderson gang.

To **handwriting expert Jeff Taylor**, for giving us advice about how to proceed with the Ferrer/Laffite handwriting samples very early in our project.

To **the very large turtle** on a two-lane blacktop in Alabama who gave his life for our cause late on an afternoon in May. We tried our best, buddy, but it was simply your time to go. Godspeed.

To **the family of wild pigs** who greeted us from the middle of the road as we rounded a curve near Liberty, Texas, on a cold and rainy January day. Thank you for the best laugh we have had in a very long time.

To our husbands, **Joe Yarbrough** and **Chris Oliphant**, for your enduring patience. We told you all those trips to New Orleans were for research and not just étouffée, and now we have the book to prove it.

ENDNOTES

CHAPTER ONE

1. Hubert Howe Bancroft, *The Works of Hubert Howe Bancroft, Vol. XVI: History of the North Mexican States and Texas*, vol. 2, *1801–1889* (San Francisco: History Company Publishers, 1889), 39.

2. William C. Davis, *The Pirates Laffite: The Treacherous World of the Corsairs of the Gulf* (Orlando: Harcourt, 2005), 2.

3. The Laffite Society spells Jean's brother's name Alexandre; however, the Laffite journal translation spells it "Alexander," and that is the way it is referenced in Chapter Eight.

4. Davis, 494.

5. Rosalie Daniels, "Fact and Legend about Jean Lafitte, Privateer of the Gulf of Mexico," *Mississippi Folklore Register* 18, no. 2 (1984): 45.

6. Jean Garrigoux, *A Visionary Adventurer: Arsène Lacarrière Latour 1778–1837, the Unusual Travels of a Frenchman in the Americas* (Lafayette: University of Louisiana at Lafayette Press, 2017), 76.

7. Minutes of the Laffite Society, February 12, 2008, the Laffite Society Collection, Texas A&M University, https://tamug-ir.tdl.org/bit-stream/handle/1969.3/28463/Minutes%202008.pdf?sequence=15.

8. Lyle Saxon, *Lafitte the Pirate* (Gretna, LA: Pelican Publishing, 1989), 288.

9. Garrigoux, 76.

10. Aya Katz, "An Interview with Pam Keyes about Jean Laffite," *Historia Obscura*, http://www.historiaobscura.com/an-interview-with-pam-keyes-about-jean-laffite/.

11. Davis, 163.

12. Inès Murat, *Napoleon and the American Dream* (Baton Rouge: Louisiana State University Press, 1976), 123.

13. Henderson King Yoakum, *History of Texas 1685–1846* (repr., North Charleston, SC: Createspace, n.d.), 1: 88.

14. Winston Groom, *Patriotic Fire: Andrew Jackson and Jean Laffite at the Battle of New Orleans* (New York: Vintage, 2006), 72.

15. *Portrait of Jean Lafitte (?)*, oil on canvas, catalog number 79.200, Rosenberg Library, Galveston, TX.

16. Eleanor Barton, interview by Ashley Oliphant.

17. Alyce Martin, *Portrait of Jean Lafitte*, oil on devoe composition board, catalog number 81.086, Rosenberg Library, Galveston, TX.

18. Paul R. Schumann, *Jean Lafitte*, oil, catalog number 76.021, Rosenberg Library, Galveston, TX.

19. Pam Keyes, "The Laffite Portrait Proves the Authenticity of the Laffite Journal," Historia Obscura, http://www.historiaobscura.com/the-laffite-portrait-proves-the-authenticity-of-the-laffite-journal/.

20. *Jean Lafitte at Dominique You's Bar*, oil, accession number 04917, Louisiana State Museum, New Orleans.

21. Karen T. Leathem, interview by Ashley Oliphant.

22. Garrigoux, xiv.

23. *The Works of Hubert Howe Bancroft, Vol. XVI*, 43.

CHAPTER TWO

1. Jean Garrigoux, *A Visionary Adventurer: Arsène Lacarrière Latour 1778-1837, the Unusual Travels of a Frenchman in the Americas* (Lafayette: University of Louisiana at Lafayette Press, 2017), 76–77.

2. William C. Davis, *The Pirates Laffite: The Treacherous World of the Corsairs of the Gulf* (Orlando: Harcourt, 2005), 9.

3. David Head, "Slave Smuggling by Foreign Privateers: The Illegal Slave Trade and the Geopolitics of the Early Republic," *Journal of the Early Republic* 33, no. 3 (Fall 2013): 433.

4. "Jean Laffite's instructions to Henri [Saybatier]," October 20, 1805, T080827.4813, Historic New Orleans Collection.

5. J. O. Dyer, "Jean Laffite in 1820," *Daily News* (Galveston, TX), May 9, 1920.

6. Davis, 21.

7. Rich Cohen, "Pirate City," *The Paris Review* 1 (Summer 2012): 152.

8. Rosalie Daniels, "Fact and Legend about Jean Lafitte, Privateer of the Gulf of Mexico," *Mississippi Folklore Register* 18, no. 2 (1984): 49.

9. Robert Tallant, *The Pirate Lafitte and the Battle of New Orleans* (Gretna, LA: Pelican Publishing, 1998), 21.

10. Cohen, 156.

11. Winston Groom, *Patriotic Fire: Andrew Jackson and Jean Laffite at the Battle of New Orleans* (New York: Vintage, 2006), 76.

12. Lionel Bienvenue, "The Short Life of Dominique You: New Orleans' Most Popular Man," *The Life and Times of Jean Lafitte*, no. 6 (1982): 2–3.

13. Charles Gayarré, "The Story of Jean and Pierre Lafitte: The Pirate-Patriots," reprint from the *Magazine of American History*, vol. 10, July–December 1883, 7.

14. Cohen, 161.

15. Davis, 157.

16. Davis, 131.

17. Michael Poll, "The Battle of New Orleans: A Masonic Perspective," *Texas Freemason* (Winter 2018): 13.

18. Davis, 176.

Chapter Three

1. Winston Groom, *Patriotic Fire: Andrew Jackson and Jean Laffite at the Battle of New Orleans* (New York: Vintage, 2006), 5.

2. Frank Lawrence Owsley Jr., *Struggle for the Gulf Borderlands: The Creek War and the Battle of New Orleans 1812–1815* (Gainesville: University Press of Florida, 1981), 109.

3. Edward Alexander Parsons, "Jean Lafitte in the War of 1812: A Narrative Based on the Original Documents," *American Antiquarian Society* (October 1940): 216.

4. William C. Davis, *The Pirates Laffite: The Treacherous World of the Corsairs of the Gulf* (Orlando: Harcourt, 2005), 173.

5. The German Coast was a settlement on the east bank of the Mississippi River above New Orleans.

6. Rich Cohen, "Pirate City," *The Paris Review* 1 (Summer 2012): 170.

7. Davis, 210.

8. Groom, 124–25.

9. Owsley, 131.

10. Owsley, 131.

11. Davis, 217.

12. Davis, 223.

13. Groom, 205.

14. Pam Keyes, "Eyewitness Pension Record Testimonies Place Jean Laffite at Battle of New Orleans," Historia Obscura, http://www.historiaobscura.com/eyewitness-pension-record-testimonies-place-jean-laffite-at-battle-of-new-orleans/.

15. Jean Garrigoux, *A Visionary Adventurer: Arsène Lacarrière Latour 1778-1837, the Unusual Travels of a Frenchman in the Americas* (Lafayette: University of Louisiana at Lafayette Press, 2017), 131.

16. Garrigoux, 140–41.

17. Charles Gayarré, "The Story of Jean and Pierre Lafitte: The Pirate-Patriots," reprint from the *Magazine of American History*, vol. 10, July–December 1883, 19–20.

CHAPTER FOUR

1. Inès Murat, *Napoleon and the American Dream* (Baton Rouge: Louisiana State University Press, 1976), 14.

2. Clarence Macartney and Gordon Dorrance, *The Bonapartes in America* (Philadelphia: Dorrance and Company, 1939), 213–14.

3. Macartney and Dorrance, 250.

4. Murat, 5–6.

5. Macartney and Dorrance, 202.

6. Macartney and Dorrance, 209–10.

7. Murat, 186–87.

8. Lyle Saxon, Edward Dreyer, and Robert Tallant, *Gumbo Ya Ya: Louisiana Folktales* (New Orleans: River Road Press, 2015), 318.

9. Steven C. Bullock, *Revolutionary Brotherhood: Freemasonry and the Transformation of the American Social Order, 1730–1840* (Chapel Hill: University of North Carolina Press, 1996), 2.

10. Glen Lee Greene, *Masonry in Louisiana: A Sesquicentennial History 1812–1962* (New York: Exposition Press, 1962), 64.

11. Michael Poll, "The Battle of New Orleans: A Masonic Perspective," *Texas Freemason* (Winter 2018): 11.

12. Bullock, 236.

13. Greene, 64–65.

14. Greene, 65.

CHAPTER FIVE

1. Pedro Luengo-Gutiérrez and Gene A. Smith, eds. *From Colonies to Countries in the North Caribbean: Military Engineers in the Development of Cities and Territories* (Cambridge Scholars Publishing, 2016), 108.

2. Jean Garrigoux, *A Visionary Adventurer: Arsène Lacarrière Latour 1778–1837, the Unusual Travels of a Frenchman in the Americas* (Lafayette: University of Louisiana at Lafayette Press, 2017), 67.

3. Garrigoux, 63.

4. Garrigoux, 90, 96.

5. Arsène Lacarrière Latour, *Historical Memoir of the War in West Florida and Louisiana in 1814–15 with an Atlas*, ed. Gene A. Smith (Gainesville: Historic New Orleans Collection and University Press of Florida, 1999).

6. Garrigoux, 74.

7. William C. Davis, *The Pirates Laffite: The Treacherous World of the Corsairs of the Gulf* (Orlando: Harcourt, 2005), 232.

8. Davis, 145.

9. Garrigoux, 141.

10. Garrigoux, 142.

11. Davis, 249.

12. Davis, 249.

13. Michael A. Morrison, ed., *The Human Tradition in Antebellum America* (Lanham, MD: Rowman & Littlefield, 2000), 96.

14. Pam Keyes, "The True Tale of Mitchell, the Zombie Pirate," Historia Obscura, http://www.historiaobscura.com/the-true-tale-of-mitchell-the-zombie-pirate/.

15. Morrison, 97.

CHAPTER SIX

1. Eugene C. Barker, "The African Slave Trade in Texas," *Texas Historical Association Quarterly* 6, no. 2 (1902): 145–46.

2. Henderson King Yoakum, *History of Texas 1685–1846: Volume 1* (repr., North Charleston, SC: Createspace, n.d.), 87.

3. Jorge Ignacio Rubio Mañé, *The Pirates Lafitte*, trans. Jeffrey P. Modzelewski, 2006, no page in translation.

4. Yoakum, 87.

5. Yoakum, 87.

6. William C. Davis, *The Pirates Laffite: The Treacherous World of the Corsairs of the Gulf* (Orlando: Harcourt, 2005), 323.

7. Eleanor Barton, interview by Ashley Oliphant.

8. David Head, "Slave Smuggling by Foreign Privateers: The Illegal Slave Trade and the Geopolitics of the Early Republic," *Journal of the Early Republic* 33, no. 3 (Fall 2013): 452.

9. Barker, 148.

10. Joe G. Taylor, "The Foreign Slave Trade in Louisiana After 1808," *Louisiana History: The Journal of the Louisiana Historical Association* 1, no. 1 (Winter 1960): 38–39.

11. Edward Alexander Parsons, "Jean Lafitte in the War of 1812: A Narrative Based on the Original Documents," *American Antiquarian Society* (October 1940): 222.

12. J. O. Dyer, "Jean Laffite in 1820," *Daily News* (Galveston, TX), May 9, 1920.

13. Davis, 371.

CHAPTER SEVEN

1. William C. Davis, *The Pirates Laffite: The Treacherous World of the Corsairs of the Gulf* (Orlando: Harcourt, 2005), 443–44.

2. David Head, "Slave Smuggling by Foreign Privateers: The Illegal Slave Trade and the Geopolitics of the Early Republic," *Journal of the Early Republic* 33, no. 3 (Fall 2013): 458.

3. Davis, 455.

4. Jean Garrigoux, *A Visionary Adventurer: Arsène Lacarrière Latour 1778–1837, the Unusual Travels of a Frenchman in the Americas* (Lafayette: University of Louisiana at Lafayette Press, 2017), 263.

5. Davis, 459.

6. Garrigoux, 264.

7. *Gaceta de Colombia* (Bogotá), April 20, 1823.

8. "The Historical Timeline of the Laffites," The Laffite Society, http://thelaffitesociety.com/Laffite_Timeline.html.

9. "Jean Laffite," Encyclopaedia Britannica Online, https://www.britannica.com/biography/Jean-Laffite.

10. J. O. Dyer, "Jean Laffite in 1820," *Daily News* (Galveston, TX), May 9, 1920.

11. Robert L. Schaadt, "The Journal of Jean Laffite: Its History and Controversy," *Provenance: Journal of the Society of Georgia Archivists* 16, no. 1 (January 1998): 26.

12. Charles Adam Gulick Jr., ed. *The Papers of Mirabeau Buonaparte Lamar: Edited from the original papers in the Texas State Library* (Austin, TX: Baldwin & Sons Printers, 1922), 38.

13. Emmet Collins, "Pirate Jean Lafitte: Blue-Eyed Natives May Hold Key to Demise of Legendary Buccaneer," Newspaper clipping, box 1, no. 7, Jean Laffite Collection, Sam Houston Regional Library (Liberty, TX).

14. "Lafitte, the Pirate," *Newark Daily Advertiser* (Newark, NJ), February 12, 1840.

15. Russell B. Guerin, "The Pirate House and Jean Lafitte," Hancock County Historical Society, http://www.hancockcountyhistoricalsociety.com/history/lafittepirate.htm.

CHAPTER EIGHT

1. Robert L. Schaadt, "The Journal of Jean Laffite: Its History and Controversy," *Provenance: Journal of the Society of Georgia Archivists* 16, no. 1 (January 1998): 29.

2. Schaadt, 29.

3. Schaadt, 31.

4. Schaadt, 32.

5. Aya Katz, "Jean Laffite and the Laflin Connection," Historia Obscura, http://www.historiaobscura.com/jean-laffite-and-the-laflin-connection/.

6. *The Journal of Jean Laffite: The Privateer-Patriot's Own Story* (Moonglow Books Reprint, 2009), 6.

7. *The Journal of Jean Laffite*, 6.

8. *The Journal of Jean Laffite*, 6.

9. *The Journal of Jean Laffite*, 7.

10. "History of Psychology: Timeline," Annenberg Learner Foundation, https://www.learner.org/series/discovering-psychology/explorations/history-of-psychology-contemporary-foundations/.

11. *The Journal of Jean Laffite*, 17.

12. *The Journal of Jean Laffite*, 17.

13. *The Journal of Jean Laffite*, 21.

14. *The Journal of Jean Laffite*, 8.

15. *The Journal of Jean Laffite*, 39.

16. *The Journal of Jean Laffite*, 12.

17. *The Journal of Jean Laffite*, 18.

18. *The Journal of Jean Laffite*, 18.

19. *The Journal of Jean Laffite*, 152.

20. Jean Garrigoux, *A Visionary Adventurer: Arsène Lacarrière Latour 1778–1837, the Unusual Travels of a Frenchman in the Americas* (Lafayette: University of Louisiana at Lafayette Press, 2017), 289.

21. Garrigoux, 289.

22. To clarify for research purposes, there is earlier correspondence between Latour in Havana and Livingston in the United States during the year 1818 that deals with an ongoing legal dispute over a land grant to the Marquis de Maison Rouge, a man who died in 1799. That land grant ended up being the source of ongoing legal battles after his death, and in the 1818 correspondence, the people involved are clearly named (and none of them are referred to as "Maison Rouge"). As far as we have been able to determine, the matter of the legal dispute involving the late Marquis de Maison Rouge and the mention of a person nicknamed or code-named *Maison Rouge* in 1829 are not connected.

CHAPTER NINE

1. William C. Davis, *The Pirates Laffite: The Treacherous World of the Corsairs of the Gulf* (Orlando: Harcourt, 2005), 17–18.

2. LaTricia M. Nelson-Easley, *Images of America: Copiah County* (Mount Pleasant, SC: Arcadia Publishing, 2007), 7.

3. Franklin L. Riley, "Extinct Towns and Villages of Mississippi," in *Publication of the Mississippi Historical Society*, vol. 5, ed. Franklin L. Riley, (Oxford, MS: Mississippi Historical Society, 1902), 332–35.

4. Dunbar Rowland, ed., *Mississippi: Contemporary Biography–Comprising Sketches of Counties, Towns, Events, Institutions, and Persons, Arranged in Cyclopedic Form*, vol. 3, *Contemporary Biography* (Spartanburg, SC: Reprint Company Publishers, 1976), 10.

5. "Public Land Sales, 1800s–1840s," Mississippi Encyclopedia, // mississippiencyclopedia.org/entries/land-sales-public-1800-1840s/.

6. "Public Land Sales, 1800s–1840s," Mississippi Encyclopedia.

7. Max Grivno, "Antebellum Mississippi," Mississippi History Now, http://www.mshistorynow.mdah.ms.gov/articles/395/antebellum-mississippi.

8. Mrs. N. D. Deupree, "Some Historic Homes of Mississippi," in *Publication of the Mississippi Historical Society*, vol. 6, ed. Franklin L. Riley (Oxford, MS: Mississippi Historical Society, 1902), 245–64.

9. Kathleen Stanton Hutchinson, "Mississippi," in *Red Book: American State, County & Town Sources*, ed. Alice Eichholz (United States: Ancestry, 2004), 366–81.

10. Grivno.

11. Edward Ball, "Retracing Slavery's Trail of Tears," *Smithsonian Magazine* (November 2015), https://www.smithsonianmag.com/history/slavery-trail-of-tears-180956968/.

12. "Slave Trade," Mississippi Encyclopedia Online, https://mississippiencyclopedia.org/entries/slave-trade/.

13. Grivno.

14. "Slave Trade," Mississippi Encyclopedia Online.

15. Eron Opha Rowland, *History of Hinds County Mississippi 1821–1922* (Jackson: Mississippi Historical Society, 1922), 16.

16. Jim Barnett and H. Clark Burkett, "The Forks of the Road Slave Market at Natchez," Mississippi History Now Online, http://mshistorynow.mdah.state.ms.us/articles/47/the-forks-of-the-road-slave-market-at-natchez.

CHAPTER TEN

1. Mississippi Department of Archives and History, Series 1202: County Tax Rolls, Copiah, 1818–1902, 7, http://da.mdah.ms.gov/series/osa/s1202/copiah/1831-combined/.

2. Loan of Louisa to George Brewer by Lorenzo Ferrer, December 27, 1831, box 2, folder 13, item 3, Henry Brewer Collection at the East Texas Research Center, Nacogdoches, TX.

3. Loan of Louisa to George Brewer by Lorenzo Ferrer, Henry Brewer Collection.

4. Loan of Louisa to George Brewer by Lorenzo Ferrer, Henry Brewer Collection.

5. Paul Cartwright, interview by Ashley Oliphant.

6. Dunbar Rowland, ed., *Mississippi: Contemporary Biography–Comprising Sketches of Counties, Towns, Events, Institutions, and Persons, Arranged in Cyclopedic Form*, vol. 3, *Contemporary Biography* (Spartanburg, SC: Reprint Company Publishers, 1976), 823.

7. *Natchez Weekly Courier* (Natchez, MS), January 22, 1840.

8. "National Register of Historic Places Multiple Property Documentation Form for the Historical and Architectural Resources of Copiah County, Mississippi," prepared by the Mississippi Department of Archives and History for the National Park Service, January 14, 1996. https://www.apps.mdah.ms.gov/t_nom/Historic%20and%20Architectural%20Resources%20of%20Copiah%20County,%20Mississippi.pdf.

9. *WPA History Copiah County Ante-Bellum Days 1823–*. Uncatalogued booklet in the local history room at the George W. Covington Memorial Library in Hazlehurst, Mississippi.

10. George Brewer to Jes ledger, box A-11, B1, folder 6, Henry Brewer Collection.

11. Clara Wright Forrest, *Hinds County, Mississippi Marriage Records, 1823–1848* (Forrest Publications, 1857).

12. Tamie Dehler, "Genealogy: Think of a Marriage Bond as an Intention to Marry," *Tribune Star Online* (Terre Haute, IN), August 11, 2007.

13. Judy G. Russell, "The Ties That Bond," The Legal Genealogist, https://www.legalgenealogist.com/2012/01/25/the-ties-that-bond/.

14. "Mississippi 'Alford' Federal Land Records," Alford American Family Association, http://www.alfordassociation.org/ACTION/aact7770.pdf.

15. Receipt for the sale of an enslaved woman named Maria, August 5, 1837, A-11, B2, folder 13, Henry Brewer Collection.

16. Copiah County Deed Book D, 189, Copia County Chancery Clerk, http://www.deltacomputersystems.com/MS/MS15/INDEX.HTML.

17. "Probable Descendants of Ferrell and Phebe Alford," Alford American Family Association, http://www.alfordassociation.org/GENEALOGY/fer770.pdf.

18. "Probable Descendants of Ferrell and Phebe Alford," Alford American Family Association.

19. George M. Mounger and Rose Diamond, interview by Ashley Oliphant and Beth Yarbrough.

20. "National Register of Historic Places Multiple Property Documentation Form for the Historical and Architectural Resources of Copiah County, Mississippi," prepared by the Mississippi Department of Archives and History for the National Park Service, January 14, 1996, https://www.apps.mdah.ms.gov/t_nom/Historic%20and%20Architectural%20Resources%20of%20Copiah%20County,%20Mississippi.pdf.

21. Jean Garrigoux, *A Visionary Adventurer: Arsène Lacarrière Latour 1778–1837, the Unusual Travels of a Frenchman in the Americas* (Lafayette: University of Louisiana at Lafayette Press, 2017), 289.

22. Box 80, folder 26, Edward Livingston Papers, Princeton University Library Special Collections.

Chapter Eleven

1. Amelia W. Williams and Eugene C. Barker, eds., *The Writings of Sam Houston 1813–1863* (Austin, TX: Jenkins Publishing Company, 1970), 141.

2. Darin Panel, interview by Ashley Oliphant.

3. *The New Handbook of Texas Vol. 3* (Austin: The Texas State Historical Association, 1996), 554.

4. John Warner Barber and Henry Howe, *Our Whole Country, or the Past and Present of the United States, Historical and Descriptive* (New York: George F. Tuttle and Henry M'Cauley Publishers, 1861), 1379.

5. William L. Sherrill, *Annals of Lincoln County, North Carolina, Containing Interesting and Authentic Facts of Lincoln County History Through the Years 1749–1937* (Baltimore: Southern Stars Chapter of Daughters of the Confederacy and Regional Publishing Company, 1967), 131.

6. Elbert L. Watson, *Tennessee at the Battle of New Orleans* (Battle of New Orleans 150th Anniversary Committee of Louisiana, 1965), 25.

7. Alexander Walker, *The Life of Andrew Jackson, to Which Is Added an Authentic Narrative of the Memorable Achievements of the American Army at New Orleans, in the Winter of 1814, '15* (New York: Derby and Jackson, 1859), 231.

8. Watson, 25.

9. *Western Democrat* (Charlotte, NC), December 1, 1854.

Chapter Twelve

1. Jay Hampton, "Lincoln County Rich in History," *Gastonia Gazette* (Gastonia, NC), November 22, 1970.

2. *Lincoln County Heritage Book, 1997*, Charles R. Jonas Library North Carolina Collection, Lincolnton, NC, 331.

3. Victor N. Fair, *The Hills of Home*, Charles R. Jonas Library (Lincolnton, NC), 220.

4. Joe Marusak, "Was Wealthy Lincolnton Man Really the Pirate Jean Lafitte?," *Charlotte Observer* (Charlotte, NC), March 11, 1990.

5. Marusak.

6. Marusak.

7. Lincoln Country Deed Book 38, February 25, 1843, Lincoln County Register of Deeds, 644–48.

8. North Carolina State Archives (Raleigh, NC), General Assembly Session Records November 1844–January 1845.

9. "Celebration of Independence at Lincolnton," *Lincoln Courier* (Lincolnton, NC), July 7, 1847.

10. "4th of July, 1848," *Lincoln Courier* (Lincolnton, NC), July 7, 1848.

11. Lincoln Country Deed Book 42, May 30, 1853, Lincoln County Register of Deeds, 415.

12. *Western Democrat* (Charlotte, NC), January 19, 1858.

13. "Some Reminiscences of the Confederate War," *Lincoln County News* (Lincolnton, NC), July 1, 1915.

14. Fair, 161.

15. Fair, 160.

16. Lincoln Country Deed Book 46, August 26, 1870, Lincoln County Register of Deeds, 400.

17. "Lorenzo Ferrer Will," 5200.40.138, North Carolina State Archives, Raleigh.

Chapter Thirteen

1. *Lincoln County Heritage Book, 1997*, Charles R. Jonas Library North Carolina Collection (Lincolnton, NC), 331.

2. Gladys Childs, "Lincolnton's Pirate: Lorendzo Ferrer," St. Luke's Episcopal Church Archives (Lincolnton, NC).

3. Robert L. Williams, *People Worth Meeting and Stories Worth Repeating* (Dallas: Southeastern Publishing Company, 2000), 55.

4. Scotti Cohn, "The Stranger from New Orleans," *It Happened in North Carolina: Remarkable Events That Shaped History* 2nd ed. (Guilford: GPP, 2000), 51.

5. Judy Ausley, "Legendary Pirate's Tomb Still a Mystery," *Alexandria Daily Town Talk* (Alexandria, LA), May 12, 1996.

6. Robert Williams, 55.

7. Childs.

8. Ausley.

9. Therne Dellinger, "Ferrer or Lafitte?" Lincoln County Historical Association (Lincolnton, NC).

10. Fair, 159–60.

11. Jim Mathews, "Was Resident a Legendary Pirate?," *Wilson Daily Times* (Wilson, NC), March 19, 1988.

12. Hubert Howe Bancroft, *The Works of Hubert Howe Bancroft, Vol. XVI: History of the North Mexican States and Texas*, vol. 2, *1801–1889*, (San Francisco: History Company Publishers, 1889), 43–44.

13. "Lorenzo Ferrer Will," 5200.40.138, North Carolina State Archives, Raleigh.

14. "Thirty-Five Years Age," *Weekly Lincoln Progress* (Lincolnton, NC), February 7, 1880.

15. Box 2, folder 13, item 3, Henry Brewer Collection at the East Texas Research Center, Nacogdoches, TX.

16. J. D. Lewis, "A History of Catawba Springs, North Carolina," https://www.carolana.com/NC/Towns/Catawba_Springs_NC.html.

17. *Lincoln Progress* (Lincolnton, NC), February 7, 1880.

18. Ann Dellinger, interview by Ashley Oliphant and Beth Yarbrough.

19. Mary-Kathryn Craft, "Plantation opens its doors for 200th birthday," *Lincoln Times-News* (Lincolnton, NC), October 16, 1998.

20. Craft.

21. Craft.

22. Diane Turbyfill, "History of Haunts," *Lincoln Times-News*, October 24, 2003.

23. Rick Ramseur, interview by Beth Yarbrough.

24. Joe Marusak, "Was Wealthy Lincolnton Man Really the Pirate Jean Lafitte?," *Charlotte Observer* (Charlotte, NC), March 11, 1990.

25. "Ferrer, Lorenzo," Caswell County Genealogy, http://caswellcountync.org/genealogy/getpersonphp?personID=I73878&tree=tree1.

26. Ann Dellinger, Readers' Forum, *Lincoln Times-News* (Lincolnton, NC), July 19, 2006.

27. Ann Dellinger, interview.

28. Cohn, 52.

29. Robert Williams, 53.

30. Childs.

31. Childs.

32. Fair, 157.

33. Robert Williams, 53.

34. Mathews.

35. William C. Davis, *The Pirates Laffite: The Treacherous World of the Corsairs of the Gulf* (Orlando: Harcourt, 2005), 52.

36. Bancroft, *The Works of Hubert Howe Bancroft, Vol. XVI,* 43–44.

37. Fair, 220.

CHAPTER FOURTEEN

1. "Thirty-Five Years Ago," *Weekly Lincoln Progress* (Lincolnton, NC), February 7, 1880.

2. Jason Harpe, *Lincoln County, North Carolina,* Images of America Series (Mount Pleasant: Lincoln County Historical Association with Arcadia Publishing, 2000), 38.

3. *Raleigh Register* (Raleigh, NC), March 22, 1851.

4. *Weekly Standard* (Raleigh, NC), March 19, 1851.

5. *Weekly Standard,* March 19, 1851.

6. *Carolina Republican* (Lincolnton, NC), April 3, 1851.

7. George G. Kundahl, ed., *The Bravest of the Brave: The Correspondence of Stephen Dodson Ramseur* (Chapel Hill: University of North Carolina Press, 2010), 10.

8. Kundahl, 48.

9. Kundahl, 49.

10. Kundahl, 49.

11. Kundahl, 65.

12. Kundahl, 66.

13. "Ferrer v. Barrett, 57 NC 455 (NC 1859)," Court Listener, https://www.courtlistener.com/opinion/3918954/ferrer-v-barrett/.

14. "Grand Lodge of the Month, February 2020: Grand Lodge of Louisiana," George Washington Masonic National Memorial, https://gwmemorial.org/blogs/gl-of-the-month/the-grand-lodge-of-louisiana?_pos=1&_sid=6408977dc&_ss=r.

15. Michael Poll, "The Battle of New Orleans: A Masonic Perspective," *Texas Freemason* (Winter 2018): 11.

16. "Lorenzo Ferrer Freemason Lodge #137 Petition," Lincoln County Historical Association files (Lincolnton, NC).

17. Deed Book 38, February 25, 1843, Lincoln County Register of Deeds, 664.

18. William L. Sherrill, *Annals of Lincoln County, North Carolina, Containing Interesting and Authentic Facts of Lincoln County History Through the Years 1749–1937* (Baltimore: Southern Stars Chapter of Daughters of the Confederacy and Regional Publishing Company, 1967), 200.

19. Brent Turner, interview by Ashley Oliphant and Beth Yarbrough.

Chapter Fifteen

1. F. F. Rowe, "Was Marshal Ney in America?," *Studies in History from the Davidson College Historical Association* (March 1898): 12–13.

2. Inès Murat, *Napoleon and the American Dream* (Baton Rouge: Louisiana State University Press, 1976), 185.

3. Robert L. Williams, *People Worth Meeting and Stories Worth Repeating* (Dallas: Southeastern Publishing Company, 2000), 33.

4. Clarence Macartney and Gordon Dorrance, *The Bonapartes in America* (Philadelphia: Dorrance and Company, 1939), 219.

5. E. Randall Floyd, *Great Southern Mysteries: Two Volumes in One* (New York: Barnes & Noble Books, 1989), 165.

6. Williams, 33.

7. Williams, 33.

8. Williams, 25.

9. Floyd, 163.

10. Rowe, 25.

11. John Kerr Fleming, *History of the Third Creek Presbyterian Church: Cleveland, North Carolina, 1787–1966, Concord Presbytery* (Raleigh: Offset Compositors and the office of Synod of North Carolina, 1967), 67.

12. Rowe, 14–15.

13. Rowe, 14.

14. Murat, 185.

15. Macartney and Dorrance, 221.

16. Williams, 28.

17. Williams, 29.

18. Harry C. West, "Peter Stuart Ney, A Schoolteacher," *NC Folklore Journal* 23, no. 3 (August 1875): 67.

19. LeGette Blythe, *Marshal Ney: A Dual Life* (New York: Stackpole Sons, 1937), 221.

20. Rowe, 9.

21. West, 67–68.

22. Rowe, 9.

23. Murat, 186.

24. Robert Williams, 54.

25. Jim Mathews, "Was Resident a Legendary Pirate?," *Wilson Daily Times* (Wilson, NC), March 19, 1988.

26. David C. Heavner, "The Story of Wallace Reinhardt," *Lincoln Times-News* (Lincolnton, NC), July 14, 1996.

27. Victor N. Fair, *The Hills of Home*, Charles R. Jonas Library Lincolnton, NC, 160.

28. Gladys Childs, "Lincolnton's Pirate: Lorendzo Ferrer," St. Luke's Episcopal Church Archives (Lincolnton, NC).

29. Blythe, 273.

30. Blythe, 219.

31. Blythe, 219.

32. Robert Williams, 30.

33. West, 67.

34. Rowe, 20–21.

35. Robert Williams, 30.

CHAPTER SIXTEEN

1. Sally Reeves, "Cruising Contractual Waters: Searching for Laffite in the Records of the New Orleans Notarial Archives," *Provenance: Journal of the Society of Georgia Archivists* 16, no. 1 (January 1998), 14.

2. Reeves, 16.

3. "Narcisse Broutin Ledger," volume 28, folio 54V, New Orleans Notarial Archives Research Center.

4. "Jean Laffite's instructions to Henri [Saybatier]," October 20, 1805, T080827.4813, Historic New Orleans Collection.

5. "Jean Laffite to James Madison," December 17, 1815, microfilm reel 17, series 1, General Correspondence, 1723–1859, James Madison Papers, Library of Congress.

6. "North Carolina General Assembly Session Records November 1844–January 1845," North Carolina State Archives, Raleigh.

7. "Lorenzo Ferrer Freemason Lodge #137 Petition," Lincoln County Historical Association, Lincolnton, NC.

CHAPTER SEVENTEEN

1. "Lorenzo Ferrer Will," 5200.40.138, North Carolina State Archives, Raleigh.

2. Victor N. Fair, *The Hills of Home*, Charles R. Jonas Library, Lincolnton, NC, 160.

3. Fair, 161.

4. Martha Helen Haywood, Hubert Haywood, Mary Hilliard Hinton, and E. E. Moffitt, *The North Carolina Booklet: Great Events in North Carolina History* 9, no. 1 (July 1909): 173.

5. Fair, 220.

6. *Lincoln Courier* (Lincolnton, NC), April 26, 1889.

7. *Lincoln Courier*, January 13, 1893.

8. Edward Alexander Parsons, "Jean Lafitte in the War of 1812: A Narrative Based on the Original Documents," *American Antiquarian Society* (October 1940): 221.

9. Mary Whisonant, interview by Ashley Oliphant.

10. Michael Trinkley, Chicora Foundation Report on the Restoration of Lorenzo Ferrer's tombstone, 2007.

11. Trinkley, Chicora Foundation Report.

12. Trinkley, Chicora Foundation Report.

CHAPTER EIGHTEEN

1. Lyle Saxon, Edward Dreyer, and Robert Tallant, *Gumbo Ya Ya: Louisiana Folktales* (New Orleans: River Road Press, 2015), 263.

2. Henderson King Yoakum, *History of Texas 1685–1846: Volume 1* (repr., North Charleston, SC: Createspace, n.d.), 93.

3. J. O. Dyer, "Jean Laffite in 1820," *Daily News* (Galveston, TX), May 9, 1920.

4. W. T. Block, "The Legacy of Jean Lafitte in Southwest Louisiana," https://www.ned.lib.tx.us/jean1.htm.

5. James and Sarah Kaserman, *Florida Pirates: From the Southern Gulf Coast to the Keys and Beyond* (Charleston: The History Press, 2011), 64.

6. Kaserman, 65–66.

7. Block.

8. Gladys Childs, "Lincolnton's Pirate: Lorendzo Ferrer," St. Luke's Episcopal Church Archives (Lincolnton, NC).

9. Carole Hoffman Howell, interview by Ashley Oliphant.

10. Childs.

11. Robert L. Williams, *People Worth Meeting and Stories Worth Repeating* (Dallas: Southeastern Publishing Company, 2000), 53–54.

12. Scotti Cohn, "The Stranger from New Orleans," *It Happened in North Carolina: Remarkable Events That Shaped History* 2nd ed. (Guilford: GPP, 2000), 51–52.

13. David C. Heavner, "The Story of Wallace Reinhardt," *Lincoln-Times News* (Lincolnton, NC), July 14, 1996.

14. Therne Dellinger, "Ferrer or Lafitte?," Lincoln County Historical Association, Lincolnton, NC.

15. Victor N. Fair, *The Hills of Home*, Charles R. Jonas Library, Lincolnton, NC, 158–59.

16. *Lincoln County Heritage Book, 1997*, Charles R. Jonas Library North Carolina Collection, Lincolnton, NC, 32.

17. Ralph Farmer, "Lorendzo Ferrer & Jean Lafitte . . . One in the Same?," *Footprints in Time* 1, year 8 (1994–1995): 13.

18. "Lorenzo Ferrer Will," North Carolina State Archives, Raleigh.

Chapter Nineteen

1. Ralph Farmer, "Lorendzo Ferrer & Jean Lafitte . . . One in the Same?," *Footprints in Time* 1, Year 8 (1994–1995): 14.

2. Lynden Berry, interview by Ashley Oliphant and Beth Yarbrough.

3. Winston Groom, *Patriotic Fire: Andrew Jackson and Jean Laffite at the Battle of New Orleans* (New York: Vintage, 2006), 161.

4. Brent Turner, interview by Ashley Oliphant and Beth Yarbrough.

5. Victor N. Fair, *The Hills of Home*, Charles R. Jonas Library, Lincolnton, NC, 161.

6. Scotti Cohn, "The Stranger from New Orleans," *It Happened in North Carolina: Remarkable Events That Shaped History* 2nd ed. (Guilford: GPP, 2000), 55.

7. Therne Dellinger, "Ferrer or Lafitte?," Lincoln County Historical Association, Lincolnton, NC.

8. Fair Whitley, interview by Ashley Oliphant.

Chapter Twenty

1. *The African Queen*, directed by John Huston, Horizon Pictures, 1951.

2. Mecca Whitesides Simmons, interview by Ashley Oliphant.

1. William L. Sherrill, *Annals of Lincoln County, North Carolina, Containing Interesting and Authentic Facts of Lincoln County History Through the Years 1749–1937* (Baltimore: Southern Stars Chapter of Daughters of the Confederacy and Regional Publishing Company, 1967), 131.

2. Sherrill, 160.

3. Sherrill, 131.

4. Daniel W. Patterson, *A Tree Accurst: Bobby McMillon and Stories of Frankie Silver* (Chapel Hill: University of North Carolina Press, 2000), 154–55.

5. Lincoln County Historical Association archives, Lincolnton, NC.

6. Sherrill, 103.

7. "4th of July, 1848," *Lincoln Courier* (Lincolnton, NC), July 7, 1848.

WORKS CITED

1790 United States Federal Census

1800 United States Federal Census

1810 United States Federal Census

1820 United States Federal Census

1830 United States Federal Census

1840 United States Federal Census

1850 United States Federal Census

1860 United States Federal Census

1870 United States Federal Census

"1850 Census: Lincoln County, North Carolina," trans. Judson Crow.

The African Queen. Directed by John Huston. Horizon Pictures, 1951.

Alexandria Daily Town Talk (Alexandria, LA).

Ball, Edward. "Retracing Slavery's Trail of Tears." *Smithsonian Magazine.* November 2015. https://www.smithsonianmag.com/history/slavery-trail-of-tears-180956968/.

Bancroft, Hubert Howe. *The Works of Hubert Howe Bancroft, Vol. XV: History of the North Mexican States and Texas*, vol. 1, *1531–1800.* San Francisco: A.L. Bancroft & Company, 1884.

———. *The Works of Hubert Howe Bancroft, Vol. XVI: History of the North Mexican States and Texas*, vol. 2, *1801–1889.* San Francisco: History Company Publishers, 1889.

Barber, John Warner, and Henry Howe. *Our Whole Country, or the Past and Present of the United States, Historical and Descriptive.* New York: George F. Tuttle and Henry M'Cauley Publishers, 1861.

Barker, Eugene C. "The African Slave Trade in Texas." *Texas Historical Association Quarterly* 6, no. 2 (1902): 145–58.

Barnett, Jim, and H. Clark Burkett. "The Forks of the Road Slave Market at Natchez." Mississippi History Now Online, last modified February 2003. http://mshistorynow.mdah.state.ms.us/articles/47/the-forks-of-the-road-slave-market-at-natchez.

Barton, Eleanor. Interview by Ashley Oliphant, July 24, 2019.

Berry, Lynden. Interview by Ashley Oliphant and Beth Yarbrough, June 28, 2019.

Bienvenue, Lionel. "The Short Life of Dominique You: New Orleans' Most Popular Man." *The Life and Times of Jean Lafitte* no. 6 (1982): 1–7.

Block, W. T. "The Legacy of Jean Lafitte in Southwest Louisiana." W. T. Block Jr. webpage, last modified 2020. http://www.wtblock.com/wt-blockjr/jean1.htm.

Blythe, LeGette. *Marshal Ney: A Dual Life*. New York: Stackpole Sons, 1937.

Boyd, Gregory A. *Family Maps of Hinds County, Mississippi*. Cross Roads, TX: Arphax Publishing, 2005.

Branley, Edward. "NOLA History: Jean Lafitte the Pirate." GoNOLA.com, last modified October 26, 2011. https://gonola.com/things-to-do-in-new-orleans/arts-culture/nola-history-jean-lafitte-the-pirate.

Brice, A. G. *Masonry: Its Great Age, Teachings, and Influence for Good. Oration Delivered at Dedication of the Masonic Temple, New Orleans, LA, June 24, 1892*. New Orleans: A.H. Hyatt, 1892.

Brown, Everett S. "Letters from Louisiana, 1813–1814." *Mississippi Valley Historical Review* 11, no. 4 (March 1925): 570–79.

Bullock, Steven C. *Revolutionary Brotherhood: Freemasonry and the Transformation of the American Social Order, 1730–1840*. Chapel Hill: University of North Carolina Press, 1996.

Buktman, Bethany Ewald. *New Orleans*. Oakland: Compass American Guides, 1994.

Carolina Republican (Lincolnton, NC).

Carpenter, Edwin H., Jr. "Arsène Lacarrière Latour." *Hispanic American Historical Review* 18, no. 2 (May 1938): 221–27.

Cartwright, Paul. Interview by Ashley Oliphant, November 24, 2018.

"Chancery Clerk Database." Madison County, Mississippi, Chancery Clerk webpage, last modified 2020. https://www.madison-co.com/elected-offices/chancery-clerk.

Charlotte Observer (Charlotte, NC).

Childs, Gladys. "Lincolnton's Pirate: Lorendzo Ferrer." St. Luke's Episcopal Church archives, Lincolnton, NC.

Cohen, Rich. "Pirate City." *The Paris Review* 1 (Summer 2012):145–75.

Cohn, Scotti. "The Stranger from New Orleans." *It Happened in North Carolina: Remarkable Events That Shaped History.* 2nd ed. Guilford: GPP, 2000. 51–55.

Collins, Emmet. "Pirate Jean Lafitte: Blue-Eyed Natives May Hold Key to Demise of Legendary Buccaneer." Jean Laffite Collection Box 1, no. 7, Sam Houston Regional Library, Liberty, TX.

Coon, Charles Lee. *North Carolina Schools and Academies, 1790–1840: A Documentary History.* New York: Wentworth Press, 2016.

Copiah County Chancery Clerk, last modified 2020, http://www.delta-computersystems.com/MS/MS15/INDEX.HTML.

Copiah County, Mississippi, Taxpayers, 1825–1841. Miami Beach: T.L.C. Genealogy, 1990.

"Copiah County Genealogy and History Network." Mississippi Genealogy and History Network, last modified 2019. https://copiah.msghn.org/.

Daily News (Galveston, TX).

Daniels, Rosalie. "Fact and Legend about Jean Lafitte, Privateer of the Gulf of Mexico." *Mississippi Folklore Register* 18, no. 2 (1984): 45–54.

Davis, William C. *The Pirates Laffite: The Treacherous World of the Corsairs of the Gulf.* Orlando: Harcourt, 2005.

Dehler, Tamie. "Genealogy: Think of a Marriage Bond as an Intention to Marry." *Tribune Star Online* (Terre Haute, IN), August 11, 2007. https://www.tribstar.com/news/lifestyles/genealogy-think-of-a-marriage-bond-as-an-intention-to-marry/article_0d-4c0f38-f3a7-5e83-a556-e75bbaca2bd4.html.

Dellinger, Ann. Interview by Ashley Oliphant and Beth Yarbrough, June 27, 2018.

Dellinger, Mary. Typed, undated document. St. Luke's Episcopal Church folder. North Carolina History Room. Charles R. Jonas Library, Lincolnton, NC.

Dellinger, Paul H. *1860 Lincoln County Census*. 1991.

Dellinger, Therne. "Ferrer or Lafitte?" Lincoln County Historical Association, Lincolnton, NC.

Denslow, Ray Vaughn. *Territorial Masonry: The Story of Freemasonry and the Louisiana Purchase, 1804–1821*. Washington, DC: The Masonic Service Association of the United States, 1925.

DePriest, Virginia Greene. *1840 Federal Census of Lincoln County, North Carolina*. 1983.

"Descendants of Lawson and Elizabeth Carruth Henderson, 1774–1843." Ancestry.com, last updated 2020. https://www.ancestry.com/boards/localities.northam.usa.states.northcarolina.counties.mecklenburg/3768.

Deupree, N. D. "Some Historic Homes of Mississippi." In *Publication of the Mississippi Historical Society*, vol. 6, edited by Franklin L. Riley. Oxford, MS: Mississippi Historical Society, 1902.

"Edward Livingston Notebook 1834–1836." Edward Livingston Papers (C0280); Manuscripts Division, Department of Rare Books and Special Collections. Princeton University Library.

Ellis, J. Tuffly. "James Pinckney Henderson." NCpedia, last modified 2020. https://www.ncpedia.org/biography/henderson-james-pinckney.

Epperson, Jean L. "Who Was Jean Lafitte?" *Laffite Society Chronicles* 17, no. 2 (2011).

Fair, Victor N. *The Hills of Home*. Charles R. Jonas Library (Lincolnton, NC).

Farmer, Ralph. "Lorendzo Ferrer & Jean Lafitte . . . One in the Same?" *Footprints in Time* 1, year 8 (1994–1995): 13–14.

Farrar, William R., and Ethel. *The Farrars*. St. Petersburg: St. Petersburg Print Company, 1964.

Fayetteville Weekly Observer (Fayetteville, NC).

"Ferrer, Lorenzo." Caswell County Genealogy, last modified 2020. https://caswellcountync.org/genealogy/getperson.php?personID=I73878&tree=tree1.

"Ferrer v. Barrett, 57 NC 455 (NC 1859)." Court Listener. https://www.courtlistener.com/opinion/3918954/ferrer-v-barrett/.

Fleming, John Kerr. *History of the Third Creek Presbyterian Church: Cleveland, North Carolina, 1787–1966, Concord Presbytery*. Raleigh: Offset Compositors and the Office of Synod of North Carolina, 1967.

Floyd, E. Randall. *Great Southern Mysteries: Two Volumes in One*. New York: Barnes & Noble Books, 1989.

Forrest, Clara Wright. *Hinds County, Mississippi Marriage Records, 1823–1848*. Forrest Publications, 1857.

Froneberger, Virginia B. "St. Luke's Episcopal Church, Lincolnton, NC: A Short History and Appreciation of St. Luke's Episcopal Church." *Lincoln Sentinel* 4, no. 3 (July–September 2002): 5–6.

Gaceta de Colombia (Bogotá).

"Gaither Schrum Papers." Lincoln County Historical Association, Lincolnton, NC.

Garrigoux, Jean. *A Visionary Adventurer: Arsène Lacarrière Latour 1778–1837, the Unusual Travels of a Frenchman in the Americas*. Lafayette: University of Louisiana at Lafayette Press, 2017.

The Gastonia Gazette (Gastonia, NC).

Gayarré, Charles. "The Story of Jean and Pierre Lafitte: The Pirate-Patriots." Reprint from the *Magazine of American History*, vol. 10, July–December 1883.

"Grand Lodge of the Month, February 2020: Grand Lodge of Louisiana." George Washington Masonic National Memorial, last modified 2020. https://gwmemorial.org/blogs/gl-of-the-month/the-grand-lodge-of-louisiana?_pos=1&_sid=6408977dc&_ss=r.

Greene, Glen Lee. *Masonry in Louisiana: A Sesquicentennial History 1812–1962*. New York: Exposition Press, 1962.

Grivno, Max. "Antebellum Mississippi." Mississippi History Now, last modified 2017. http://www.mshistorynow.mdah.ms.gov/articles/395/antebellum-mississippi.

Groom, Winston. *Patriotic Fire: Andrew Jackson and Jean Laffite at the Battle of New Orleans*. New York: Vintage, 2006.

Guerin, Russell B. "Book B–Analysis." Hancock County Historical Society, last modified 2020. http://www.hancockcountyhistoricalsociety.com/ reference/deed-book-B-analysis.htm.

———. "The Pirate House and Jean Lafitte." Hancock County Historical Society, last modified 2020. http://www.hancockcounty historicalsociety.com/history/lafittepirate.htm.

———. "The Pirate House Revisited." Hancock County Historical Society, last modified 2020. http://www.hancockcountyhistoricalsoci-ety.com/history/lafittepirate-part2.htm.

Gulick, Charles Adam, Jr., ed. *The Papers of Mirabeau Buonaparte Lamar: Edited from the original papers in the Texas State Library.* Austin, TX: A.C. Baldwin & Sons Printers, 1922.

Harpe, Jason. *Lincoln County, North Carolina.* Images of America Series. Mount Pleasant: Lincoln County Historical Association with Arcadia Publishing, 2000.

Haywood, Martha Helen, Hubert Haywood, Mary Hilliard Hinton, and E. E. Moffitt. *The North Carolina Booklet: Great Events in North Carolina History* 9, no. 1 (July 1909).

Hazlehurst, Copiah County, Mississippi: Its Early Settlers and Families. Edited by Hartwell Cook and Meredith Bass. Jackson: AAA Printing, 1985.

Head, David. "Slave Smuggling by Foreign Privateers: The Illegal Slave Trade and the Geopolitics of the Early Republic." *Journal of the Early Republic* 33, no. 3 (Fall 2013): 433–62.

"Henderson, First Governor of Texas Was Lincoln Man." Undated clipping *Lincoln Times-News* (Lincolnton, NC). Charles R. Jonas Library North Carolina Collection, Lincolnton, NC.

Hendrix, Mary Louise Flowers. *Mississippi Court Records from the Files of the High Court of Errors and Appeals 1799–1859.* Greenville, SC: Southern Historical Press, 1999.

"The Historical Timeline of the Laffites." The Laffite Society. http://the laffitesociety.com/Laffite_Timeline.html.

"History of Psychology: Timeline." Annenberg Learner Foundation, last modified 2020. https://www.learner.org/series/discovering-psychology/ explorations/history-of-psychology-contemporary-foundations/.

Hodges, Dr. and Mrs. T. L. Hodges. "Jean Lafitte and Major L. Latour in Arkansas Territory." *Arkansas Historical Quarterly* 7, no. 4 (Winter 1948): 237–56.

Howell, Carole Hoffman. Interview by Ashley Oliphant, July 1, 2019.

Howells, John L. "The Journals of Jean Laffite." 1–11.

Hutchinson, Kathleen Stanton. "Mississippi." In *Red Book: American State, County & Town Sources*. Edited by Alice Eichholz, 366–81. United States: Ancestry, 2004.

"James Pinckney Henderson." Lone Star Junction, last modified 1996. www.lsjunction.com/people/hendersn.htm.

Jenkins, John H., ed. *The Papers of the Texas Revolution 1835–1836 Volume 8*. Austin, TX: Presidial Press, 1973.

"Jean Laffite." Encyclopaedia Brittanica Online, last modified 2020. https://www.britannica.com/biography/Jean-Laffite.

"Jean Laffite's instructions to Henri [Saybatier]." October 20, 1805. T080827.4813. Historic New Orleans Collection.

"Jean Laffite to James Madison." December 17, 1815, Microfilm Reel 17, Series 1, General Correspondence, 1723–1859, James Madison Papers, Library of Congress. https://www.loc.gov/item/mjm018032/.

"Jean Lafitte." National Park Service, US Department of the Interior, last modified 2020. https://www.nps.gov/jela/index.htm.

Jean Lafitte at Dominique You's Bar, oil. Accession number 04917. Louisiana State Museum, New Orleans, LA. https://louisianadigitallibrary.org/islandora/object/tahil-aaw%3A762.

The Journal of Jean Laffite: The Privateer-Patriot's Own Story. Moonglow Books Reprint, 2009.

Kaserman, James and Sarah Kaserman. *Florida Pirates: From the Southern Gulf Coast to the Keys and Beyond*. Charleston: The History Press, 2011.

Katz, Aya. "An Interview with Pam Keyes about Jean Laffite." Historia Obscura, last modified September 30, 2013. http://www.historiaobscura.com/an-interview-with-pam-keyes-about-jean-laffite/.

———. "Jean Laffite and the Laflin Connection." Historia Obscura, last modified April 28, 2013. http://www.historiaobscura.com/jean-laffite-and-the-laflin-connection/.

———. "Was the Journal of Jean Laffite an Original, a Copy or a Forgery?" Historia Obscura, last modified October 19, 2013. http://www.historiaobscura.com/tag/the-journal-of-jean-laffite/.

Keever, Elsie. Interview by Ashley Oliphant, June 20, 2018.

Keyes, Pam. "Beverly Chew: The Man Behind the Curtain in Early New Orleans." Historia Obscura, last modified November 19, 2015. https://www.historiaobscura.com/beverly-chew-the-man-behind-the-curtain-in-early-new-orleans/.

———. "Eyewitness Pension Record Testimonies Place Jean Laffite at Battle of New Orleans." Historia Obscura, last modified February 21, 2018. http://www.historiaobscura.com/eyewitness-pension-record-testimonies-place-jean-laffite-at-battle-of-new-orleans/.

———. "The Laffite Portrait Proves the Authenticity of the Laffite Journal." Historia Obscura, last modified December 1, 2015. http://www.historiaobscura.com/the-laffite-portrait-proves-the-authenticity-of-the-laffite-journal/.

———. "The True Tale of Mitchell, the Zombie Pirate." Historia Obscura, last modified March 11, 2016. http://www.historiaobscura.com/the-true-tale-of-mitchell-the-zombie-pirate/.

Kundahl, George G., ed. *The Bravest of the Brave: The Correspondence of Stephen Dodson Ramseur*. Chapel Hill: University of North Carolina Press, 2010.

Kramer, Joyce. "Jean Lafitte–Life as a Pirate." The Post Searchlight, last modified July 25, 2011. https://www.thepostsearchlight.com/2011/07/25/jean-lafitte-life-as-a-pirate/.

Latour, Arsène Lacarrière. *Historical Memoir of the War in West Florida and Louisiana in 1814–15 with an Atlas*. Edited by Gene A. Smith. Gainesville: Historic New Orleans Collection and University Press of Florida, 1999.

Leathem, Karen T. Interview by Ashley Oliphant, August 19, 2019.

Le Plongeon, Alice D. *Here & There in Yucatan*. New York: The Publishers Book Composition and Electrotyping Company, 1886.

"Letter from Arsène Latour to Edward Livingston May 23, 1829." Edward Livingston Papers (C0280); Manuscripts Division, Department of Rare Books and Special Collections. Princeton University Library.

Lewis, J. D. "A History of Catawba Springs, North Carolina," last modified 2007. https://www.carolana.com/NC/Towns/Catawba_Springs_NC.html.

Lincoln County Heritage Book, 1997. Charles R. Jonas Library North Carolina Collection (Lincolnton, NC).

Lincoln County News (Lincolnton, NC), June 14, 1910.

Lincoln Courier (Lincolnton, NC).

Lincoln Times-News (Lincolnton, NC).

Lincoln County Register of Deeds, last modified 2020. http://www.co.lincoln.nc.us/index.aspx?NID=214.

Lincoln Lodge #137 A.F. & A.M. record books, Lincolnton, NC.

"Lorenzo Ferrer Freemason Lodge #137 Petition." Lincoln County Historical Association, Lincolnton, NC.

Lorenzo Ferrer Will." Record ID 5200.40.138, North Carolina State Archives, Raleigh.

Luengo-Gutiérrez, Pedro, and Gene A. Smith, eds. *From Colonies to Countries in the North Caribbean: Military Engineers in the Development of Cities and Territories.* Cambridge Scholars Publishing, 2016.

Macartney, Clarence, and Gordon Dorrance. *The Bonapartes in America.* Philadelphia: Dorrance and Company, 1939.

Mañé, Jorge Ignacio Rubio. *The Pirates Lafitte.* Translated by Jeffrey P. Modzelewski, 2006.

Martin, Alyce. *Portrait of Jean Lafitte,* oil on devoe composition board. Catalog number 81.086. Rosenberg Library, Galveston, TX. https://rosenberg.pastperfectonline.com/webobject/5A266474-F7DF-48E9-9B99-546374721010.

"McBee Family Papers, 1754-1937." ID 2263. Louis Round Wilson Library Special Collections. UNC Chapel Hill.

McBee, May Wilson. *Mississippi County Court Records.* Baltimore: Clearfield, 2008.

McCarthy, Kevin M. *Twenty Florida Pirates.* Sarasota: Pineapple Press, 1994.

"Meeting Notes of The Laffite Society." February 12, 2008. Galveston, TX.

"Milton, North Carolina." Wikimapia.org, last modified 2014. http://wikimapia.org/8917634/Milton-North-Carolina.

"Milton State Bank Building." Caswell County Historical Association webpage, last modified December 19, 2007. https://ncccha.blogspot.com/2007/12/milton-state-bank-building-sold-1924.html.

Minutes of the Laffite Society, February 12, 2008. The Laffite Society Collection. Texas A&M University. https://tamug-ir.tdl.org/bitstream/handle/1969.3/28463/Minutes%202008.pdf?sequence=15.

"Mississippi 'Alford' Federal Land Records." Alford American Family Association, last modified summer 2007. http://www.alfordassociation.org/ACTION/aact7770.pdf.

Mississippi Department of Archives and History, last modified 2020. http://www.mdah.ms.gov/new/.

Mounger, George M., and Rose Diamond. Interview by Ashley Oliphant and Beth Yarbrough, May 21, 2019.

Morning Star (Houston, TX), February 8, 1842.

Morrison, Michael A., ed. *The Human Tradition in Antebellum America.* Lanham, MD: Rowman & Littlefield, 2000.

Murat, Inès. *Napoleon and the American Dream.* Baton Rouge: Louisiana State University Press, 1976.

Muster Rolls of the Texas Revolution. Austin, TX: Daughters of the Republic of Texas, Inc., 1986.

"Narcisse Broutin Ledger." Volume 28, folio 54V. New Orleans Notarial Archives Research Center.

Natchez Weekly Courier (Natchez, MS), January 22, 1840.

"National Register of Historic Places Multiple Property Documentation Form." Historical and Architectural Resources of Copiah County, Mississippi, January 14, 1996. https://www.apps.mdah.ms.gov/t_nom/Historic%20and%20Architectural%20Resources%20of%20Copiah%20County,%20Mississippi.pdf.

Nelson-Easley, LaTricia M. *Images of America: Copiah County.* Mount Pleasant, SC: Arcadia Publishing, 2007.

The New Handbook of Texas Vol. 3. Austin: The Texas State Historical Association, 1996.

Newark Daily Advertiser (Newark, NJ).

"North Carolina General Assembly Session Records November 1844–January 1845." North Carolina State Archives, Raleigh.

North Carolina Reports. Cases in Equity, Argued and Determined in the Supreme Court of North Carolina, from June Term, 1858, to August Term, 1859 Volume IV, 1859.

The Official Federal Land Records Site. US Department of the Interior, Bureau of Land Management, last modified 2020. glorecords.blm.gov.

"On the Watery Trail of Jean Lafitte." *Southern Living*. February 1990.

Orians, G. Harrison. "Lafitte: A Biographical Note." *American Literature* 9, no. 3 (November 1937): 351–53.

Owsley, Frank Lawrence, Jr. *Struggle for the Gulf Borderlands: The Creek War and the Battle of New Orleans 1812-1815*. Gainesville: University Press of Florida, 1981.

Panel, Darin. Interview by Ashley Oliphant, May 1, 2019.

Papers of William Alexander Graham: Volume 1, North Carolina Digital Collections of the North Carolina State Archives, North Carolina Department of Archives and History, Raleigh.

Parsons, Edward Alexander. "Jean Lafitte in the War of 1812: A Narrative Based on the Original Documents." *American Antiquarian Society* (October 1940): 205–24.

Patterson, Daniel W. *A Tree Accurst: Bobby McMillon and Stories of Frankie Silver*. Chapel Hill: University of North Carolina Press, 2000.

Peele, William Joseph. *Lives of Distinguished North Carolinians*. Raleigh: North Carolina Publishing Society, 1898.

"Poem found at the home of Lorenzo Ferrer after this death." Bette Morris Collection, Lincoln County Historical Association, Lincolnton, NC.

Poll, Michael. "The Battle of New Orleans: A Masonic Perspective." *Texas Freemason* (Winter 2018): 10–13.

Portrait of Jean Lafitte (?), oil on canvas, Catalog number 79.200, Rosenberg Library, Galveston, TX. https://rosenberg.pastperfectonline.com/webobject/C42618F0-83B1-4B88-A4C2-609916579343.

Potter, John S., Jr. *The Treasure Diver's Guide*. Revised Edition. Garden City: Doubleday & Company, 1972.

Powell, William, and Virginia. *St. Luke's Parish in Lincolnton, NC, founded, November 29, 1841: a record of the first one hundred years of services of the parish*. Lincolnton: St. Luke's Vestry, 1941. University of North Carolina at Chapel Hill.

Pratt, Willis W., ed. *Galveston Island, or, A Few Months off the Coast of Texas: The Journal of Francis C. Sheridan 1839–1840*. Austin: University of Texas Press, 1982.

"Probable Descendants of Ferrell and Phebe Alford." Alford American Family Association, http://www.alfordassociation.org/GENEALOGY/fer770.pdf.

Pruitt, A. B. *Lincoln County, NC Tax List, 1837*. 1998.

"Public Land Sales, 1800s–1840s." Mississippi Encyclopedia, last modified April 14, 2018. https://mississippiencyclopedia.org/entries/land-sales-public-1800-1840s/.

Raleigh Register (Raleigh, NC), March 22, 1851.

Ramseur, Rick. Interview by Beth Yarbrough, May 12, 2019.

Reeves, Sally. "Cruising Contractual Waters: Searching for Laffite in the Records of the New Orleans Notarial Archives." *Provenance: Journal of the Society of Georgia Archivists* 16, no. 1 (January 1998).

———. "Searching for Lafitte the Pirate." NewOrleansFrenchQuarter. com, last modified 2020. http://www.frenchquarter.com/jeanlaffitte/.

Riley, Franklin L. "Extinct Towns and Villages of Mississippi." In *Publication of the Mississippi Historical Society*, vol. 5. Edited by Franklin L. Riley, 332–35. Oxford, MS: Mississippi Historical Society, 1902.

Roth, Stacy Flora. *The Edward Livingston Papers: A Finding Aid*. Princeton: Department of Special Collections, Princeton University Libraries, 1989.

Rowe, F. F. "Was Marshal Ney in America?" *Studies in History from the Davidson College Historical Association* (March 1898): 4–28.

Rowland, Dunbar, ed. *Mississippi: Contemporary Biography–Comprising Sketches of Counties, Towns, Events, Institutions, and Persons, Arranged in Cyclopedic Form Volume III*. Spartanburg, SC: The Reprint Company Publishers, 1976.

Rowland, Eron Opha. *History of Hinds County Mississippi 1821–1922*. Jackson: Mississippi Historical Society, 1922.

Russell, Judy G. "The Ties That Bond." The Legal Genealogist, last modified January 25, 2012. https://www.legalgenealogist.com/2012/01/25/the-ties-that-bond/.

"Samuel Lander Ledgers, 1838–1865." ID 5449, Louis Round Wilson Library Special Collections, UNC Chapel Hill.

Sanborn Map of Downtown Lincolnton, Lincoln County Historical Association, Lincolnton, NC.

Saxon, Lyle. *Lafitte the Pirate*. Gretna, LA: Pelican Publishing, 1989.

Saxon, Lyle, Edward Dreyer, and Robert Tallant. *Gumbo Ya Ya: Louisiana Folktales*. New Orleans: River Road Press, 2015.

Schaadt, Robert L. "The Journal of Jean Lafitte: Its History and Controversy." *Provenance: Journal of the Society of Georgia Archivists* 16, no. 1 (January 1998): 23–54.

Schumann, Paul R. *Jean Lafitte*, oil. Catalog number 76.021, Rosenberg Library, Galveston, TX. https://rosenberg.pastperfectonline.com/web-object/B77FA8B6-A2F4-4470-8FB6-280004783510.

Scot, James B. *Outline of the Rise and Progress of Freemasonry in Louisiana*. The Grand Lodge of Louisiana, 1912.

Selin, Shannon. "Jean Lafitte: The Mexican Gulf Pirate and Privateer." Imagining the Bounds of History, last modified 2020, https://shannonselin.com/2014/04/jean-laffite-mexican-gulf-pirate-privateer/.

Sherrill, William L. *Annals of Lincoln County, North Carolina, Containing Interesting and Authentic Facts of Lincoln County History Through the Years 1749–1937*. Baltimore: Southern Stars Chapter of Daughters of the Confederacy and Regional Publishing Company, 1967.

Simmons, Mecca Whitesides. Interview by Ashley Oliphant, May 12, 2019.

Skowronek, Russell K., and Charles R. Ewen, editors. *X Marks the Spot: The Archaeology of Piracy*. Gainesville: University Press of Florida, 2007.

"Slave Trade." Mississippi Encyclopedia Online, last modified 2020. https://mississippiencyclopedia.org/entries/slave-trade/.

St. Luke's Episcopal Church record books, Lincolnton, NC.

St. Luke's Parish in Lincolnton, NC, founded, November 29, 1841: a record of the first one hundred years of service of the parish. Forgotten Books, 2018.

Tallant, Robert. *The Pirate Lafitte and the Battle of New Orleans*. Gretna, LA: Pelican Publishing, 1998.

Tanner, Henry Schenck, cartographer. *Map of Trade Routes in Eastern United States in 1835*. https://www.loc.gov/resource/g3700.rr000030 /?r=-0.32,0.388,1.593,0.975,0.

Tate, Al. "A Brief History of Freemasonry in North Carolina and Lincoln County." *Lincoln Sentinel* 4, no. 4 (October–December 2002): 20–24.

Taylor, Joe G. "The Foreign Slave Trade in Louisiana After 1808." *Louisiana History: The Journal of the Louisiana Historical Association* 1, no. 1 (Winter 1960): 36–43.

Trinkley, Michael. Interview by Ashley Oliphant, January 28, 2019.

———. *Chicora Foundation Report on the Restoration of Lorenzo Ferrer's tombstone*. 2007.

Turner, Brent. Interview by Ashley Oliphant and Beth Yarbrough, September 3, 2019.

Vogel, Robert C. "Letter to Reginald Wilson dated 18 June 2001." Jean Laffite Archives, Liberty, TX.

———. "Pierre and Jean Laffite: Going to the Primary Sources." *The Laffite Chronicles* 7, no. 2 (October 2001): 7–12.

Walker, Alexander. *The Life of Andrew Jackson, to Which Is Added an Authentic Narrative of the Memorable Achievements of the American Army at New Orleans, in the Winter of 1814, '15*. New York: Derby and Jackson, 1859.

"Wallace Reinhardt House." *The Lincoln Sentinel* 10, no. 1 (Spring 2007): 10–13.

Watson, Elbert L. *Tennessee at the Battle of New Orleans*. The Battle of New Orleans 150th Anniversary Committee of Louisiana, 1965.

The Weekly Lincoln Progress (Lincolnton, NC).

Weekly Standard (Raleigh, NC), March 19, 1851.

West, Harry C. "Peter Stuart Ney, A Schoolteacher." *NC Folklore Journal* 23, no. 3 (August 1875): 67–69.

Western Democrat (Charlotte, NC).

Whisonant, Mary. Interview by Ashley Oliphant, February 2, 2019.

Whitley, Fair. Interview by Ashley Oliphant, July 10, 2019.

Williams, Amelia W., and Eugene C. Barker, eds. *The Writings of Sam Houston 1813–1863*. Austin, TX: Jenkins Publishing Company, 1970.

Williams, Robert L. *People Worth Meeting and Stories Worth Repeating*. Dallas: Southeastern Publishing Company, 2000.

Wilson Daily Times (Wilson, NC).

WPA History Copiah County Ante-Bellum Days 1823–. Uncatalogued booklet in the local history room at the George W. Covington Memorial Library, Hazlehurst, MS.

Yoakum, Henderson King. *History of Texas 1685–1846*, vol. 1 of 2. Reprint, North Charleston, SC: Createspace, n.d.

Zimmerman, Thomas. "The Mystery of the Final Years of Jean Lafitte." JeanLafitte.net, last modified 2009. http://jeanlafitte.net/end.htm.

ABOUT THE AUTHORS

Dr. Ashley Oliphant and Beth Yarbrough are a mother-daughter research team from Lincolnton, North Carolina.

Oliphant is an associate professor of English at Pfeiffer University, where she has taught in the English Department since 2007. She is the author of four books: *Hemingway and Bimini: The Birth of Sport Fishing at the "End of the World"* (2017, Pineapple Press), *Hemingway's Mixed Drinks: An Examination of the Varied Representation of Alcohol Across the Author's Canon* (2007, UNC-Greensboro Dissertation), *Shark Tooth Hunting on the Carolina Coast* (2015, Pineapple Press), and a novel called *In Search of Jimmy Buffett: A Key West Revival* (2018, Warren Publishing). She is an active member of the Hemingway Society, having presented at its international conferences and published in the *Hemingway Review*.

Beth Yarbrough is a nationally known artist and photographer whose depictions of historic homes and structures across the South are featured on her website *Southern Voice* and in her extensive collection of published calendars. Both Oliphant and Yarbrough travel all over the country to promote their books and art, respectively. They are lifelong Lincolntonians with a passion for preserving local history.